When Will It Be

Lean-Agile Forecasting To Answer Your Customers' Most Important Question

Daniel Vacanti

When Will It Be Done?

Lean-Agile Forecasting To Answer Your Customers' Most Important Question

Daniel Vacanti

ISBN 978-0-9864363-7-6

Leanpub

This is a Leanpub book. Leanpub empowers authors and publishers with the Lean Publishing process. Lean Publishing is the act of publishing an in-progress ebook using lightweight tools and many iterations to get reader feedback, pivot until you have the right book and build traction once you do.

© 2017 - 2020 ActionableAgile Press, Daniel S. Vacanti

Also By Daniel Vacanti

Actionable Agile Metrics for Predictability

For Sicily. Forever.

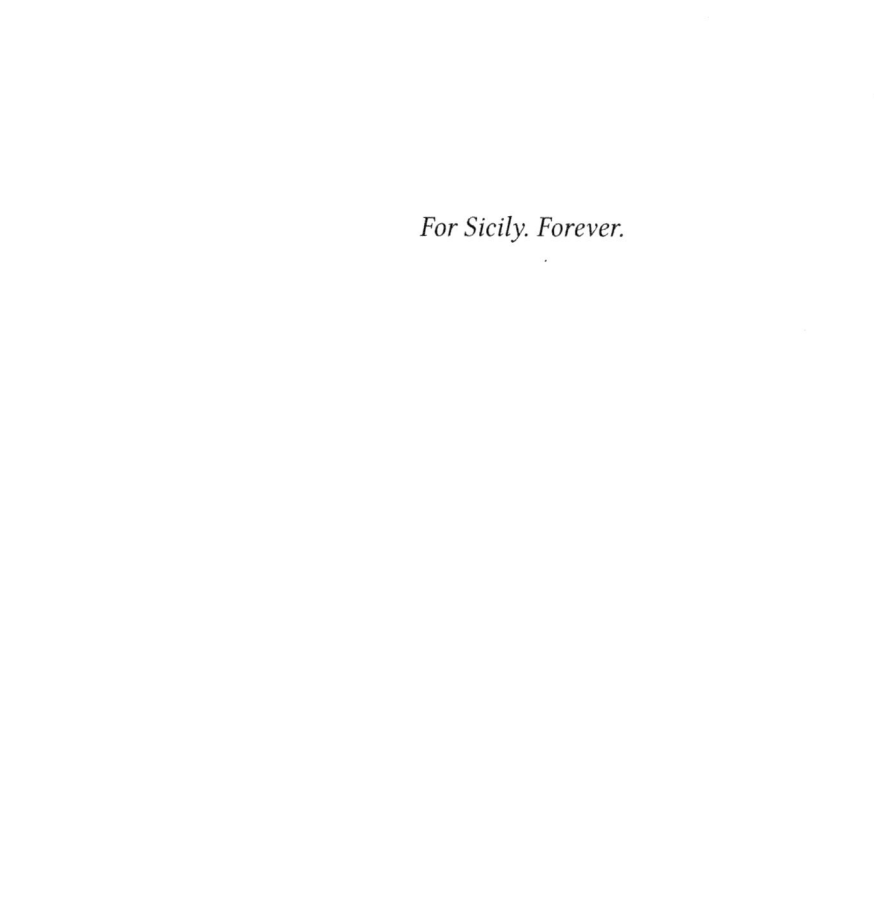

Contents

Preface 1
    Why Write This Book 2
    Assumptions 2
    Who Should Read This Book 3
    Conventions Used 3
    How to Read 3
    ActionableAgile.com 5

Section I: Forecasting 7

Chapter 1: The Basic Principles of Forecasting 9
    Some Basic Principles of Forecasting 18
    The answer to WWIBD is a forecast! 24
    Conclusion 25
    Key Learnings and Takeaways 26

Section II: Forecasts for Single Items 27

Chapter 2: How To Make A Forecast For A Single Item . . 29
    Cycle Time 30
    Cycle Time Scatterplots 36
    Percentiles Are Forecasts! 40
    Conclusion 41

CONTENTS

    Key Learnings and Takeaways 42

Chapter 3: Improving Single Item Forecasts - What To Do 45
    The Most Important Chart That You Have Never Heard
        Of (And How to Use It) 46
    Reforecast When You Get More Information 52
    Flow Efficiency 54
    Internal and External Variability 57
    Another Way To See the Effects of Improved Forecasts . 60
    Conclusion 65
    Key Learnings and Takeaways 65

**Chapter 4: Improving Single Item Forecasts – What Not
To Do** 67
    Never Communicate a Forecast in Terms of an Average 68
    The Most Likely Outcome Is Not Very Likely 69
    Your Data Is Not Normal 71
    Do Not Waste Time Estimating and Planning 74
    Do Not Ignore Pull Policies 79
    Conclusion 85
    Key Learnings and Takeaways 85

Section III: Forecasts for Multiple Items 87

Chapter 5: How To Make A Forecast For Multiple Items . 89
    A Quick Thought Experiment 90
    Probabilistic Thinking Redux 91
    Forecasts for Multiple Items 101
    Conclusion 108
    Key Learnings and Takeaways 109

**Chapter 6: How To Improve Forecasts For Multiple Items
– What To Do** 111
    Consistent Throughput 111

Reforecast Based on New Information 119
Consider Different Selection Techniques for Inputs . . . 122
Pay Attention to Your Model's Assumptions 124
Conclusion 125
Key Learning and Takeaways 125

Chapter 7: How to Improve Forecasts for Multiple Items – What Not to Do 127
Do Not Use Averages 129
Do Not Use Little's Law for Forecasting 132
Do Not Estimate 133
Forget Curve Fitting 134
Conclusion 137
Key Learnings and Takeaways 137

Section IV: How To Know If You Can Trust Your Forecasts 139

Chapter 8: Process Stability As Defined by Little's Law . . 141
A Little's Law Refresher 142
We Need a Little Help 143
Conclusion 158
Key Learnings and Takeaways 159

Chapter 9: How to Visualize System Stability 161
What makes a CFD a CFD? 161
Constructing a CFD 169
Work In Progress 172
Approximate Average Cycle Time 173
Average Throughput 178
Conclusion 181
Key Learnings and Takeaways 184

Chapter 10 - Improving System Stability 187
Matching Arrivals to Departures 187

One Way or Another, Finish All Work That is Started . . 194
Do Not Let Items Age Unnecessarily 196
Key Learnings and Takeaways 204

Section V: Putting It All Together 205

Chapter 11: How to Get Started 207
   A Recipe for Getting Started 207
   Some Other Things to Consider When Getting Started . 213
   Conclusion 218
   Key Learnings And Takeaways 218

Chapter 12: Putting It All Together 219
   Standups for Predictability 219
   Retrospectives for Predictability 220
   How to Do Release Planning 221
   Some Other Ideas 223
   Segmenting WIP 223
   Other Forecasting Techniques 224
   But What If I Don't Care About Predictability? 225
   Key Learnings and Takeaways 225

Section VI: Case Studies 227

Chapter 13: Case Study - Ultimate Software 229
   Ultimate Software 229
   Starting With Scrum 230
   Problems With Scrum Adoption 232
   Progression to Kanban 234
   Results with Kanban 235
   Organization Wide Impact 243
   Probabilistic Release Planning (Monte Carlo) 244
   Release Tracking 246
   Daily Product Review 248

    Feature Visualization 251
    Next Steps 254
    Moving Beyond Development 255
    Key Learnings And Takeaways 257

Chapter 14: Case Study - Linear Projections vs Monte Carlo Simulation **259**
    The Setup 259
    The Analysis 261
    Conclusion 264
    Key Learnings And Takeaways 265

Chapter 15: Case Study - Siemens HS **267**
    Introduction 267
    History 268
    Actionable Metrics 272
    How Metrics Changed Everything 281
    Conclusion 286
    Key Learnings and Takeaways 287

Acknowledgments **289**

About the Author **291**

Bibliography 293

Preface

They are the five words that product development teams hate to hear most: "When will it be done?" To answer that accurately requires an ability to predict the future, and most people—myself included—are not renowned for their prognostication skills. Product development teams are particularly infamous for their inability to make reliable forecasts. It is a little-known fact that all software engineers carry a gene that make them wholly inept at predicting the future. That's right: they are genetically predisposed to be absolutely crap at estimating when things will be done. As they cannot rely on their own innate abilities to make accurate forecasts, software teams have been taught to use other proxy methodologies as a "good enough" first approximation.

The problem is that most of these estimation hacks have not served us well. In fact, they have performed the dual role of not only making our processes less predictable, but also causing no end of confusion for our customers (honestly, what is a "Story Point", really?).

The great downfall of most current Agile forecasting practices is that they are rooted in 20th century thinking. It is not that that thinking was wrong per se, but rather that our current modes of working need to be updated to reflect the contemporary aspects of the environment we live in. That is to say, if we are going to continue to improve, we need a new forecasting paradigm that will work well into the 21st century.

To that end, there are several innovative techniques available that will enable us to make more accurate forecasts. This book is not intended to be authoritative on any of these topics; rather, it is here to give you a no-nonsense introduction and enough information to get you started. It is roadmap for better process performance and efficiency. But, mostly, this book is a call to action. We need a scientific revolution in Agile forecasting, and it starts here now.

Why Write This Book

Admittedly, my previous book "Actionable Agile Metrics for Predictability" reads more like a textbook rather than as an approachable guide to forecasting. Believe it or not, that tone was actually on purpose as one of my main goals in writing it was to correct much of the erroneous literature that had been previously published on flow metrics and their associated analytics. As such, that book did a pretty good job of explaining *why*–if built properly–flow analytics can be used as actionable evidence for better process predictability. Unfortunately, however, that book did not do such a good job of explaining *how* those flow analytics are actionable. This book is an attempt to remedy some of that.

Additionally, Chapters 14 and 15 of my previous book introduced some concepts of forecasting but those chapters were in many ways unfinished or incomplete thoughts on the subject. This book will do a much deeper dive into forecasting and will show how flow analytics can be not only used for better predictability but for better overall process efficiency as well.

Assumptions

For this book, I am going to assume you are familiar with the concepts of my previous book, "Actionable Agile Metrics for Predictability" (AAMFP). Specifically, I am going to assume that you have a well-defined process with well-defined boundaries. I am going to assume that you have a basic understanding of flow and the metrics of flow. And I am going to assume you have some familiarity with flow-based analytics.

There are some parts of AAMFP that are repeated here, and I will call those repeat sections out as necessary, but AAMFP remains the authority on the topics it covers.

Who Should Read This Book

Anyone who has ever been asked to give an estimate or otherwise make a time-sensitive forecast should read this book. Likewise, anyone who has ever asked for an estimate should read this book.

Analysts, developers and testers need to know how to stop giving estimates and how to start making accurate predictions.

Product owners, project managers, and executives need to know what makes for a meaningful prediction and how to hold teams accountable to make those predictions.

Conventions Used

All metrics and analytics will be capitalized. For example: Work In Progress, Cycle Time, Throughput, Cumulative Flow Diagram, Scatterplot, etc. I am also going to capitalize all methodology names: Agile, Scrum, Kanban, etc.

I am also generally going to use the words "process" and "system" interchangeably. I will try to make the distinction clear when a distinction is necessary.

How to Read

This book is intended to be read in order as the concepts in later chapters are built on the concepts developed in earlier ones. However, each chapter can stand alone, and, where possible, when I re-examine a concept that has already been explained, I will try to reference the part of the book that contains the more detailed explanation. As mentioned above, there is some repeat of information that I have already published in my previous book. Again, where possible, I will callout repeat information so that those of you who are already familiar with the material in AAMFP can safely skip those repeated sections without loss of overall continuity (although, it would not hurt you to reread that information!).

Section I – When Will It Be Done?

Chapter 1 covers the basics of forecasting including its fundamental definition and what goes into making a forecast.

Section II – Forecasts for Single Items

Chapter 2 is an introduction to how to make forecasts for single items. This approach might be very different to what you have been introduced to before.

Chapter 3 gives you tips on what to do in order to improve the forecasts for single items.

Chapter 4 gives you tips on what not to do in order to improve the forecasts for single items.

Section III – Forecasts for Multiple Items

Chapter 5 an introduction to how to make forecasts for multiple items. Monte Carlo Simulation is discussed in-depth.

Chapter 6 gives you tips on what to do in order to improve the forecasts for multiple items.

Chapter 7 gives you tips on what not to do in order to improve the forecasts for multiple items.

Section IV – How to Know If You Can Trust Your Forecasts

Chapter 8 defines system stability in terms of Little's Law. If you want to make accurate forecasts, you have to understand why Little's Law works. Period.

Chapter 9 introduces Cumulative Flow Diagrams and how to use them to visualize system stability.

Chapter 10 discusses how to use the assumptions behind Little's Law as an aid to improve overall process stability

Section V – Putting It All Together

Chapter 11 gives you some tips on how to put all of these ideas together in terms of actions you can take every day to improve the accuracy of your forecasts.

Chapter 12 gives you tips on how to roll this out and get started making your first probabilistic forecasts.

Section VI – Case Studies

Chapter 13 is a cases study in process improvement at Ultimate Software–the world's leading company in the Human Capital Management space and one of the most progressive and innovative Agile adopters out there.

Chapter 14 is a brief case study using real data in the difference between Linear Projections and Monte Carlo Simulation.

Chapter 15 re-examines a previously published case study from Siemens Health Services. This case study has been updated with an emphasis on how Siemens put into practice all of the principles in this book. It has been republished here for completeness for those who have not read my first book.

I believe the concepts presented throughout are relevant regardless of your chosen Agile implementation. Where applicable, I will try to point out how actions might differ based on a specific Agile methodology.

Additionally, this book has a distinct software development bent to it, but you need not be in the software product development industry nor do you need to be familiar with any Agile methodology to understand these principles. They can be equally applied to any process regardless of domain.

ActionableAgile.com

Finally, and unless otherwise noted, all of the images of the analytics charts and graphs that are presented in this book were built using the ActionableAgileTM Analytics tool. In the interest of a full disclaimer, this analytics tool is one that my company has developed and can be found at:

https://www.actionableagile.com

You can find a fully functional free demo of the tool as well as sign up for a free trial of the software for use with your own process data at that website. Accompanying blog posts, book updates and errata, videos, etc. can also be found there.

Happy Forecasting!

Section I: Forecasting

Chapter 1: The Basic Principles of Forecasting

The mid-Atlantic Ocean—especially between the Equator and the Tropic of Cancer—is renowned for its severe weather activity. Any storm that forms in this area is given the official title of "tropical wave". After formation, a tropical wave will typically track to the west and north in accordance with the prevailing winds in this part of the world. Tropical waves that form between June 1 and November 1 and that follow a typical track usually find favorable conditions to grow into much larger storms. You know these storms by their much more familiar name: hurricanes.

Unfortunately for the United States, its geography lends itself to being regularly hit by hurricanes. The U.S., therefore, has a vested interest in determining as early as possible when a tropical wave has formed, and once one has formed, immediately attempting to predict if:

(a) the newly formed storm is on track for a direct hit of the U.S.; and, if so,

(b) the tropical wave will mature into a much larger storm or hurricane.

As such, the U.S. has created an organization called the National Oceanographic and Atmospheric Administration (NOAA). Within NOAA, there is another organization called the National Hurricane Center (NHC) that is responsible for identifying, tracking, and forecasting the paths of any and all tropical waves.

On October 22, 2012 NHC began tracking one such storm. This particular tropical wave had formed just south of Jamaica and at the time seemed to be of no immediate interest. After a mere six hours of existence, however, this tropical wave had quickly grown into a tropical storm (a tropical storm is one "level" below hurricane) and only two days after that, it had matured into a hurricane. Within a week, this once insignificant weather system had grown into the largest Atlantic hurricane ever recorded. Its name was Hurricane Sandy.

The numbers behind Hurricane Sandy were (are) astounding. It was:

- the largest Atlantic hurricane in history—as measured by diameter—with storm-strength winds spanning 1,100 miles (1,800 km);
- estimated to have caused about $75 billion (2012 USD) in damages—making it the second-costliest hurricane in United States history (second only to Hurricane Katrina);
- massive in scope, impacting 24 U.S. states and the District of Columbia.

No one living in the U.S. would have guessed any or all of these outcomes when Sandy first formed as a minor storm in late October 2012. In fact, when Sandy was first upgraded to a tropical storm, it was not even projected to hit the U.S. at all. That first day of Sandy's existence, NOAA put out an initial forecasted storm track as shown in Figure 2.1:

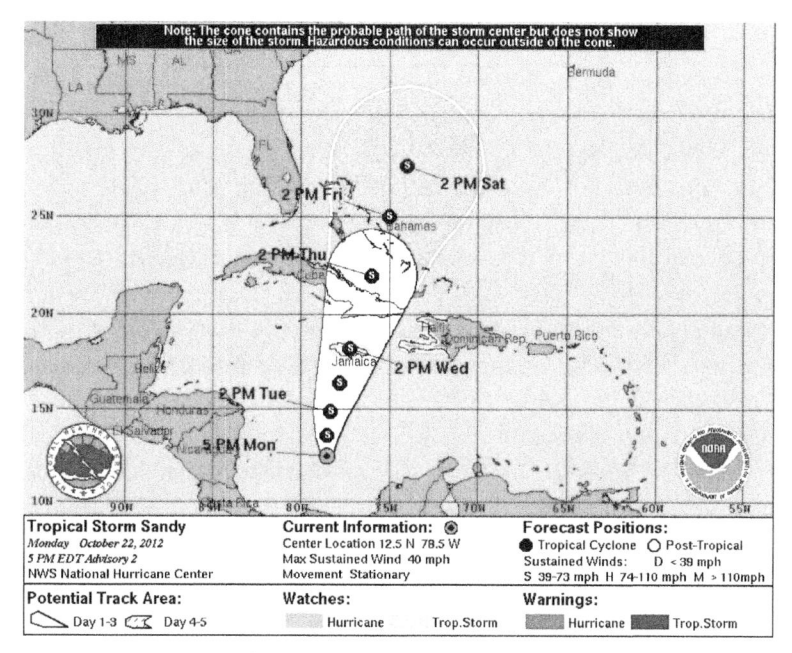

Figure 1.1 – Tropical Storm Sandy Forecasted Path on October 22, 2012

If you have ever come across a hurricane forecast before (you people in South Florida know what I am talking about) then you have probably seen a picture much like Figure 1.1. At first glance, Figure 1.1 makes it look like Tropical Storm Sandy is going to track straight through the Greater Antilles and then head out into the Northern Atlantic—thus missing the U.S. entirely. In fact, if you were someone living in New Jersey or Pennsylvania, then after looking at this picture you probably would not have even given this storm a second thought (we will come back to the great states of New Jersey and Pennsylvania in a minute).

The overall track notwithstanding, let's examine just exactly what Figure 1.1 is telling us. First and foremost, take a look at the "cone" (the white shaded area and extended white dashed area) that is labeled as the "Potential Track Area". Most people assume this cone represents the size of the storm as it progresses. That is absolutely not true—as is stated by the text in the black box at the top of the picture which reads, "Note: The cone contains the probable path of the storm center but does not show the size of the storm. Hazardous conditions can occur outside of the cone." The website of the National Hurricane Center (the department within NHC specifically designated to track hurricanes) further describes the cone this way: "the entire track of the center of the tropical storm can be expected to remain within the cone roughly 60-70% of the time." To be clear, what the National Hurricane Center (NHC) is telling us is that the cone does not represent the areas that will be impacted by the storm but rather it represents *the possible range of paths that the center of the storm *could take**. In fact, the NHC makes it very clear that the impact of any particular forecasted storm could be—and usually is—felt far in excess of the boundaries outlined by the projected cone.

For example, if the center of the storm tracked on the far western edge of the cone shown in Figure 1.1 (or even outside of that edge as that is a distinct possibility) then you would surmise that most of Florida could be impacted. If it tracked on the far eastern side of the cone, then Florida most likely would be spared.

But getting back to the cone description itself, you will notice that the NHC's explanation contains two very important elements. First, it conveys a range; i.e., the area described by the cone. Second, it conveys a probability for that range; i.e., a "roughly 60-70%" chance that the center of the storm will pass through the cone. So why does the NHC publish a forecast that is a range of probabilities and not a single line forecast that represents the exact path that the center of the storm is expected to take?

The answer to that question should be intuitively obvious. Think of all the variables that go into projecting the future path of a hurricane: the speed of the storm itself, surface water temperature, other weather systems in area, prevailing wind direction and speed, etc. Those variables can change over time and can combine in any number of ways to give a multitude of possible outcomes that the actual path of the storm could take. For example, what if the wind direction suddenly changed and caused the storm to track more to the west than to the east? What if the storm moved more slowly than predicted and was able to strengthen more than expected? What if a high pressure system settles in over the southeastern U.S. and pushes the storm harmlessly out to sea?

Those potential outcomes and many more like them are all possible when predicting a future hurricane track. So how does the NHC account for all of these scenarios? More importantly, how do they turn all of those outcomes into a credible forecast? It turns out that they run several different computer simulation models to come up with range of paths that ultimately make up their published forecast. Each successive run of a simulation results in a different predicted path. The multiple possible paths that are produced by these models are shown in Figure 1.2:

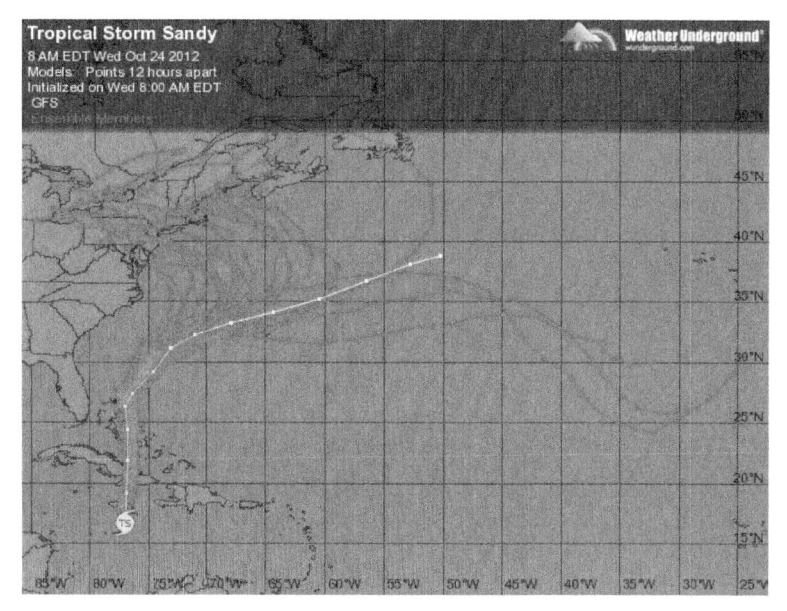

Figure 1.2 – Different Possible Paths of Tropical Storm Sandy on October 24, 2012

Each pink line in Figure 1.2 represents one possible path that the center of Hurricane Sandy could have taken based on the information available to the NHC on October 24th, 2012. In other words, each pink line represents a particular combination of the variables that I mentioned earlier to make up a possible path. Because there are many possible permutations, there are many possible projected paths. The NHC consolidates these possible paths into the projected cone that you see in Figure 1.1. It then publishes that cone as its official forecast.

We have a word that we use to describe any situation like weather forecasting where more than one possible future outcome exists: uncertainty. Most people assume that highly uncertain situations are unpredictable. Not true. In fact, we will explore several situations in this book that are highly uncertain but still very predictable. There is actually a science that deals with uncertainty and that science is called probability (more on this a little later). The forecasters at the NHC understand uncertainty very well which means they also understand what it means to think probabilistically about hurricane forecasting. That is why they put out probability-based projections like the cone depicted in Figure 1.1 instead of, for example, a single line forecast like the white line in Figure 1.2. They understand better than anyone that to publish only one outcome (the single line) when many exist is not only foolhardy but dangerous.

If the first thing you noticed from Figure 1.1 was the cone, then possibly the second thing you noticed was how the cone gets wider over time. At the part of the picture marked "8AM Wed" the cone is much more narrow than at the part of the picture marked "8AM Sun". Any guess as to why that is? Again, the answer is very straightforward. The further out into the future you get, the more uncertainty you are likely to encounter. The more uncertainty that you have, the wider the range of possible outcomes. This should make intuitive sense and should not require much explanation. You have already encountered this phenomenon thousands of times in your life when you looked at any weather forecast. The weather forecast for later today is more likely to be correct than the weather forecast ten days from now. Near term forecasts are almost always more predictable than more distant ones.

Now, let me ask you this: do you think the forecasters at the NHC put out that initial forecast on Monday, October 22nd and then closed up shop saying, "That's the path. Our job is done."? Of course, not. Rather, the very next day (October 23rd) they put out another forecast that looked like Figure 1.3:

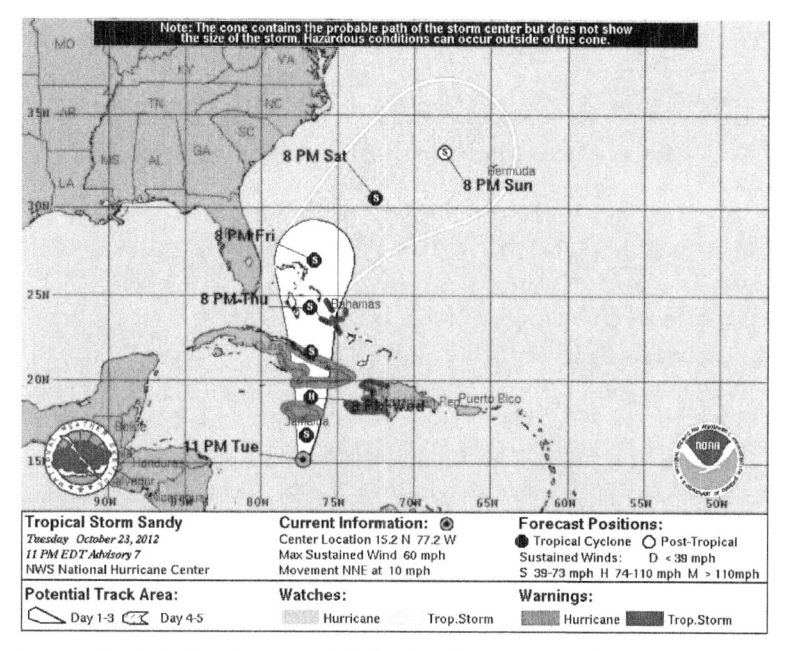

Figure 1.3 – Updated Forecast Path for Tropical Storm Sandy on October 23, 2012

Notice anything different? Let me put the two pictures side by side for you:

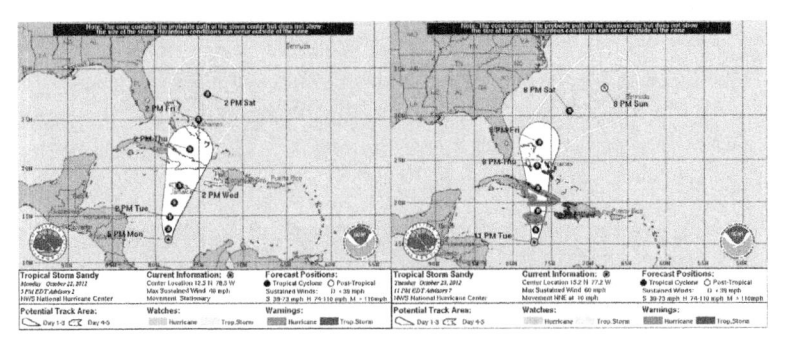

16   Chapter 1: The Basic Principles of Forecasting

Figure 1.4 – Side by Side Comparison of Forecasted Sandy Paths

Now what's different? You can see that in the second forecast (the one on the right in Figure 1.4) that it looks as if the storm is going to shift even further to the east and head out to sea. You might even breathe a huge sigh of relief if you lived in the Carolinas once you saw this updated forecast. But should you? And why did the NHC forecasters alter their forecast? Why wasn't that first one good enough?

I opened this chapter talking about the damage that Hurricane Sandy made landfall in New Jersey, causing massive destruction there. Imagine if the only forecast the NHC put out was Figure 1.3. If you were a government emergency official in either NJ would you have taken any action? If you were an emergency official of any state on the eastern seaboard would you have taken any action? Would you have even paid attention to the storm? Probably not. Worse, what if the original path had shown a direct hit to Florida or the Carolinas? Based on that information lots of time, money, and energy would have been spent on hurricane preparedness in those states, unnecessarily disrupting lives and business. You would have a situation then where mitigation plans were put into effect in one area of the country at great cost and no benefit and no mitigation plans would have been put in place where they were truly needed (again, at great cost).

This point is best illustrated by the forecast for Sandy that the NHC put out on October 25th (which was only a day after the forecast in Figure 1.3 that showed Sandy heading out to sea):

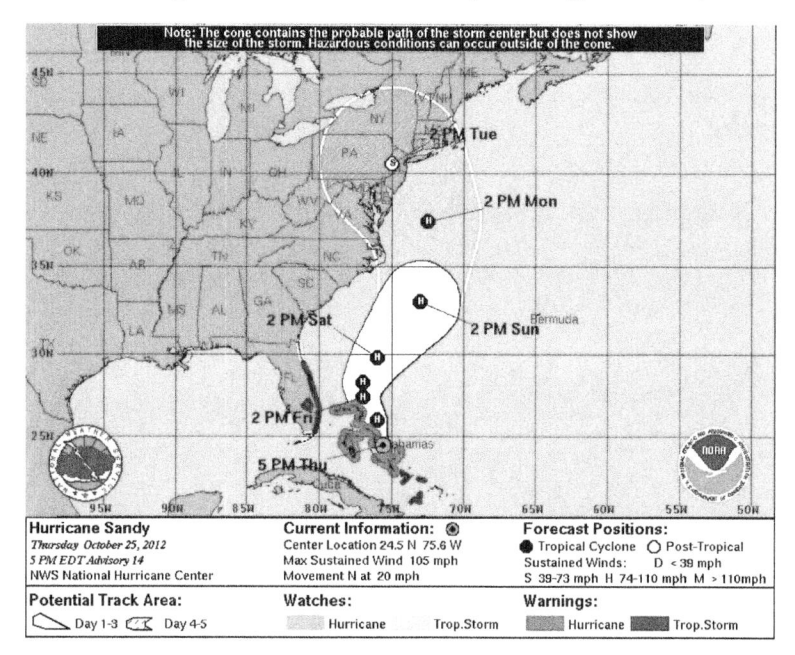

Figure 1.5 – Hurricane Sandy Projected Path on October 25, 2012

Now what do you see? If you live in New Jersey or Pennsylvania you are probably very nervous now. In the particular case of Sandy, it got worse. As the hurricane approached the waters off the coast of New Jersey, it merged with a fast southeastward-moving cold air mass, which ultimately drew Sandy westward over land. The storm's westward shift coincided with a full moon that made tides 20% higher than they normally would have been. All of these factors combined to allow Hurricane Sandy to produce waves as high as 29 feet (9 meters) and a storm surge of 6 feet (2 meters). As you can imagine coastal flooding was horrendous.

That combination with a cold air mass also caused Sandy to morph into what was later called a "Superstorm". It was this combination that turned Sandy into the largest hurricane (by diameter) ever recorded to hit the U.S. Again, would you have guessed any of this by just looking at the forecasts shown in Figure 1.1?

By the way, as all of this was happening, the NHC continued to publish updated forecasts for Sandy. It is their policy to produce updated forecasts every 8 hours at a minimum while they are tracking an active storm. Some of those updated forecasts are shown in Figure 1.6:

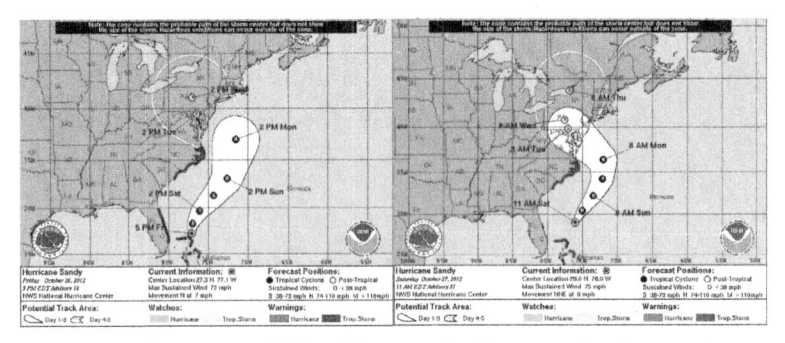

Figure 1.6 – Updated forecasts for Hurricane Sandy

You can see how quickly these forecasts converged on the actual path as the NHC got more and more data. It was the accuracy of these forecasts that prevented the extreme loss of life that would have otherwise been associated with the largest hurricane in history.

Some Basic Principles of Forecasting

How does all of this apply to us? What can we learn from the NHC about how to make accurate forecasts? As you have probably already guessed, the key to making a credible forecast is to copy all the practices that the NHC employs when making theirs:

1. Think probabilistically and not deterministically
2. Make short and long term forecasts with the understanding that shorter forecasts will be more accurate than longer ones
3. Reforecast when you get more information

Let's explore each of these in more detail as they pertain to our world.

Think probabilistically and not deterministically

This is probably the most important point and one that I will stress for the rest of this book. Forecasts are all about describing the future. The future, however, is full of uncertainty. Uncertainty manifests itself as a multitude of possible outcomes for a given future event. As I mentioned earlier, the good news is that we have a branch of science that deals specifically with uncertainty (situations where multiple possible future outcomes exist). That science is called probability. Whenever many possible outcomes are involved, one must take a probabilistic approach—as opposed to a deterministic one. To me, the essence of probabilistic thinking can be summed up in one, concise statement:

"To think probabilistically means to acknowledge that there is more than one possible future outcome."

A simple way to explain this type of thinking is to consider rolling two fair, six-sided dice. It is impossible to predict with 100% certainty the outcome of any given roll before the dice have been cast. That does not mean, however, that results of rolling two dice are completely unpredictable. Actually, there are several things that we can say with complete certainty about each throw:

- There is a 0% chance of rolling 1 or 13
- The possible outcomes are any whole number between 2 and 12 (inclusive)
- The most likely outcome of any given roll is 7
- There is a specific probability associated with rolling exactly 7. In fact, the chance of getting exactly 7 is...do you know the chance of this happening? For those of you who want to read ahead, the answer is in Chapter 4

Acknowledging that the future must be described in terms much like these is precisely what we are going to need to do in order to provide more practical forecasts.

From my previous book (AAMFP), we know the necessary elements of a valid forecast:

> A forecast is a calculation about the future that includes both a range and a probability of that range occurring.

You will note from the Hurricane Sandy story that the NHC faithfully adheres to this definition for its forecasts. Recall that the cone on the projected path is defined as the area that "the entire track of the center of the tropical storm can be expected to remain within roughly 60-70% of the time." That definition gives a range (the cone) and a probability (60-70%). The NHC does not guarantee that the center will remain within that projected area. Nor does it give an exact, single path that the storm will take either inside or outside of that area. Rather, it acknowledges that due to a multitude of variables there are many possible tracks that the storm could take. Thus, they describe their forecast probabilistically. Not only is this the practical way to communicate a forecast, it is the responsible one.

This concept can be very uncomfortable to people who are used to being given deterministic forecasts. By a "deterministic forecast", I mean a single-valued forecast where 100% certainty is assumed. "The project will be done on June 1st" is a classic example of one such forecast. It is going to be hard for those people to give up determinism even though those types of forecasts are almost always wrong. We must be forever vigilant and remember that forecasting is not a deterministic trade. Whenever you see a forecast in terms of a single number or a single result you can almost guarantee that the forecaster has taken a deterministic approach. In Chapter 3 and Chapter 6 I will show you two approaches that you can use to figure out all the possible outcomes of your individual work item or project. Just like the NHC, after reading those chapters you will have all the tools you need to not only make a practical forecast but also a responsible one.

By the way, the problem of deterministic forecasting is further compounded by the fact that the single, deterministic result is usually represented by an average. Forecasting is based on averages is a very dangerous trade because it puts us squarely in the realm of the "Flaw of Averages". Simply put, the Flaw of Averages can be stated as "plans based on average fail on average". I will discuss the Flaw of Averages in much more detail in Chapter 3.

Above all else, the ability to think probabilistically is going to be what is required to make accurate forecasts. As I stated when I opened this section, the entirety of the rest of this book is built upon this assumption.

Shorter timeframe predictions are better than longer term ones

Working with a client recently, I was asked to employ the techniques outlined in this book to come up with a three-year plan. Specifically, they wanted to know how many User Stories they would get finished in the next three years. The thinking was this number would help them to come up with a hiring plan and product roadmap. Now there is nothing inherently wrong with asking for a three-year plan and there is nothing inherently wrong with putting one together (assuming, of course, that it does not take you four years to come up with the three-year plan). However, you must understand going in that the shelf life of that three-year plan is about three minutes. I exaggerate, of course, but think about all of the assumptions that would go into making that three-year plan: rates of hiring, rates of attrition, productivity increases (or decreases), changes in the business environment, changes in priorities, etc. The chances of all of those initial assumptions staying exactly true over the next three years is minuscule. [As an aside, it is this exact phenomenon why practitioners of flow focus so much on reducing the time it takes to deliver customer value. The shorter the delivery timeframe, the higher the chance that our notion of value matches the customer's perception of value. The shorter the delivery timeframe as well, the smaller chance of an item being delayed by some unforeseen circumstance. Delay begets delay.]

This is why it is so important to keep the timeframe of your forecasts as short as possible. The longer the timeframe, the more uncertainty you will encounter. As I just pointed out above, more uncertainty manifests itself as more possible future outcomes. More possible outcomes ultimately could mean that you have to give a range of probability that is so wide as to be impractical or unusable.

Furthermore, as the future becomes reality, we gain information. That information will either validate or invalidate assumptions that put into our forecast model. Either way, the fact that we now have new information necessitates that we incorporate that new information into a new forecast. Which is a nice segue into the next important aspect of forecasting.

Reforecast when you get more information

I did not specifically call this out above, but the NHC actually states on its website that any forecast they give is only valid until they put out their next forecast. This is yet another aspect to probabilistic forecasting the NHC understands very well: it is almost always necessary to update a forecast whenever new information is obtained. How many times have you set a plan at the beginning of a Project, Release, or Sprint and then never altered that plan even when new information was gained? "We made our plan and no matter what happens we are going to stick to the plan!" There are few things in traditional project management that are more ridiculous to me than this type of thinking.

It is easy to see why this type of thinking is dangerous. Let's look at the early days of Hurricane Sandy again (this is the same picture as was shown in Figure 1.3) as compared to the final full path of the storm:

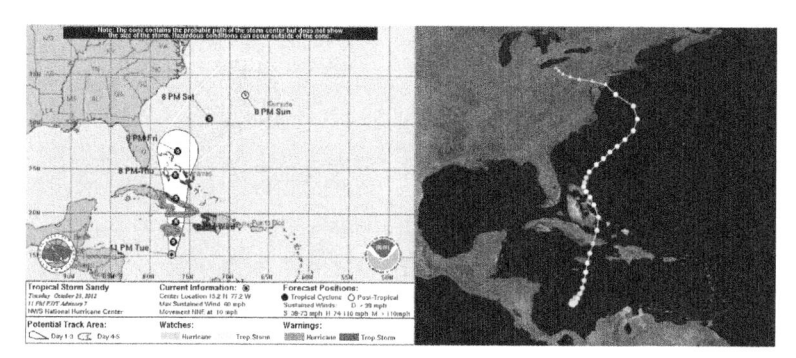

Figure 1.7 – An Early Forecast of Hurricane Sandy Versus the Actual Path It Took

Comparing the picture on the left side of Figure 1.7 (the initial forecast) to the picture on the right side (the actual path) we can see that the initial forecast did not have the storm moving as far to the east as it did when it got close to Florida. The initial forecast also had the storm moving much further out to sea. But you can also see that the early forecast got the path for the first few days almost exactly right. The storm headed straight through Jamaica and straight through the eastern side of Cuba—almost exactly as forecast by the NHC.

These failings of the early forecasts are mitigated by the fact the NHC put out new forecasts at a minimum of every 8 hours and that those new forecasts overrode the predictions made by previous ones. Take a look at a sample of some of the updated forecasts again as compared to the ultimate final path:

Figure 1.8 – Various Hurricane Sandy Forecasts as Compared to the Final Path

In each case of Figure 1.8, you can see how the updated forecast was correct for a day or two out but less so further out. However, each new forecast brought their prediction closer in line with the ultimate path of the storm.

As you will learn in Chapter 3 and Chapter 6, re-forecasting in the face of new information is paramount to making accurate predictions. The earliest forecasts that we make are usually based on the most imperfect or most incomplete data. As a Project or Feature or User Story progresses, new information is gained. That new information could take the shape of better data about duration, team productivity, dependencies, technology short comings, etc. This new information should not be looked at as a hindrance or a bother but as a distinct benefit. This new data is going to help us get closer to our goal of a more accurate forecast. Not reforecasting in the face of gathered data is not only incorrect, it is reckless. In order to make correct predictions, you are going to want to take advantage of any and all relevant information available to you—regardless of when that information was received.

Ultimately, when you get really good at this—and if you have the right tooling—you will be able to do continuous forecasting. Chapter 13 outlines a case study where a client of mine who did just that.

The answer to WWIBD is a forecast!

I mentioned in the Preface that the most important question that our customers will ask us is "When Will It Be Done?". It should be obvious to you now that answering that question will require you to make a forecast. The forecast you must make is fraught with all of the same problems as forecasting hurricanes. Thus, it will require a similar approach. Even so, it is quite probable that the type of forecasting that you are going to do will not be a matter of life or death. Nevertheless, my hope is this chapter has changed the way you think about how you might go about producing an accurate forecast. In the chapters to come, we will get into the specifics of how to apply the principles presented here to make daily predictions.

Conclusion

No one—and I mean no one—could have predicted the size and scale of Hurricane Sandy when it formed as a tropical wave in late October 2012. To you give you a final idea of the magnitude of Hurricane Sandy, consider this excerpt from Wikipedia: "In the United States, Hurricane Sandy affected the entire eastern seaboard of the U.S. from Florida to Maine and west across the Appalachian Mountains to Michigan and Wisconsin, with particularly severe damage in New Jersey and New York. Its storm surge hit New York City on October 29, flooding streets, tunnels and subway lines and cutting power in and around the city. Damage in the United States amounted to $71.4 billion (2013 USD)."

As scary as the storm became, its impact could have been much, much worse. By applying the principles outlined in this chapter, the U.S. National Hurricane Center probably saved lives. At last count, Sandy accounted for 72 deaths in the United States. While tragic, consider that the storm made landfall in the New Jersey/New York/Pennsylvania corridor—one of the most populous areas of the U.S. Without the accurate forecasting made by the NHC, the loss life could have been horrific.

The Two Faces of "When Will It Be Done?"

But before we get to all that, I feel that I must come clean. Up until now I have been misleading you. I have let you believe that there is just one type of the WWIBD question. Strictly speaking, that is not true. What I have failed to mention is that there are actually two flavors of the WWIBD question—the answer to each is going to require its own particular metric and its own particular forecasting method.

The first type of WWIBD calls for a forecast for a single item. For example, "When will User Story X be complete?" "When will Epic Y be complete?" "When will Defect Z be complete?" And so on.

The second type of WWIB is when you are asked to make forecasts for multiple items. For example, "We have 100 items left in our backlog, when will they all be complete?" "How many items can you get finished by date X?" And so on.

We need to begin somewhere, so we will tackle first case first.

Key Learnings and Takeaways

- There are at least three basic principles to remember when making an accurate forecast:
    - Think probabilistically instead of deterministically.
    - Shorter timeframe predictions are generally better than longer term ones.
    - Reforecast as new information is received.
- Thinking probabilistically means acknowledging there is more than one possible future outcome.
- Shorter time frame forecasts mean potentially taking lots of uncertainty out of play.
- A reforecast is probably in order when new information arrives that either validates or invalidates initial assumptions in place when the original forecast was made.
- New information should be viewed as a benefit and not a detriment.
- All forecasts should include a range, a probability for that range, and time to live for the forecast.

Section II: Forecasts for Single Items

Chapter 2: How To Make A Forecast For A Single Item

> **Please Note**: before proceeding, it would be helpful if you could review the definitions of the basic metrics of flow from my previous book, "Actionable Agile Metrics for Predictability" (AAMFP)—specifically, Chapter 2. For your convenience, I will restate some of those definitions as I work my way through the rest of this text; however, I will assume that you have at least a passing familiarity with these metrics. Further, there is some repeat of information presented in Chapter 10 of AAMFP.

How long does it take you to get to work in the morning? For those of you who commute to work, this seems like straightforward question. Perhaps you immediately thought of a single value, say, 25 minutes. But upon reflection, does it really take you that long, *every single day*? My guess is your true answer is "it depends".

If you drive to work, what are some factors that affect your drive time? Traffic, road work, accidents, departure time, can all make a difference. If you take the train to work, your travel time might depend on how busy the trains are, whether there is work being conducted on the lines, or an occasional worker strike.

As a thought experiment, suppose we were to begin timing your commute to work every day. If we define the start of your commute as the moment when you step out the door of your home, and we define the end of your commute as the moment you step into the door of your workplace, then we simply need to collect the timestamps at those two points and build a table like the one shown below:

Day	Start Time	End Time
1	07:17	07:43
2	07:35	08:03
3	07:22	07:44
4	07:44	08:58
5	07:12	07:37

Figure 2.1 - Sample Commute Data

Given the example data in Figure 2.1, how long does it take for this person to get to work? Take a moment to come up with your answer. Now that you have it, let me take a guess at how you came up with your answer. Did you take End Time and subtract Start Time to come up with a total elapsed time for each day? For example, on Day 1 did you take 07:43 minus 07:17 to come up with a travel time of 26 minutes? Good. Once you had all of the elapsed times, did you then average them to come up with your daily commute time? Not so good. If you were mathematically savvy, maybe you even calculated the standard deviation or a standard error to come up with a confidence level? That is potentially even less good.

I mentioned previously that reducing a forecast to a single number is questionable, and having that single number take the form of an average usually makes things even worse. I will explain why in more detail a little later, but for now let's get back to the example at hand. The reason I asked you about your commute times is because it so concisely exemplifies all of the aspects of the most fundamental forecast we can make: the forecast for a single item.

Cycle Time

In Chapter 1, I proposed that the first question our customers will ask of us once we start to work on something is "When Will It Be

Done?" I further suggested that they are expecting a very specific form of an answer to that question: a date or number of days (in elapsed time). What follows is probably the most radical idea of this whole book. If our customers care about how long it takes for things to get done, then we should track how long it takes for things to get done! In other words, we need to do for our own process exactly what we did for the commute example. We need to first define what it means to have started (or committed to) work, and we need to define what it means for work to have finished. With those two points defined, we will take a timestamp when work crosses the starting point and we will take another timestamp when work crosses the finish point, just like we did in the commute example.

> For the purposes of work item forecasting, if you track nothing else, track these two things: the timestamp for when work begins on an item and the timestamp for when work finishes on an item.

Start date and end date are the only two pieces of data that you will need to track. Really, that's all you need. All metrics, analytics, and forecasts that I will produce for you for the rest of this book will be based on those two pieces of information only. Of course, you may wish to capture other data for additional analysis, but for basic forecasting all you need is start and end timestamps for each item that you work on. And here is some even better news: whether you know it or not you probably have all of this data available to you already. Certainly, if you use some type of Agile tooling like Jira or Trello, then you can easily go in and mine these timestamps. (You can find more information on tracking and mining data in Chapter 11).

Interestingly, many Agile Methodologies focus solely on the definition of "Done" for work items. The definition of "Start" in these frameworks is for the most part ignored. I want to emphasize that the definition of start in your process is just as important as the definition of done. You cannot measure elapsed time unless you have clear definition of both the start point and the end point.

Once we have those two timestamps we can calculate the duration, which in flow metrics we call Cycle Time:

> **Cycle Time** is the amount of elapsed time that it takes for work to complete.

For example, in your context, your timestamp tracking might look like this:

Work Item ID	Arrived	Departed
1	01/01/2016	01/03/2016
2	02/02/2016	03/03/2016
3	01/02/2016	03/04/2016

Figure 2.2 – Sample Timestamp Data

I hope the non-Americans out there will forgive the use of American-style, month-first dates in Figure 2.2. Turning the data from the above table into Cycle Time is actually very straightforward. The calculation to do that is:

> **Cycle Time = End Time – Start Time + 1**

Applying this calculation to Figure 2.2 give us:

Work Item Id	Arrived	Departed	Cycle Time (days)
1	01/01/2016	01/03/2016	3
2	02/02/2016	03/03/2016	31
3	01/02/2016	03/04/2016	63

Figure 2.3 – Example Cycle Time Data

If you do the above calculations yourselves, you should come up with the same Cycle Time answers that I did. I actually tried to do the math in my head first (never a good idea for me) and got the third answer wrong when I checked myself with excel. I had forgotten that 2016 was a leap year!

By the way, if you are wondering where the "+ 1" comes from in the calculation, it is because we count every day in which the item is worked as part of the total. For example, when an item starts and ends on the same day, we would never say that it took zero time to complete. So we add one, effectively rounding the partial day up to a full day. What about items that don't start and finish on the same day? For example, let's say an item starts on January 1st and finishes on January 2nd. The above Cycle Time definition would give an answer of two days (2 − 1 + 1 = 2). I think this is a reasonable, realistic outcome. Again, from the customers' perspective, if we communicate a Cycle Time of one day, then they could have a realistic expectation that they will receive their item on the same day. If we tell them two days, they have a realistic expectation that they will receive their item on the next day.

You might be concerned that the above Cycle Time calculation is biased toward measuring Cycle Time in terms of days. In reality, you can substitute whatever notion of "time" that is relevant for your context (that is why up until now I have kept saying track a "timestamp" and not a "date"). Maybe weeks is more relevant for your specific situation. Or hours. Or even sprints. For a Scrum team, if you wanted to measure Cycle Time in terms of sprints, then the calculation would just be End Sprint − Start Sprint + 1. The point here is that this calculation applies in all contexts.

Some Other Thoughts On Cycle Time

An even better definition for Cycle Time that I offered in my first book is "the amount of time that an item spends as Work In Progress". This definition will become much more useful when we discuss Little's Law and system stability in Chapter 8.

I should probably add a quick word about nomenclature. You have maybe come across the debate about how certain flow metrics are defined and what they are called. In my opinion, what matters is that you define a specific entry point and exit point for your process, and use a consistent naming

> convention. I will call it Cycle Time.

I have made all of this fuss about Cycle Time because, believe it or not, Cycle Time is the sole metric we need to make forecasts for single items.

> 💬 Cycle Time is the flow metric you use to make forecasts for single items.

How do we make forecasts using Cycle Time? Returning to our commute experiment, once we have collected all of our Cycle Time data, we plot it in a specific type of chart. In this chart, the X-axis is the calendar date, and the Y-axis is Cycle Time. For each commute, on the chart we find the date of the commute on the X-axis, and then we plot a dot on the Y-axis that corresponds to the Cycle Time for that commute. If you do this for several days, you will get a chart that looks something like:

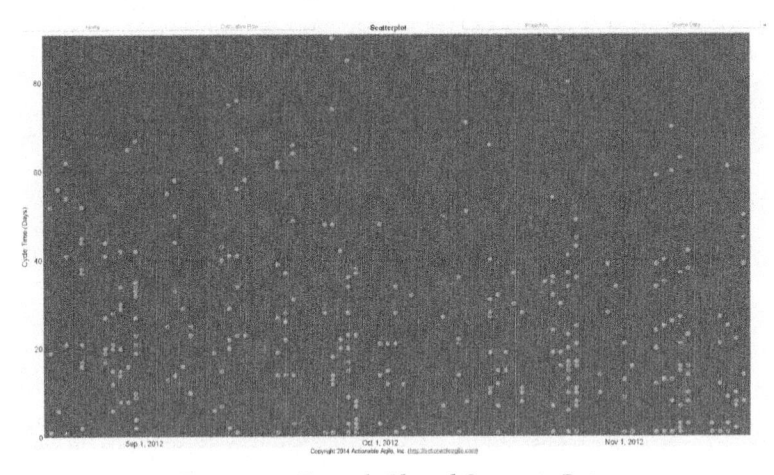

Figure 2.4 – Example Plotted Commute Data

You will note that Figure 2.4 looks like a random collection of dots. Here is the punchline: it is a random collection of dots.

Your commute Cycle Times are the result of a random process; thus, your data will fit many traditional definitions of randomness. When you step out of your door each morning, it is impossible (yes, impossible) for you to know beforehand (deterministically) exactly how long it is going to take you to get to work. If you drive, you do not know exactly how many red lights you will make or miss. You do not know exactly how much traffic will slow you down. You do not know if there will be an accident on the way. You do not even know if your commute will go perfectly smoothly with no interruptions or delays whatsoever. In other words, before you get into your car to drive to work, there are many possible outcomes in terms of how long it will take you. From Chapter 1, we know that whenever we are in a situation with many possible future outcomes, we must take a probabilistic approach to forecasting.

The same is true for your Lean-Agile process. For your own process you must do exactly what you did for the commute experiment. That is, you must calculate a Cycle Time for every item that finishes according to the defined start and end points of your system, and then plot your results on a chart like Figure 2.4. The result will look like Figure 2.5:

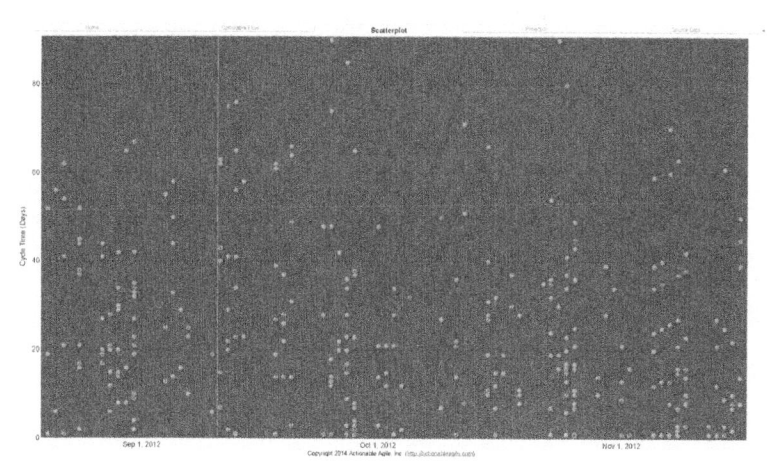

Figure 2.5 – Example Plotted Process Data

Figure 2.4 and Figure 2.5 look very similar, do they not? That is because—just like your commute times—the Cycle Times for your system are the result of a random process. In fact, it may help you to think of your process as a random Cycle Time generator. As was the case in the commute example, when an item is sitting in your backlog, it is impossible for you to know how long it will take to complete once you start to work on it (it is even potentially impossible to know if it will ever be worked on at all!). Once started, an item could at some point be blocked for many reasons—an external dependency, a lack of resources, a technological problem, misunderstood requirements, etc. Or it could sail through your process completely unimpeded and finish in a much shorter time than you were expecting. When that item is sitting in your backlog, it has multiple possible outcomes in terms of how long it would take to complete. Again, this scenario calls for a probabilistic approach.

So how do we take a probabilistic approach with the data shown in Figure 2.5?

Cycle Time Scatterplots

The chart in Figure 2.5 is known as a Cycle Time Scatterplot. In my first book, I go into great detail about what Cycle Time Scatterplots are, how to construct them, and how to interpret them (specifically, AAMFP Chapters 10 and 11). For our purposes here, it is enough to point out that the anatomy of a Cycle Time Scatterplot is calendar time across the X axis and Cycle Time up the Y axis. Each dot on the chart therefore indicates the cycle time and date of an item that has finished. So how do we make sense of all these points?

Percentile Lines on a Scatterplot

The first thing that we can do to gain a better understanding of our process's Cycle Time performance is to draw a percentile line on our Scatterplot. A percentile line is a horizontal line for which that percent of dots fall on or below the line. For example, referring again to the chart shown in Figure 2.5, the 50th percentile line is drawn across the chart at a cycle time such 50% of the dots on the chart fall on or below that line. This calculation is shown in Figure 2.6 below.

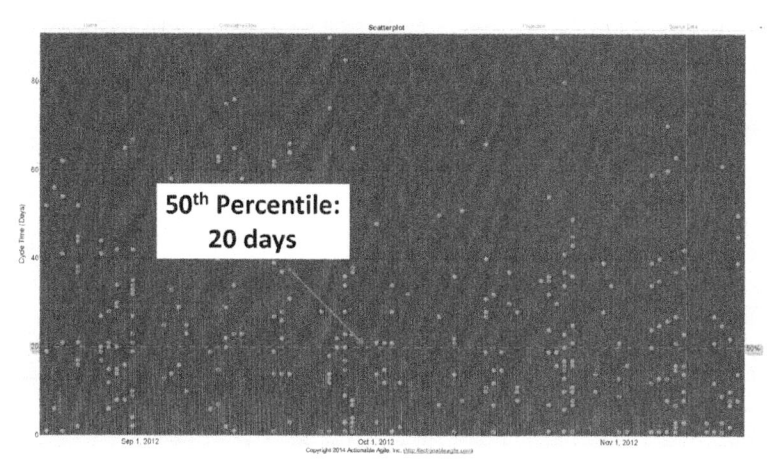

Figure 2.6 - The 50th Percentile Line added to a Scatterplot

In Figure 2.6, the 50th percentile line occurs at twenty days. That means that 50% of the work items that have flowed through our process took twenty days or less to complete. So we can say that when a work item enters our process it has a 50% chance of finishing in twenty days or less. That is without doing any estimation! (More on this concept a little later).

We can use any percentile for our lines. A commonly used percentile is the 85th. Again, this line represents the amount of time it took for 85% of our work items to finish. In Figure 2.7 below you can see that the 85th percentile line occurs at 43 days. That means that 85% of the dots on our chart are on or below that line, and 15% of the dots on our chart are above that line. This percentile line tells us is that when a work item enters our process it has an 85% chance of finishing in 43 days or less, again, with no estimation!.

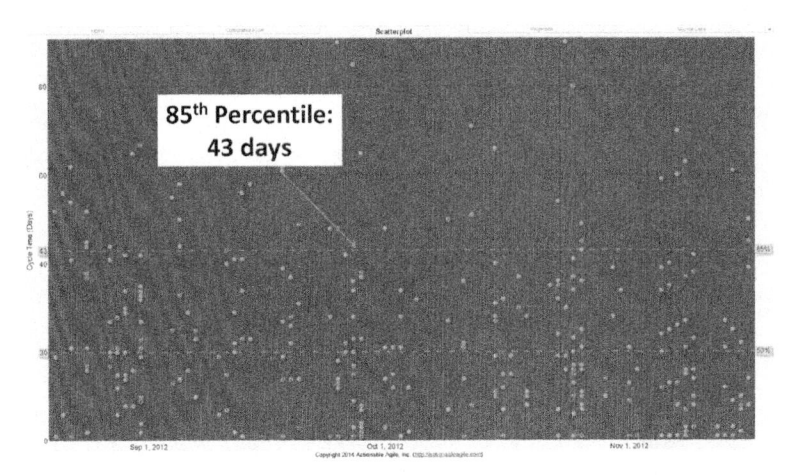

38   Chapter 2: How To Make A Forecast For A Single Item

Figure 2.7 - The 85th Percentile Line Added to a Scatterplot

Another common percentile is the 95th. In Figure 2.8 below the 95th percentile line occurs at 63 days and tells us that our work items have a 95% chance of finishing in 63 days or less.

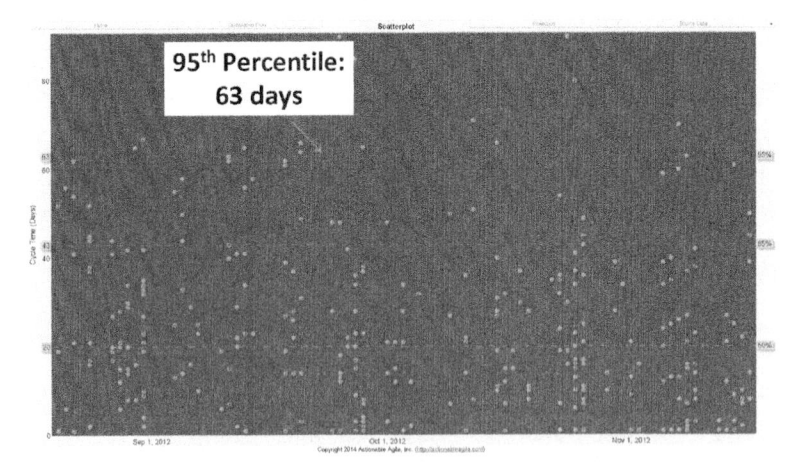

Figure 2.8 - The 95th Percentile Line added to a Scatterplot

The 50th, 85th, and 95th percentiles are probably the most popular "standard" percentiles to draw. You may see other percentiles, though, so I have included Figure 2.9 with two more. Note the 30th percentile is 11 days and the 70th percentile is 32 days:

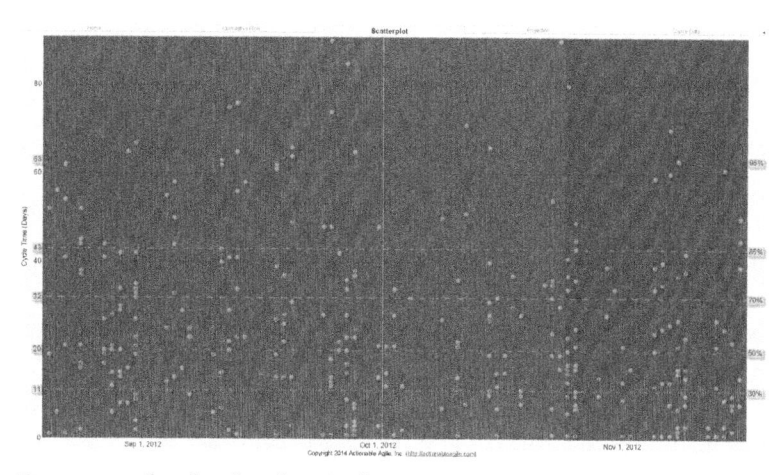

Figure 2.9 -30th, 50th, 70th, 85th, and 95th Percentile Lines all shown on Scatterplot

I am sure you have noticed that as we increase our level of confidence we must increase the amount of time it takes for work items to complete. This is due to the variability (randomness) inherent in our process. No matter how hard we try to drive it out, variability will always be present. Later I will discuss how we want to understand how much of that variability is self-imposed, and how much of that variability is outside of our control, and I will give you ways to identify each of these cases and strategies with which to handle them.

Why Percentiles Are Preferred

There are at least three reasons why I like the percentile line approach to segmenting Scatterplot data. First, notice that when I described how to draw the standard percentile lines on a Scatterplot, I never made one mention of how the underlying Cycle Time data might be distributed. And that is the beauty of it. To draw those lines, I do not need to know how your data is distributed. These percentile line calculations work independent of any underlying distribution.

Second, percentiles are extremely easy to calculate. You simply count up all the dots and multiply by percentages. No advanced degree in statistics is required!

Third, percentiles are not skewed by outliers. One of the great disadvantages of a mean and standard deviation approach (other than the false assumption of normally distributed data) is that both of those statistics are heavily influenced by outliers. You have probably heard the saying, "If Bill Gates walks into a bar, then on average everyone in the bar is a millionaire". Obviously average is no longer a useful statistic in that case. The same type of extreme outlier phenomenon happens in our world. However, when you do get those extreme Cycle Time outliers, your percentile lines will not budge all that much. This robustness in the face of outliers is a strong advantage for percentile lines in Cycle Time analysis.

Percentiles Are Forecasts!

As discussed in Chapter 1, valid forecasts come in the form of a range of outcomes and a probability associated with that range. The percentile lines on our Scatterplot fit that definition exactly! For example, in Figure 2.7 above, let's say our customer requires a forecast confidence of 85%. Therefore, when an item entered our system we would communicate our completion time forecast as "43 days or less, with an 85% confidence". It is really that simple.

A couple of things to note, here, though. First, you have to decide which past data to include. The dirty little secret of all of the probabilistic forecasting methods is that the future that you predict is going to resemble the past that you used to predict it. That means in order to make meaningful forecasts, you are going to have to choose a relevant set of historical data that you think will roughly mirror the future that you are trying to predict. This practice is more art than science. Sometimes you may want to use all past data that you have. Or, you may want to select a relevant subset of data, such as the past six months. In short, there is no right answer here. You will just want to select the past data set that is going to most resemble the future. To accomplish this selection, it is usually easiest to use a flexible tool that will facilitate the easy, immediate selection of different sets of past data to explore what future outcomes those disparate sets predict. That way you can play around with different historical datasets and see the instantaneous impact of the selected past data on your percentiles. What past data to select, and how much data you need, will be covered in a little more detail in Chapter 11.

Second, you have to decide which percentile confidence is appropriate for your context. Again, this is more art than science. The placement of percentile lines helps you understand the timeline risk associated with items that run through your process. Most customers and mangers are very risk averse, so they will immediately jump to removing all risk altogether. "I want 100% confidence!", they will say. This, of course, is not possible. Once they realize 100% is not a possibility, then they will jump to "I want 99% confidence!". Fair enough, but you have to realize there is a trade-off between confidence and range—the two are directly correlated. Higher confidence means a higher range of outcomes that must be included in the forecast. In the percentile example above, a 50% confidence forecast would be 20 days or less while a 95% confidence would be 60 days or less. Consider that for a second. To go from a 50% confidence to a 95% confidence you have to more than triple the associated range of possible outcomes! The question you have to ask yourself, then, is "is the higher confidence worth the bigger range of possible Cycle Times?"

Conclusion

The steps to forecasting WWIBD for a single item are:

1. Build a Cycle Time Scatterplot for completed items (which items you include in your Scatterplot is up to you)
2. Decide how much confidence you need in your forecast
3. Calculate Percentile Lines for your Scatterplot

4. Communicate your forecast in terms of the range and probability of your required confidence.

Cycle Times communicated as percentiles meet the full definition of a forecast. Further, they are short term in nature. That is, a Cycle Time forecast is only valid for a given item once that specific enters your process. The next item that enters your process could have a completely different percentile forecast based on new data. Which brings us to the third point that Cycle Times forecasts should be updated as new information comes along. We will cover that in the next chapter.

Speaking of predictability, earlier I mentioned the need to increase the range of possible outcomes if a higher confidence forecast is required. I even gave a specific example of how moving from a 50% confidence to a 95% confidence would require a more than tripling of the range of possible outcomes. You may be wondering why that is. This extreme increase in range is due to the long tail of your Cycle Time distribution. I said earlier that you do not need to understand the underlying distribution of your Cycle Time to make accurate forecast—and that is true. You may, however, need to understand the shape of your Cycle Time distribution when you want to learn how to improve your forecasts. That is an important topic that we shall cover next.

Key Learnings and Takeaways

- Cycle Time is the amount of elapsed time it takes to complete work.
- Cycle Time is the metric we use to make forecasts for single items.
- A forecast for a single item (a User Story, or an Epic, or a Feature, etc.) is the most fundamental forecast you can make.
- If you track nothing else for forecasting, track the timestamp for when work begins on an item and the timestamp for when work finishes on an item.

- Use a Cycle Time Scatterplot and Percentile Lines to understand forecast risk.
- Communicate a forecast based on those percentile lines.
- The Percentile Lines and the associated ranges and probabilities represent your forecast for a single item moving through your process.

Chapter 3: Improving Single Item Forecasts - What To Do

Disclaimer: There is some repeat of material from my last book in this chapter, but the information presented here is mostly a new take on most of the repeated ideas.

Using a Cycle Time Scatterplot with percentile lines to make forecasts for single items is actually the easy part. The real challenge is the longer-term struggle to make more accurate forecasts. Here is a bit of good news for you: the practices that will improve your predictions will also to improve the health and efficiency of your process overall. That's right, as you follow the steps in this chapter to make your process more predictable, you will get better overall process performance for free. In fact, the argument should be made that what you should really care about is better process performance, because if you focus on that, the forecasting side will take care of itself. Either way, that is the best two-for-one deal that you will see all day.

What do I mean when I say "a more accurate forecast"? It is a reduction of the range of possible outcomes associated with the forecast. Simply put, a more accurate forecast has percentile lines that are closer together, and in most cases, all your percentile lines will move down as well. Instead of "35 days or less at the 85th percentile", a more accurate forecast might be "15 days or less at the 85th percentile", and raising your confidence to 95% will require a smaller increase in your forecast cycle times.

Also, as we are about to see, improving forecasts is going to be a two-sided optimization. You will need to have a good understanding both of what to do and what not to do. In this chapter

I will explore what to do. In the next, what not to do.

The Most Important Chart That You Have Never Heard Of (And How to Use It)

The single most important thing that you can do to improve single item forecasts is be proactive about how long it takes for items to complete.

> The single most important thing that you can do to improve single item forecasts is be proactive about how long it takes for items to complete.

You must monitor an item's progress in real time and take action when an intervention is warranted. However, the analytical chart that I have showed you thus far–the Cycle Time Scatterplot–is completely inept at providing preemptive information. By definition, a dot does not show up on a Scatterplot until an item has finished. However, if you wait until an item has finished to do something about it, it is too late. What we need, therefore, is a view into our process data while items are still in progress. The view we require is something called an Aging Work In Progress chart (or "Aging Chart" for short).

To understand an Aging chart, let's consider a process workflow that looks like this:

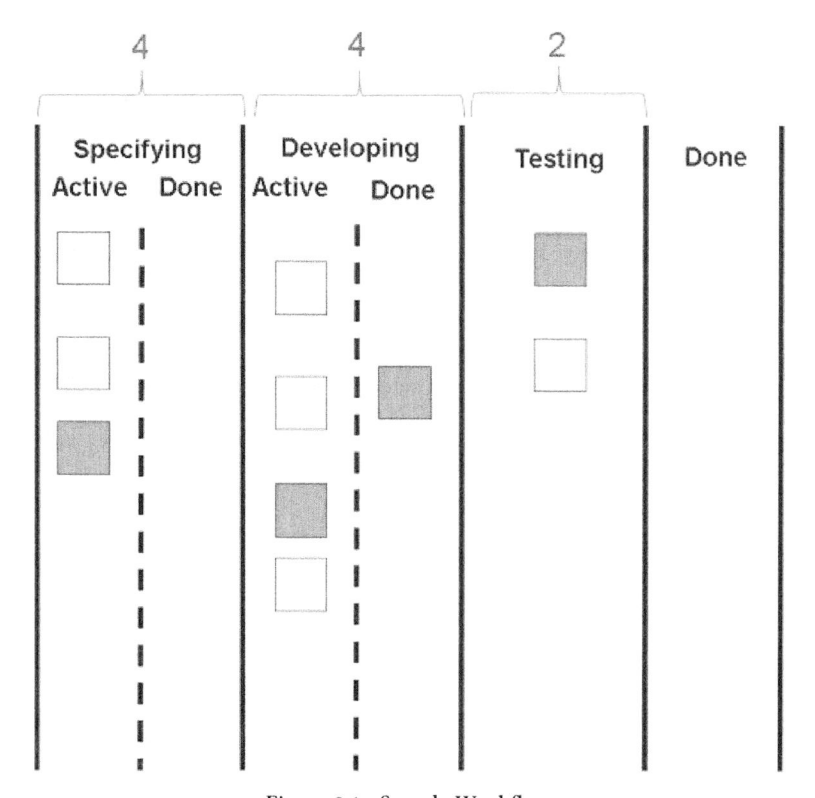

Figure 3.1 - Sample Workflow

An example of an Aging Work In Progress chart for this particular workflow might look like Figure 3.2:

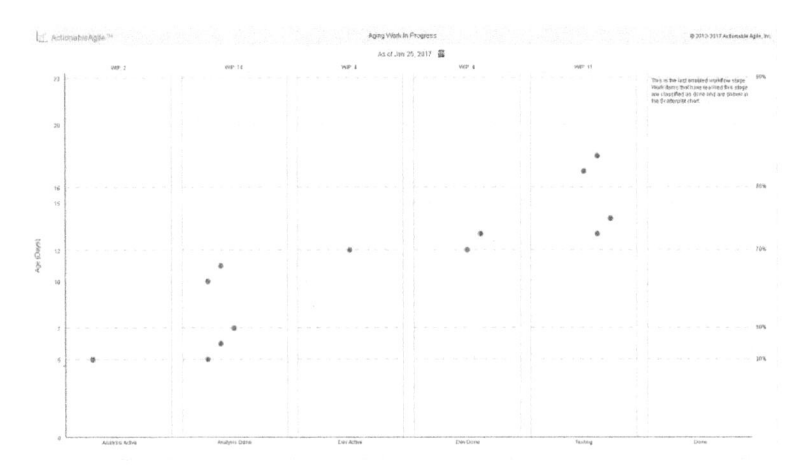

Figure 3.2 - Aging Work In Progress Chart for Sample Workflow

Before I get into how this chart should be used, let me quickly go over the anatomy of the chart so you know what you are looking at. Unlike the Scatterplot, you can see that across the bottom all of the states of your workflow have been mapped out in exactly the same order as their appearance in Figure 3.1. In fact, the whole chart itself has been segmented into columns to match your process's workflow (much like a Kanban board). Up the side of the chart is the Age of work items. Age is defined as the amount of elapsed time that an item has spent inside the workflow.

> Work Item Age is the total amount of time that has elapsed since an item entered a workflow. By definition, Work Item Age applies only to items that have entered but not exited the workflow.

Remember that Age in this context is different from Cycle Time on the Scatterplot. What we are representing on this chart (Figure 3.2) is the total elapsed time that an item has spent started but not completed (Age) as opposed to the total elapsed time it took for an item to complete (Cycle Time). However, just like Cycle Time, for Age you can use whatever time units you want: days, weeks, months, sprints, etc. Thus, every dot on the chart represents an item that has entered the process but has not exited the process. To plot a dot, you simply find the workflow stage that it is currently in and then subtract today's date from the item's start date (remember you should have tracked the timestamp for when the item entered your process!).

You will also see percentile lines on the Aging Chart. These percentile lines are exactly the same lines that we calculated for our Scatterplot. You overlay percentiles lines on the Aging Chart so that you can see how current items in progress are progressing as compared to the total amount of time it took previous items to complete. In other words, as items Age, we gain information about them. Are they taking too long? Are they spending too much time in one column? Have their chances of violating our forecast changed? This new information provides the actionable evidence we need to proactively improve single item forecasts. The percentiles from our Scatterplot work as perfect checkpoints to discuss if intervention is needed.

How does this work? Let's talk about the 50th percentile first. And let's assume for this discussion that our team is using an 85th percentile for its forecast. Once an item remains in progress to a point such that its Age is the same as the 50th percentile line of the Scatterplot, we can say a couple of things. First, we can say that, by definition, this item is now larger than half the work items we have seen before. That might give us reason to pause. What have we found out about this item that might require us to take action on it? Do we need to swarm on it? Do we need to break it up? Do we need to escalate the removal of a blocker? The urgency of these questions is due to the second thing we can say when an item's Age reaches the 50th percentile. When we first pulled the work item into our process it had a 15% chance of violating its forecast (that is the very definition of using the 85th percentile as a forecast). Now that the item has hit the 50th percentile, the chance of it violating its forecast has doubled from 15% to 30%. Even if that does not cause concern, it should at least cause conversation.

When an item has aged to the 70th percentile line, we know it is bigger than more than two-thirds of the other items we have seen before. And now its chance of missing its forecast has jumped to 50%. Flip a coin. The conversations we were having earlier (i.e., when the item hit the 50th percentile line) should now become all the more urgent.

And they should continue to be urgent as that work item's Age gets closer and closer to the 85th percentile. The last thing we want is for that item to violate its forecast—even though we know it is going to happen 15% of the time. We want to make sure that we have done everything we can to prevent a violation occurring. The reason for this is just because an item has breached its forecast does not mean that we all of a sudden take our foot off the gas. We still need to finish that work. Some customer somewhere is waiting for their value to be delivered.

However, once we breach our forecast we are squarely in unpredictable land because now we cannot communicate to our customers when this particular item will complete. For example, take a look at the Figure 3.3 below:

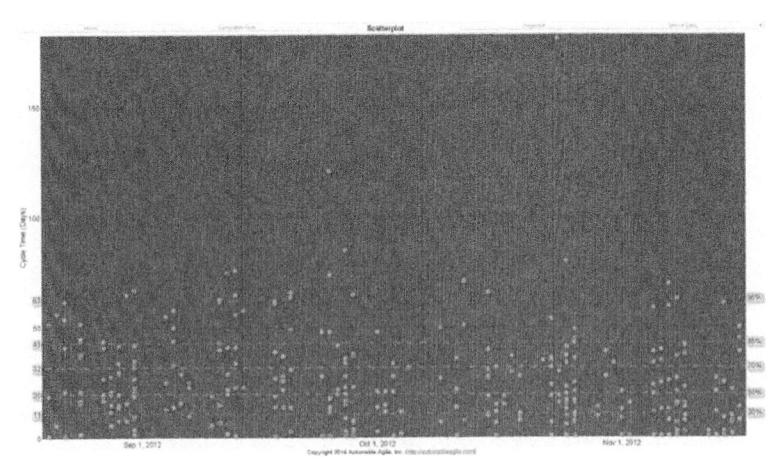

Figure 3.3: The Danger of Breaching our Forecast

You can see in this chart that the 85th percentile is 43 days. But there is an item in late October that took 181 days to finish (do you see that isolated dot right at the top of the chart?). That no man's land between 43 days and 181 days (and potentially beyond) is a scary place to be. We want to do whatever we can not to have items fall in there.

You can see how you can (should) leverage this type of information in your standups. In fact, the two things that I tell my clients to look at during their standups are their board(s) and their Aging Chart(s). Again, how to run a standup is beyond the scope of this book, but just know that—from a forecasting perspective—a team's focus should be on working as a group to complete work and not on examining the productivity of any individual member. The fact that an item as aged to a point that it is in danger of missing its forecast (or, worse, has already violated its forecast) means that the whole team has failed. This problem must be resolved by the whole group and not just by an individual.

Once you start to pay attention to work item age, and more importantly, once you start to take action on the information that aging gives you, then you will inevitably begin to complete items faster. Faster completion times will have the effect of over time lowering the percentiles on your Scatterplot. Lower percentile lines mean that we have smaller ranges of possible outcomes for the same percentile confidence. And that, if you recall, is exactly what we are after.

One last thing: you will note that I have tried very hard not to use the term "Service Level Agreement" (SLA) in this section. I talk a lot about SLAs in the AAMFP book because I do believe they are a very important concept to master in the management of flow (however regrettable the nomenclature). For those of you familiar with SLAs and the use of SLAs to manage flow, you will immediate recognize that an SLA is a forecast. As this is a book about forecasting, I will continue to use the term "forecast" in favour of the term "SLA". Just know that they are essentially the same thing.

Reforecast When You Get More Information

Recall the original forecast that the NHC put out for Hurricane Sandy (Figure 1.1). Based on the information at the time, the forecasters at the NHC thought Sandy would progress through the Caribbean and then drift harmlessly out to sea. In the days after that first forecast was put out, however, wind speeds and directions shifted, new weather systems formed in the storm's path, and, most importantly, the forecasters got to see exactly where and how the hurricane had tracked so far. As was their practice, the NHC compiled all of this new information, used it as inputs into their new models, re-ran their simulations, and published a new forecast. In fact, the NHC publishes a new forecast every 8 hours or so whenever they are tracking an active storm system.

Imagine the NHC had ignored all of this new information. I asked you to consider such a scenario in Chapter 1. Without a new forecast, the states of New York, New Jersey, and Pennsylvania would not have been prepared. Worse, with out a new forecast, there likely would have been an unspeakable increase in the loss of life and property.

In our world, we get new information about how long it takes for our work items to complete every day. Take a look at the Scatterplot in Figure 3.4:

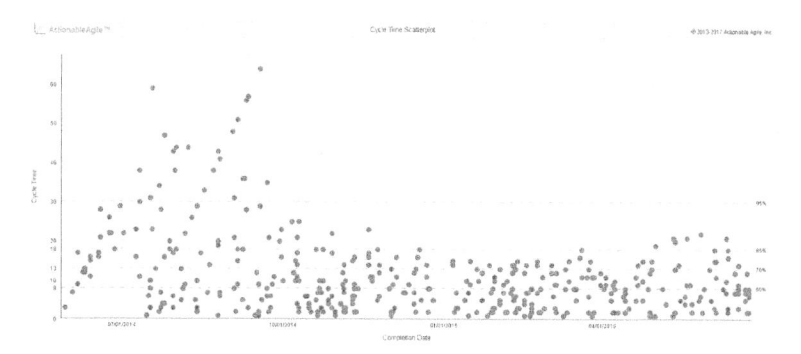

Figure 3.4 - Example Scatterplot

It should be very obvious to you that you something happened to this team around the beginning of October 2014. Imagine the team created initial forecasts based on the first four months of this data–from June to September. Figure 3.5 shows what the percentiles look like for those two months:

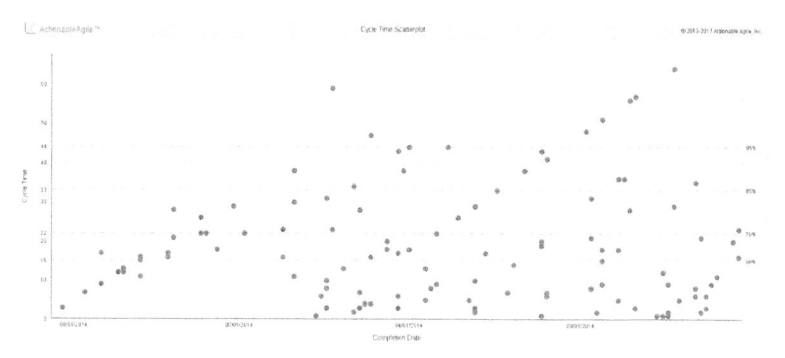

Figure 3.5 - Filtered Scatterplot

If this team wanted predictability with 85% confidence, then based on this data, they would communicate a forecast of "33 days or less 85% of the time". However, if you fast forward to the last three months of data that this team has, their percentiles now look like:

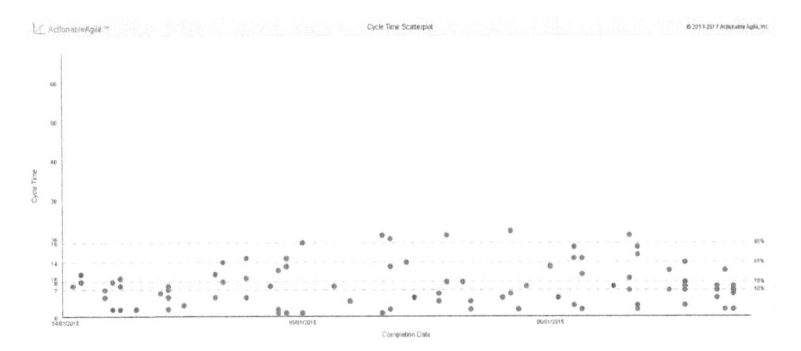

Figure 3.6 - Filtered Scatterplot

Their 85th percentile has now dropped to 14 days or less. By ignoring this new information and sticking with their old data, this team would be missing out on a tremendous opportunity to make much more accurate forecasts. Not only that but the forecasts they would give with old data would be misleading in terms of the range associated with each percentile.

The bottom line here is make sure to update (or at least consider updating) your predictions in the face of new information. Your customers will thank you for it.

Flow Efficiency

If you buy into the whole argument that you should track Cycle Time for forecasts, then it stands to reason that improving single items forecasts is all about controlling the factors that affect Cycle Time itself. At its most basic level, Cycle Time can be broken down into two constituent parts: active time and wait time. As an item flows through a process, it can be in only one of two existential states. It is either actively being worked on or it is not actively being worked on. Examples of situations where an item is not being actively worked on is it is blocked by some external dependency (team, vendor, etc.), or it is queuing waiting to be pulled. In both of those examples, an item is accumulating Cycle Time but no progress toward completion is being made.

It should seem obvious, then, that to improve the accuracy of our forecasts we need to minimize wait time and maximize active time. A measure exists that will aid in this endeavor. That measure is called Flow Efficiency. Flow Efficiency is the ratio of the total active time that a finished item was worked on to its total Cycle Time that it took to complete. To get Flow Efficiency, therefore, you take the Total Cycle Time, subtract out inactive time and then divide that result by the Total Cycle Time:

$$FlowEfficiency = \frac{ActiveTime}{CycleTime}$$

or

$$FlowEfficiency = \frac{CycleTime - WaitTime - BlockedTime}{CycleTime}$$

It is not uncommon for teams who have never measured Cycle Times before to have initial Flow Efficiencies in the 15% range. Think about that for a second. If a User Story took 20 days to complete and had a Flow Efficiency of 15% that means that it spent only 3 days having someone actively work on it and it spent 17 days in some type of inactive state. If a User Story took only 3 active days of work yet had 17 days of inactivity built into its Cycle Time, where do you think you should focus your process improvement efforts? It is probably going to be very hard to improve on that 3 days of active time, but my guess there are tons of opportunities to get that 17-day number down. Any reduction of inactive time will by definition improve overall Cycle Time. Looking at wait time is usually the best, easiest, cheapest area to investigate for process improvement.

Let's extend the above example a little further and let's say that the 85th percentile of your process is actually 20 days. As we just calculated, if your Flow Efficiency for that process is 15% then your active time is only 3 days. Let's say that you attack the wait time in your process and you are able to reduce wait time significantly while still being able to keep your active time to 3 days. Let's further say that you get your wait time down such that your new Flow Efficiency is 50%. If Flow Efficiency is 50% and active time is 3 days, then overall Cycle Time at the 85th percentile will be roughly 6 days. I say roughly because we are dealing with percentiles here and not absolute numbers–but you get the gist.

This point is so important that it bears repeating. Increasing Flow Efficiency from 15% to 50% while keeping active time constant means that you have approximately dropped your 85th percentile from 20 days to 6 days! When a customer asks you for a forecast now, you can give them the much more accurate "6 days or less" answer as opposed the much less desirable "20 days or less".

However incredible, this result is absolutely correct. In fact, this is the approach that most teams who focus on flow take when starting out (see the case study in Chapter 13). That being the case, you are probably wondering how you can reduce the wait time in your process to achieve such dramatic results. Unfortunately, a full discussion of process improvement steps is beyond the scope of this book. However, I will cover some topics in the coming chapters. For the rest, you can see my previous book as well as some of the references listed at the end of this one. A short list of some things you can do to reduce wait times is:

- Control Work In Progress (more on this in Chapter 8)
- Minimize the time an item spends blocked while on its way to completion
- Rethink poor policies (more on this in Chapter 10)

You might also be wondering what to do when Flow Efficiency gets high–say, greater than 50%. A that point, active time is the larger percentage of total Cycle Time so you should focus your forecast improvement activities there. You have a few options to consider. To improve active time, you might consider putting in place changes like automation, pairing, lowering WIP, etc. But maybe the high Flow Efficiency is signaling to you that it is time to expand the scope of your process. For example, considering bringing some upstream steps (ideation, sales, marketing, etc.) into the boundaries of your process. Or considering bringing in some downstream steps (operations, support, etc.). Either way an expansion of the boundaries of your process will almost certainly cause Flow Efficiency to plummet which will force you to go through these improvement steps all over again.

By the way, not only can you calculate Flow Efficiency for each individual completed item, but you can also calculate the Flow Efficiency of your process overall. To this, simply sum up the active times for all items that have finished and divide that result by the total Cycle Times for all the same items. This approach is far superior to the "average all of the Flow Efficiencies of the individual items" method. I will leave it as an exercise for the reader to prove why (or to prove me wrong!).

Just like with the Aging chart, increasing Flow Efficiency while keeping active time constant will allow you to complete items faster. Faster completion times will lower your percentiles lines. Lower percentile lines mean that you have smaller ranges of possible outcomes for the same percentile confidence. Again, this is exactly the goal we are aiming for.

Internal and External Variability

I mentioned in the last chapter that a Scatterplot just looks like a random collection of dots on a chart. The reason that Scatterplots look the way they do is because of the variation that exists in your process. The first thing to know about variation is that it will always exist. From a predictability perspective, the point is not to always try to drive variation out; rather, the point will be to understand the causes of that variation in an attempt to make your process more predictable.

For example, take a look at Figure 3.7:

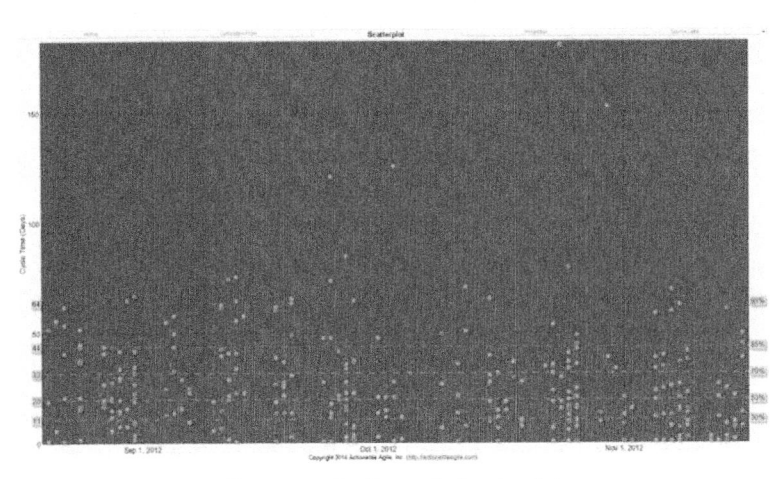

58   Chapter 3: Improving Single Item Forecasts - What To Do

Figure 3.7: An Example Scatterplot

At first glance you might be inclined to dismiss those dots at the top of the Scatterplot as extreme outliers that should be excluded from your data. You might even (if you did not like yourself very much) do some further quantitative analysis to prove that those dots are not statistically significant. And you know what, if you made those observations then I probably would not argue with you too strenuously. I would say, though, that while those points are outliers, they obviously happened. Something caused those items to take longer than they should have and that "something" probably warrants some deeper investigation. I would further say that, while potentially statistically insignificant, there might be some good contextual or qualitative reasons to keep them in from an analysis perspective.

To illustrate this point, consider what the chart in Figure 3.7 is communicating to us. The 50th percentile of Cycle Time is 20 days and the 85th percentile is 44 days. But you can see there is a work item on this chart that took 181 days! Can you think of some reasons that would have caused that particular work item to take so long? Maybe the team had a development dependency on an external vendor or a dependency on some other internal development team. Maybe the team did not have a test environment immediately available to them. Maybe the customer was not immediately available for sign-off. The shared theme for all of these reasons is that those work items took so long to complete due to reasons outside of the team's control. And that is generally what you will find as you move "up the stack" of dots on a Scatterplot. More often than not, those outliers will be caused by circumstances that are outside of the team's control.

The opposite is also generally true. As you move "down the stack" of dots, the work items that took less time to complete were generally due to reasons that were totally under the team's control. For example, reconsider that work item that I just mentioned that took 181 days to complete. Do you really think that item would have taken 181 days if it was totally under control of the team that was working on it? Maybe, but probably not (by the way, the "maybe" is potentially bad data—i.e., the team forgot to mark an item as closed in a timely manner and it sat open unnecessarily for long period of time). Additionally, look at those dots that just barely violated that 85th percentile line. Do you think that there were things that the team could have done to ensure that the violation did not happen? Probably. Swarm or break up the item are two ideas that come immediately to mind. This is where paying attention to the Aging chart as mentioned in the section above would have helped.

I hope that you are getting a feel for the type of variability analysis that I am asking you to perform with these Scatterplots. Will all outliers be due to external causes? Certainly not. Maybe the team allowed an item that ended up being too big into the process. Maybe the team ignored an item once it had been pulled and did not bother to work on it for days or weeks. Maybe, as I just suggested, the team simple forgot to mark the item as closed. Likewise, will there be external issues hiding in the shorter Cycle Times? Almost certainly. But at least I have shown you how to use a Scatterplot with percentile lines to begin the conversations about how to address those issues.

Those of you who are reading closely have probably recognized themes from the theory of variation (e.g., "special cause" and "common cause"). I have tried very hard not to use that language as I want you focused on the concepts and mechanics of improving forecasts rather than getting lost in theoretical lingo. You will also note the distinct absence of words like "Statistical Process Control" and "Control Charts". What Control Charts are and why they are probably not suited for our forecasting purposes will be covered in the next chapter.

Minimizing the number of extreme outliers as well as managing the variability in your process that is under your control will over time shift the dots on your Scatterplot down. Again, when the dots on the Scatterplot shift down the percentile lines will shift down too. As was the case with the Aging Chart and Flow Efficiency, lower percentile lines mean that we have smaller ranges of possible outcomes for the same percentile confidence and thus we can make more accurate forecasts!

Another Way To See the Effects of Improved Forecasts

First and foremost, let me say that I prefer Scatterplots for the visualization of Cycle Time data. Having said that, though, I would be remiss if I did not mention another chart available to us as a pictorial view of Cycle Time. A Histogram displays all the same data as a Scatterplot yet it displays that data as a frequency bar chart rather than a random set of dots.

The data that makes up the Scatterplot in Figure 3.4 can also be displayed as the Histogram shown in Figure 3.8

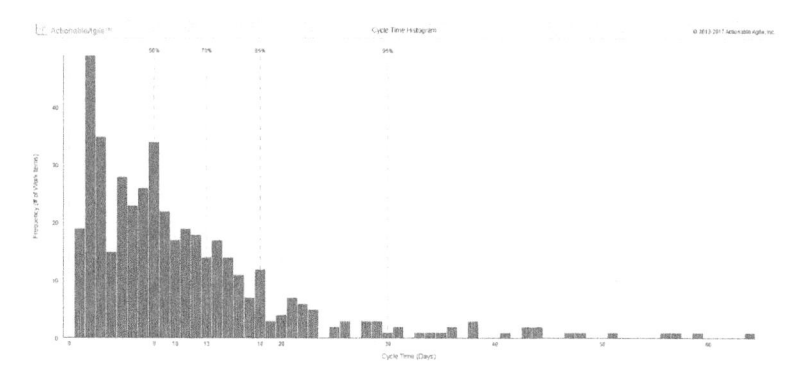

Figure 3.8 - An Example Histogram

Figure 3.8 shows frequency on the vertical (or Y) axis and Cycle Times on the horizontal (or X) axis. To construct a Histogram, every time an item finishes, you find the Cycle Time of the item on the X axis and then increment that frequency by one. For example, let's say the dataset we have has 9 items that have finished with a Cycle Time of exactly 12 days. Then on our histogram at the X-axis point of 12 days there would be a bar of height nine. Let's further say we have another item that finishes with a Cycle Time of exactly 12 days. To adjust the Histogram for this new data, we would go across the X-axis to find the Cycle Time of 12 days and then adjust the bar height for Cycle Time 12 by one—increasing the height from 9 to 10. Once you have your Histogram drawn, then you can overlay the same percentile lines that you used on your Scatterplot. These lines are calculated in exactly the same way, the only difference between the charts is that on the Histogram the percentile lines are drawn vertically (as in Figure 3.8) while in the Scatterplot, the percentile lines are drawn horizontally.

The advantage of the Histogram is that it gives you an overall idea of the distribution of your underlying data. I have mentioned several times before that knowing the underlying distribution of your data is not necessary to make accurate forecasts, and I stand by this statement. However, visualizing your data in a Histogram is a powerful image to get you to understand one of the most important facts of forecasting. The Histogram–the whole chart–represents the Cycle Time of your process. Because your process is a random Cycle Time generator, you have to think of your Cycle Time in terms of the whole Histogram. More precisely stated you have to think the Cycle Time as a shape and not a number.

> Think of your process's Cycle Time as a shape not a number

It is this concept exactly that will get you to thinking in probabilistic terms and not in deterministic ones. It is impossible to reduce the Cycle Time of your process to single value. Rather, the Cycle Time of your process is many values each with their own probability of occurring. This is exactly why asking the question WWIBD is the wrong thing to ask. Answering that question is all but impossible. As I mentioned in the previous chapter, the only question you can hope to answer is "what are the chances of getting item X done by date Y". The Histogram is the pictorial evidence as to why this is the case.

By the way, you might be interested to know that in knowledge work, a Cycle Time Histogram usually looks much like what is shown in Figure 3.8. That is to say, Histograms our data usually have a big hump on the left and a long tail to the right. In other words, they are not normally distributed. You might be wondering why. Unfortunately, I am not going to answer that question. The reason why is that for our analysis purposes it does not matter. You may have heard about mathematical methods that allow you to "fit" your data to well-known statistical curves. You can safely ignore all of those. They are at best a red herring and at worst a confusing and complete waste of time. I will spend more time on this topic in Chapter 7, but, for now please know that you should never have to any type of curve fitting.

The point of mentioning Histograms here is to give you yet another tool to understand if your forecasts are getting more accurate. I concluded each of the sections in this chapter by pointing out how the interventions that I recommend will lead to fewer possible outcomes for each percentile. On the Scatterplot, this phenomenon took the shape as more dense dots toward the bottom of the graph and fewer dots toward the top. The percentile lines themselves were shifted down toward the bottom of the graph as a result.

This same effect can be seen on Histograms. However, on a Histogram the result is a shorter, taller shape on the chart. For example, let's consider data from the Siemens HS case study that I included at the end of my first book. Before paying attention to Cycle Time (when they were running a more "traditional" Agile process) their Histogram looked like this:

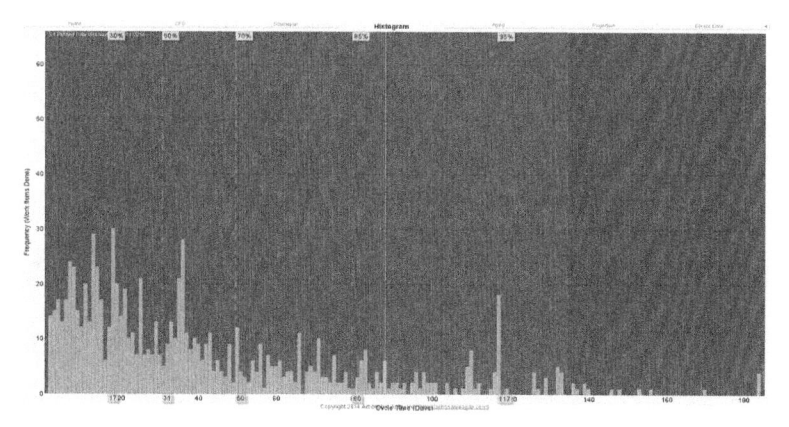

Figure 3.9 - A Less Predictable Histogram

After undertaking many of the improvements recommended in this chapter, their Histogram looked like:

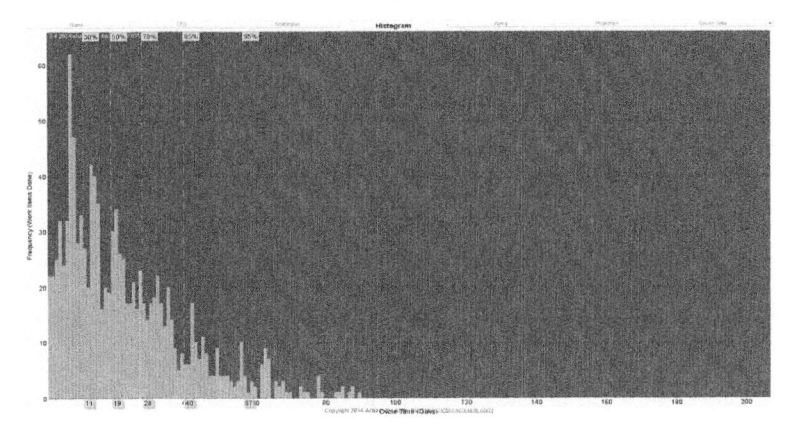

64   Chapter 3: Improving Single Item Forecasts - What To Do

Figure 3.10 - A More Predictable Histogram

To get a better feel for what really happened, let's look at these two charts side by side:

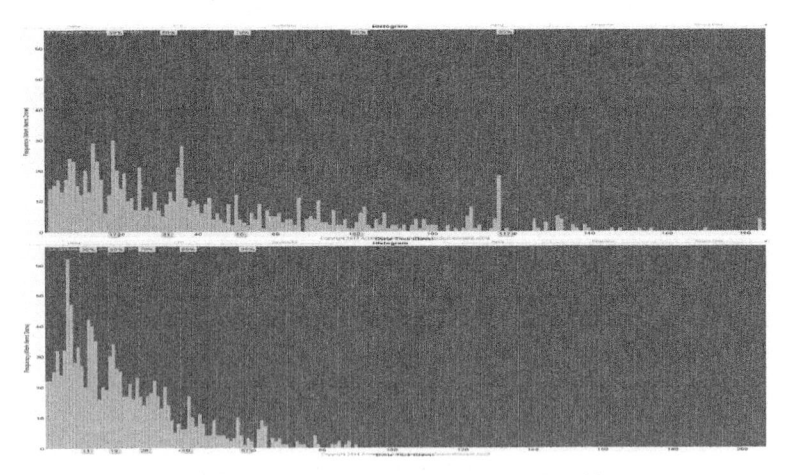

Figure 3.11 - A Comparison of More and Less Predictable Histograms

You can see from Figure 3.9 that the bottom Histogram—the one after they made Cycle Time improvements—is much narrower and taller than the top one (before they made improvements). As you can see the percentile lines shifted dramatically to the left which is exactly what we would expect. The bottom Histogram in Figure 3.9 is clear evidence of a much more predictable process. In other words, it is a process that we can make much more accurate forecasts for.

Conclusion

In this chapter, we have gone over several things to do in order to improve single item forecasts. I also demonstrated how proof of these improvements will reveal themselves on various charts. However, I mentioned at the outset that forecast improvement is a two-sided optimization. Not only do we need to understand what to do in order to improve forecasts, we also need to understand what not to do. We will explore what not to do next.

Key Learnings and Takeaways

- Forecasting is not just about gathering data to make projections—it is about the actions you take every day to ensure the predictability of your process.
- The single most important thing that you can do to improve single items forecasts is be proactive about how long it takes items to complete.
- Use an Aging Chart to continuously monitor how well items are flowing through your process.
- Consider incorporating the Aging Chart into your standup.
- Flow Efficiency is the ratio of Active Time to Cycle Time for an item or process.
- Use Flow Efficiency to determine where to look for process improvement.
- Scatterplots qualitatively show the variability in your process that can suggest further process improvement.
- Think of Cycle Time as a shape and not a number.
- Another way to see improved predictability is by a shrunken, taller histogram.

Chapter 4: Improving Single Item Forecasts – What Not To Do

Let's revisit the commute data from Chapter 2:

Day	Start Time	End Time
1	07:17	07:43
2	07:35	08:03
3	07:22	07:44
4	07:44	08:58
5	07:12	07:37

Figure 4.1 - Sample Commute Data

When I introduced this data, you may have calculated an average commute time of 24 minutes. I then asked you if you would use that average to answer the question "how long does it take you to get to work in the morning?" I suggested that an average may not be such a good number to use as a forecast. Let's examine why that is. For example, what if asked you: "Given the data above, what time would you leave your home if you needed to be at work for an 8:00am meeting with the CEO of your company?" In this scenario, would you still give yourself an average amount of time to get to work? Absolutely not. Assuming you do not want to be late for a meeting with your CEO you are most likely going to adjust your commute timing to remove as much chance as possible from being late. Instead of giving yourself 24 minutes for a commute, you will probably give yourself 60 minutes or more. You will do this because you implicitly understand that to give yourself a higher confidence of being on time, you need to leave yourself a much wider range of travel time.

Which brings us to the first point of what not to do when providing a forecast...

Never Communicate a Forecast in Terms of an Average

In Chapter 2, I made a passing reference to "The Flaw of Averages" (FoA). "The Flaw of Averages" is a book written by computer scientist and statistician, Dr. Sam L. Savage. The basic premise of FoA is that "plans based on average fail on average". Forecasting work item completion is no exception.

The Flaw of Averages

To explain this concept, I'd like to use the same example the Dr. Savage uses in many of his talks. Let's assume there is a 9:00am business meeting with 10 people invited and that all attendees must be present before the meeting can begin. Let's further assume that, on average, all participants have a history of arriving to meetings on time (for this example we'll say that average means a 50% on-time record). What are the chances that the meeting will start on time?

Again, you might think the answer to this question is easy. If, on average, everyone has a history of arriving on time, then it is reasonable to assume that there is an average chance that the meeting will start on time. Unfortunately, again, this answer is wrong. If everyone has the same chance of arriving on time as arriving late, then there is actually only a 0.1% chance that the meeting will start on time. Think of it this way: since every invitee has a 50% chance of arriving on time, then you could use the flip of a coin to model if a given attendee will arrive punctually—heads he does and tails he doesn't. Remember the meeting can only start when all participants arrive. Therefore,

> the case where the meeting starts on time is the equivalent of flipping 10 heads in a row—flipping only one tails means that participant is late and the meeting itself starts late. The chance of flipping 10 heads in a row is 0.1% ($1/2^{10}$)—or about 1 in 1,000. There is virtually no chance the meeting starts on time—which is significantly worse than average.
>
> If there is one book that you need to read (other than this one!) about why forecasts fail it is "The Flaw of Averages".

Take Figure 2.4 from Chapter 2, for example. If you had taken the average for the data in this Scatterplot you would have come up with 26 days. However, the percentile associated with a Cycle Time of 26 days or less is about 64%. That means if you had used 26 days or less as your forecast you would have been wrong 36% percent of the time. That is not very accurate!

Distilling a random variable like Cycle Time down to a single number masks all the uncertainty inherent with your process. By definition, an average is only a measure of the central tendency of your distribution. But your Cycle Time is not simply a central tendency. This is one of the reasons why I showed you the Cycle Time Histogram in the previous chapter. Remember that your Cycle Time is the entire Histogram—it is a shape and not just a single value. The whole point of drawing percentile lines on Scatterplots and Histograms is to give the risk profile associated with finishing individual items within a certain amount of time.

The Most Likely Outcome Is Not Very Likely

Which brings me to another reason why you do not forecast based on average: an average by itself does not communicate percentage confidence of completion. As was stated in Chapter 1, a forecast requires two parts: a range and a probability. Even if you argue that a single value (an average) could constitute a range, what is still completely missing from an average forecast is the probability associated with that number. It so happens that I previously calculated that probability of an average for you in the specific example above, but most do not calculate a percentage nor do they even know how to. Presenting a forecast in terms of a single value (average) communicates a level of determinism and certainty that is simply not present in our world.

You should know that other measures of central tendency suffer these same fatal flaws. For example, I have seen some Agile tooling present the most common Cycle Time value (i.e., on the Histogram, the x-axis value with the highest bar) as its forecast. The thinking is that since this is the most common Cycle Time that as occurred then it is the most likely to happen in the future. If it is the most likely outcome, then, surely, it is safe to base our forecasts on it. This approach is even worse than the arithmetic mean disaster above. The reason is because the most likely outcome is not very likely.

> The most likely outcome is not very likely.

In Chapter 1, I used the example of rolling two, fair six-sided dice. Though itself a random process I discussed several observations that make rolling dice predictable. One observation I pointed out was that rolling a seven is the most likely outcome. However, I did not tell you what the chances are of rolling exactly seven. Do you remember your answer when I asked you that question? Did you Google it? You could have reasoned that since seven is the most likely outcome, then on average we can expect to throw a seven on any given toss. Thus, if seven is our expected value, then the probability of getting seven is somewhere around 50%. I think this flawed reasoning has to do with the whole confusion around how the most likely outcome is an average and the assumption that average automatically means 50%. However, in this example, that is not the case. The chances of rolling exactly seven is only about 17%. Are you surprised by that result? Remember, the most likely outcome is not very likely.

Take a look at Figure 4.3 below. In this Histogram, the most likely outcome is 84 items. However, the chances of exactly 84 items occurring is only 16.8%. Again, not very likely. Long story short, the most likely outcome is a terrible basis for a forecast.

Your Data Is Not Normal

When I started talking about percentiles and ranges, did you expect me to start talking about averages and standard deviations? Did you assume that the lines on the chart that I was talking about were going to be the arithmetic mean line and lines that represented the mean plus or minus one or more standard deviations? Were you surprised that I did not mention mean or standard deviation at all?

For the uninitiated, let me explain the oft-cited process I am talking about. For a given set of data:

1. Calculate the mean
2. Calculate the standard deviation
3. Take the mean and add one standard deviation to it to get a number
4. Take the mean and subtract one standard deviation from it to get a second number
5. The range between the first number and the second number supposedly contains about 68% of the total items in the dataset
6. The range between the mean plus two standard deviations and minus two standard deviations supposedly contains about 95% of the total items in the dataset
7. The range between the mean plus three standard deviations and minus three standard deviations supposedly contains about 95% of the total items in the dataset

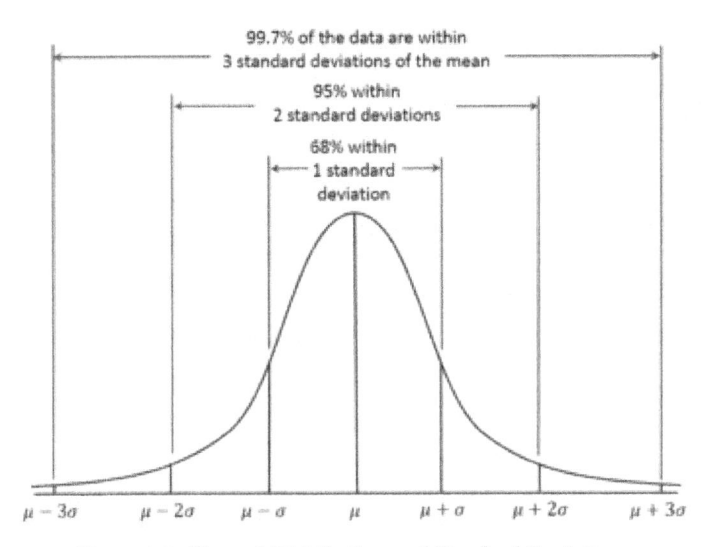

72 Chapter 4: Improving Single Item Forecasts – What Not To Do

Figure 4.2 - **Normal Distribution and Standard Deviations**

I say "supposedly" because there is only one problem with the above, and it is a big problem. The approach outlined here assumes that your data is normally distributed. A normal distribution is the commonly referred to "bell curve" shape that can be seen on the Histograms like Figure 4.3:

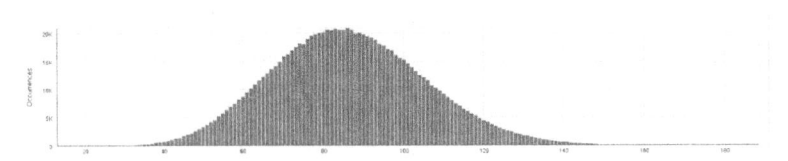

Figure 4.3 - **Histogram of a Normal Distribution**

But remember the Histogram that I showed you earlier from a typical knowledge work process?

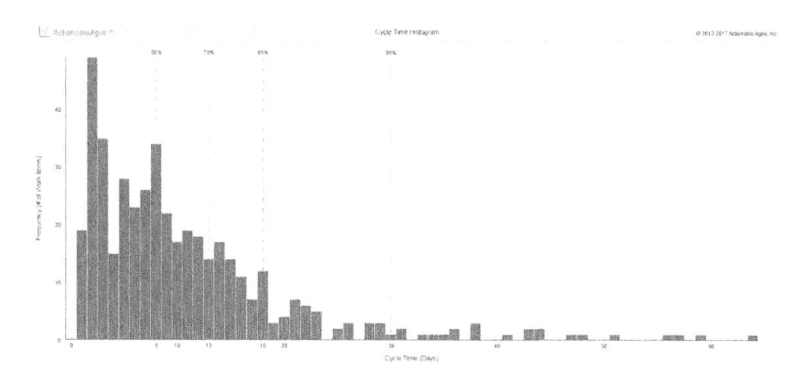

Figure 4.4 - Typical Knowldege Work Cycle Time Histogram

These two distributions do not look alike do they? That is because they are not the same. Your Cycle Time data is not normally distributed! That is not an opinion, by the way, that is a fact. When you mine your process data and put it in a Histogram, you will get a shape that looks more like Figure 4.4 than Figure 4.3. The fact that your data is not normally distributed completely rules out the exact use of the mean plus or minus one standard deviation formula above.

Many electronic tools will draw arithmetic mean and standard deviation lines on their Scatterplots instead of drawing the standard percentile lines as described in Chapter 2. They will draw a "Control Chart" containing a top standard deviation line called the "Upper Control Limit" (UCL), and a bottom standard deviation line the "Lower Control Limit" (LCL).

As described above, such charts will claim 68.2% of the dots fall between the plus one standard deviation line and the minus one standard deviation line. They might further go on to say that over 99% of the dots fall between the +3 standard deviation in the -3 standard deviation lines, and that you should segment your data this way to visually display whether you process is in control or not (hence the name Control Chart). Any dots that fall above the UCL or below the LCL, it is argued, signify the points in your process that are out of control.

What is being called a Control Chart here is supposedly inspired by the work of Walter A. Shewhart while employed at Bell Labs in the 1920s. Shewhart's work was later picked up by W. Edwards Deming who became one of the biggest proponents of that type of visualization. However, by drawing lines based on means and standard deviations using data that is not normally distributed, they have corrupted its use.

The use of this normal distribution method is pervasive because it is the type of statistics that that most of people are familiar with. One very important consequence of working in the knowledge work domain is that most people's statistics training is not applicable. We do not live in a world of normal distributions.

The point here is that when forecasting you must dump any use of the term "average". Using any semblance of an average is the first, biggest anti-pattern to providing accurate forecasts.

Do Not Waste Time Estimating and Planning

Do you not find it odd that in a book about forecasting I have not yet spent a significant amount of time discussing planning and estimation? The reason why is simple. Don't do it. Really, don't do it. Strange as it may sound, estimating and planning usually serve to make you less predictable, not more.

Think about it this way: during all of the time that you spend on estimation and planning, what are you not doing? Working. That time could otherwise be spent delivering customer value. The more time you spend planning and estimating the less value you are able to deliver. In fact, if you interrupt work to do estimation, as so many companies do, estimation is actually making you less predictable. Think about how many times you are interrupted for an estimate and how much time that costs. How much value did you get for that cost?

Do Not Use Story Points for Forecasting

Nonetheless, organizations spend more and more time trying to come up with better and better estimation schemes. Schemes that in the end provide no predictive value. For example, let's take a look at one of Agile's most popular estimation hacks: Story Points. "Clearly," the reasoning goes, "relative complexity is the best predictor of how long something will take to complete. We, as software engineers, understand the relative complexity of the items we are working on, so we will use that as our preferred method for estimation." Seems logical enough. After all, does it not stand to reason that if we perceive Story A to be more complex than Story B then surely Story A will take more time to complete than Story B. Right?

Wrong. And not just a little wrong. A lot wrong.

Remember that what customers are really asking when they say "when will it be done?" is "give me the total elapsed time from now until when my request will be completed". But what does this have to do with the relative complexity debate? It turns out there is often little or no correlation between a relative complexity estimate and the actual amount of elapsed time (Cycle Time) it takes for an item to complete. Let's look at what actually happens in the real world to explain why.

In this first example (Figure 4.5), you see a plot of Story Point Estimates against actual Cycle Times for several work items (this data is taken from a Siemens Health Services Case Study published in 2014 and included as Chapter 13 of this book). At first glance, this plot might be what you expect. As Story Point estimates get higher, Cycle Time durations get longer. Or do they? Look at the data for estimates of 3 Story Points. You'll see that on this team an item that was initially estimated at 3 points could wind up taking anywhere from 5 days to 45 days to complete. That's not very predictable. Worse still, look at the dots around the 40 day Cycle Time duration. You'll see that items that took about 40 days to complete were originally estimated anywhere from 2 Story Points

76 Chapter 4: Improving Single Item Forecasts – What Not To Do

to 11 Story Points. Again, not very predictable.

Cycle Time versus Estimate

Cycle Time (Analysis to Done)

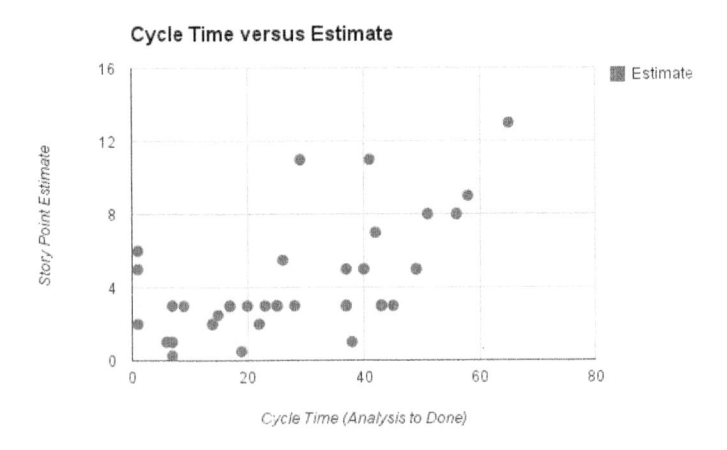

Figure 4.5: Story Point Estimates vs. Elapsed Time in Days

This next example (Figure 4.6) again shows Story Points vs. Cycle Time but in a slightly different format (this data is taken from an Ultimate Software Case Study published in 2016 and included as Chapter 15 of this book). In this chart, data is categorized by initial Story Point Estimate (on the left) and average number of days to completion (Cycle Time) for all items assigned that original point estimate (on the right). For example, you'll see on the left there were 19 items that were assigned an initial estimate of 3 Story Points, and all those items took on average 17.00 days to complete. Again, at first glance this chart might suggest a strong correlation between estimates and duration—that is until we, again, take a closer look. We just said that 3 Story Point items took on average 17.00 days to complete, but if you look at the line directly below that, 5 Story Point items took on average only 13.00 days to complete. Think about what that means for a second. Those items that were originally estimated to be roughly twice as complex as other items (5 to 3) took on average 4 less days to complete! It's potentially even worse than that. Imagine this team was doing typical two weeks sprints in Scrum. What this data would tell us was that we could pull any item estimated at 5 points into a sprint, but no items estimated at 3 points!

	Stories		Points	InProgress	Ready for QA	QA	Ready for Acceptance	Acceptance	Holding	Total Days
Total Closed	157	Total Closed	182	2.82	0.57	1.34	0.53	0.04	0.55	5.85
0 Points	9									
Half Point	86	Half Point	43	0.95	0.48	0.59	0.47	0.02	0.35	2.86
1 Points	25	1 Points	25	2.60	0.56	1.40	0.36	0.04	0.44	5.40
2 Points	12	2 Points	24	5.50	0.42	2.00	0.33	0.00	0.42	8.67
3 Points	19	3 Points	57	8.00	1.21	4.47	1.32	0.05	1.95	17.00
5 Points	5	5 Points	25	9.20	0.40	2.60	0.20	0.00	0.60	13.00
8 Points	1	8 Points	8	25.00	0.00	2.00	0.00	0.00	0.00	27.00
12 Points	0	12 Points	0							

Figure 4.6: **Story Point Estimates vs. Elapsed Time in Days**

The point here is to reinforce what should be intuitively obvious: that an upfront relative size estimation has almost no correlation to the total amount of elapsed time that it takes for an item to complete. A similar analysis can be done to disprove any positive correlation between level of effort estimates and Cycle Time, ideal days and Cycle Time, etc. In short, upfront size estimates do not matter!

Many times, however, I hear that the real value in estimating Story Points is the conversations, not the number. I actually applaud that sentiment, but in that case what we are really talking about is analysis, not estimation. If Story Points help you to "discover" your requirements, then by all means use them for that purpose. But if that is all Story Points are good for, then ask yourself this: why are you tracking them in Burn Down Charts? Why do you base your Sprint forecasts on the number of Story Points you can get done? How many times have you been in a Sprint planning meeting where there have been endless arguments over whether a Story is 2 points or 3 points?

It is rather easy to understand why estimation in general does not work. When prompted for an estimate, most people will only consider the active time that it takes to finish an item. But from our discussion in the last chapter, we know that the vast majority of elapsed time is wait time. In the estimation process, this wait time is generally wholly ignored. So, if your estimate only accounts for about 15% of the total time, then you can expect estimates to be off by 85% or more. This is not too far off from what we see in the real world.

The moral of the story is that you should abandon Story Points in favor of the other forecasting techniques I advocate in this book. In the end, your process will be better for it.

Right Sizing vs. Same Sizing

Another fallacy you may have heard regarding Cycle Time is that in order to use this approach for forecasting you must make all items the same size. Nothing could be further from the truth. By implementing the techniques in this book, you will see that your process will converge to a notion of a "right size" for items. That right size will essentially be the range of possible outcomes as dictated by the percentile confidence that you have chosen. For example, from a forecasting perspective, if you care about the 85th percentile, and your 85th percentile is 12 days or less, then the right size for items to flow your process is 12 days or less. For sizing, then, all you need to do before you pull an item into your process is have a quick conversation about whether—based on what you know right now—you can get the item done in 12 days or less. If the answer is yes, then the conversation is over and you pull the item in and start working on it. If the answer is no, then you talk about how you can redefine the work item such that it is of the right size. Maybe you need to break it up. Maybe you need to tweak the acceptance criteria. Maybe you need to do spike to get more information. Whatever the case, take the action you need beforehand and only pull the item in once you are 85% confident you can finish it in 12 days or less.

Some of you may be arguing that right-sizing is a form of estimation. I would agree. Estimation doesn't go away–instead, it should be minimized. More estimation leads to less predictability. Use data to do your estimation for you and do not get hung up on endless subjective arguments about an item's size.

Do Not Ignore Pull Policies

I have said several times before that forecasting is not just about gathering a bunch of process data and putting it in fancy charts. Quite the opposite. Accurate forecasting is about doing the little things right every day so that you do not sabotage your own process's predictability.

One of the most damaging things you can do from a predictability perspective is to ignore your process's pull policies. I go into great detail around what good pull policies are and are not in my previous book (AAMFP Chapter 13), so I will not spend a lot of time here repeating myself. But some key points bear reviewing.

Let's say you are working on items in your process and your Agile board looks like this:

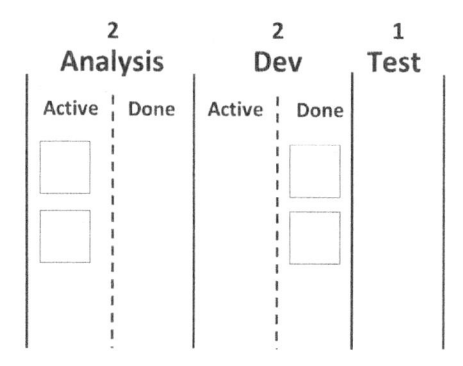

Figure 4.7 - Example Agile Board

You can see immediately from Figure 4.7 that we have a bit of a conundrum. We have two items that are finished the Dev Done

80 Chapter 4: Improving Single Item Forecasts – What Not To Do

column, but we only have space to pull one of them into the Test stage. The obvious question is "which one do we pull?" The rules around how you answer this question are what are called "pull policies"

Pull Policies: the policies or rules (either explicit or implicit) around the order in which you pull items through your process.

Some examples of pull polices might be First In First Out (FIFO), First In First Served (FIFS), ad hoc/random (where there are no explicit policies decided beforehand), etc.

When you have rules attached to certain types of work then those rules are called Classes of Service (CoS). Perhaps you have heard of the Expedite CoS in Kanban systems? Expedites work something like Figure 4.8:

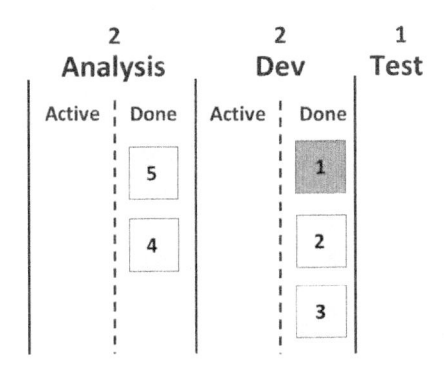

Figure 4.8 - Example Agile Board With An Expedite*

In Figure 4.8, we have a situation much like Figure 4.7 where we now have three items in Dev Done but only capacity to pull one of those items into Test. In this case, the green work item has an Expedite CoS. An Expedite CoS generally means that when possible you always pull expedited items in preference to all other items. In the situation depicted in Figure 4.8, the team will choose Work Item #1 and they will leave items #2 and #3 to sit in Dev Done to wait to pulled at some later date.

Proponents of CoS will tell you that CoS adds predictability to you process. It should be apparently obvious to you, though, how the opposite is actually true. All CoS does is bring predictability to highest level CoS items. It actually reduces predictability for all lower level CoS items. Figure 4.8 demonstrates why this is. Because of the CoS in place Items #2 and #3 have to sit and wait arbitrarily (remember our discussion of minimizing wait times from the last chapter?). However, the whole time those items are waiting they are aging. The increased age ultimately manifests itself as a longer Cycle Time than normal. Longer Cycle Times than normal mean that we have introduced additional possible outcomes to our process. More possible outcomes mean less accurate forecasts.

Other examples of poor pull policies:

- ignoring blocked items
- ignoring (or not having implemented) WIP limits
- not having explicit definitions of done at each step of your process (thus potentially causing needless rework), etc.

All of these will cause items to age unnecessarily and thus result in longer Cycle Times than normal. Generally speaking, when it comes to increasing the accuracy of forecasts, examining the pull policies that you do or do not have in place yields the best bang for the buck.

I have only scratched the surface of how your rules around pull affect predictability, so, again, I invite you to read Chapter 13 of AAMFP for a much fuller discussion. I do, however, have one more little historical anecdote to share with you to demonstrate of the perils poor pull policies:

How an Expedite Request Sunk the Titanic

Most people know that *RMS Titanic* was a British passenger ship that struck an iceberg and sank in the North Atlantic on the morning of April 15, 1912 resulting in the loss of over 1,500 lives. However, most people don't know that an expedite request caused a chain of events that directly led to the sinking of the ill-fated vessel.

First, a little background. *Titanic* was commissioned by the White Star Line as one of three ships designated as "Olympic-class ocean liners". The other two Olympic-class boats were the *Olympic* and the *Britannic (II)*. At the time of their building, these three ships were to be among the largest in the world (*Olympic* was, in fact, the largest ship in the world when she was launched). Of the three, the *Olympic* was built first (beginning in 1908) and placed into service first (in 1911). *Titanic* was second in line and her construction began in Belfast in 1909 with a scheduled maiden voyage of early 1912.

This is where things get interesting. As *Titanic* neared completion, it was given an initial sailing date of March 20, 1912. However, in February 1912, *Olympic* (which, remember, was already in service) lost a propeller blade and was immediately returned to Belfast for repairs. To get *Olympic* back in service as quickly as possible, the ship builders decided to pull resources off of *Titanic* in order to place them into service repairing *Olympic*. This expedite request caused an inevitable delay in the completion of *Titanic*. Thus, *Titanic's* maiden voyage was rescheduled from March 20, 1912 to April 10, 1912.

This delay might seem otherwise benign but for two important consequences. The three-week postponement now meant *Titanic* was going to be sailing during peak iceberg season in the North Atlantic—that is, the time of year when most icebergs appear in the major shipping lanes between Europe and North America. The chances of a boat hitting an iceberg are substantially higher in mid-April than they are in mid-March.

Further, the delay caused a reshuffling of *Titanic's* crew. As the captain now had the more experienced *Olympic* officers available to him (remember *Olympic* was still laid up for repairs) he opted to utilize that more senior crew in preference to the previously selected *Titanic* crew. In particular, the Chief Officer of the *Olympic* became the new Chief Officer of the *Titanic*. Which meant that the originally selected Chief Officer of the *Titanic* now became the new First Officer, and the original First Officer of *Titanic* now became the new Second Officer. The result of these cascading demotions was that the original Second Officer of *Titanic* was told that his services were not needed and he was asked to leave the ship. Again, these changes may seem inconsequential; however, one of the duties of the Second Officer was to be in charge of the binoculars used by the crow's nest lookouts to spot icebergs. When the original Second Officer was asked to leave after the crew shake-up, he mistakenly took the key to the locker where the binoculars were held with him. That meant that—for the duration of the journey—the lookouts had to rely only on regular sight to spot icebergs. It is now widely believed that if the lookouts had indeed had their binoculars that they would have been able to spot the fatal iceberg in plenty of time for the *Titanic* to take evasive maneuvers.

There is widespread advice given in the Lean-Kanban community that implementing Class of Service is an essential part of proper system design. This advice is built on the premise that process must be optimized for value and that it is obvious that items of higher value should be allowed to "jump the queue" and be given preferential treatment for completion. The guidance usually goes so far as to recommend the stealing of resources from lower priority items in progress to expedite the completion of the higher value ones, as was demonstrated by the *Titanic* example.

I absolutely agree with optimizing a process for value. However, I firmly believe that value is only truly determined by the end customer. While an item is sitting in a backlog, it is almost impossible to know its true value. To illustrate, let's examine the decision making process of the *Titanic's* ship builders. When *Olympic* was damaged, they made the decision that repairs to an in-service vessel (*Olympic*) were of higher value than the completion an unfinished ship (*Titanic*). Therefore, they took the action to steal resources from *Titanic* to put on *Olympic*. Now, don't you think that if the owners of *Titanic* had known that this reallocation of resources would directly lead to the loss of their flagship vessel and 1,500 lives that they would have made a different decision?

I would argue that the best way to optimize for value over the long term is to operate as predictable of a process as possible. And here's the thing: predictable processes do not use Classes of Service!

As a final thought, there was another application of Class of Service on *Titanic* that helped to doom the ship. This particular case concerns the wireless operators on board. As you might expect, one of the jobs of the wireless operators was to relay weather reports and ice warnings to the captain. However, what actually paid these workers' salary during the voyage was the sending and receiving of wireless messages for the wealthy passengers on board. Consider this: if, as a wireless operator, you got paid—and paid well—for every personal message you sent or received and you did not get paid at all for any ice report you relayed, which items do you think would you prioritize? Me too. The preferential treatment given to paid messages (expediting) caused a substantial delay in receiving many ice warnings. Some warnings were even discarded altogether. In fact, the last ice warning that actually made it into the captain's hands was at 5:30pm on the day of the sinking. Titanic struck its iceberg at 11:40pm.

Think about that the next time someone asks you to expedite a request for them...

Conclusion

In the past couple of chapters I have outlined several things that you should do and should not do to improve the forecasts for single items. If you are interested in knowing WWIBD for a given User Story, Feature, Epic, etc., then follow the practices outlined in this section.

But what if I have 100 items in my backlog and I want to know when all 100 will be completed? To answer that question we will need a completely different metric and a completely different forecasting technique. Both will be explained in detail in the next chapter.

Key Learnings and Takeaways

- Never use an average to communicate a forecast.
- Never use the most likely outcome to communicate a forecast; the most likely outcome is not very likely.
- Your Cycle Time data is not normally distributed so do not assume so when making forecasts.
- Estimation and planning usually serve to make your process less predictable and not more predictable.
- There is almost no correlation between a Story Point Estimate and the elapsed time it takes for an item to complete.
- There is no need to same size items for forecasting.
- Much if not most of the unpredictability in your process is down to poor pull policies.
- Implemented incorrectly, your process's pull policies will be about as successful as Titanic.

Section III: Forecasts for Multiple Items

Chapter 5: How To Make A Forecast For Multiple Items

On November 4, 1979, a group of Iranian revolutionaries stormed the US Embassy in Tehran and took fifty-two Americans hostage. After initial diplomatic attempts to secure the hostages' release failed, U.S. President Jimmy Carter ordered the American Armed Forces to devise a plan to rescue the captives via a clandestine military operation. The name given to this rescue mission was "Operation Eagle Claw".

The plan for Operation Eagle Claw called for U.S. Special Forces to initially be flown by helicopter from aircraft carriers in the Persian Gulf to a desert staging area south of Tehran. At this staging area, the helicopters would be refueled—to ensure there was enough fuel for the return journey—and then flown to the U.S. Embassy building in Tehran to extract the hostages. In devising this scheme, one of the most important decisions that the military had to make was to determine the required number of helicopters to send to ensure the operation's success. At a minimum, obviously, the planners had to send enough airships to carry all freed hostages and all necessary military personnel required for the mission. Based on the payload of the model of helicopter chosen, the military knew they needed at least six working helicopters to reach Tehran in order to get everyone out.

But is the minimum number the right number to send? The military understood better than anyone that in the real-world things go wrong and sending just six helicopters would leave absolutely no margin for error. Consider some of the things that could possibly go wrong with the helicopters during the operation:

- Some aircraft could crash on the journey from the gulf to the desert staging area.
- Some aircraft could develop mechanical issues during flight and be deemed not airworthy.
- A storm could come along and knock some helicopters off course.

Any reasonable amount of reflection yields several possibilities of things that could lead to a mission failure. That is in addition to the fact that absolutely nothing could go wrong and all aircraft could perform perfectly throughout the mission.

The question "how many helicopters do we send?" is a classic example of a multiple item forecast.

A Quick Thought Experiment

Let's say you have just started a project and in two weeks you have finished ten items. Let's further say that there are fifty items remaining in the project, some of which are in progress. When your customer asks, "When will the project be done?", how would you calculate how long it will take to complete those fifty items?

"Easy," you say, "since we have completed ten items in two weeks that means that we get five items done per week. At a rate of five items per week it will take us ten weeks to finish the remaining 50 items."

I want to come back to this answer in a second, but I first want to point out what should be an obvious fact about the original question: we were being asked "When will it be done?", but in this case, "it" is not a single item (e.g., Story, Epic, Feature, etc.), but the fifty items sitting in our backlog.

Let's reconsider your answer given this new information. In re-examining your response, I would like to suggest that there was one thing that was correct in your answer, and one thing that was wrong. Very wrong. The first correct part of your answer was the metric you used to calculate your projection. You calculated the rate at which you were getting items done–five per week. In the language of flow, this metric is called Throughput.

Throughput is a measure of how fast items depart a process. Stated slightly differently, Throughput is the number of work items that are completed per unit of time. The unit of time can be any unit that is useful to you–you can measure items done per day, per week, per Sprint, etc. Note also that you are counting items. This is very different from the Scrum metric of "Velocity", which is measured in Story Points per Sprint or iteration. I point this out because many agile coaches and consultants use the words "Velocity" and "Throughput" interchangeably, and this is a source of confusion.

The thing you did wrong in your calculation was to simply divide the remaining work (fifty items) by the Throughput (five items per week) to get your forecast (10 weeks). This type of thinking is yet another classic example of the "Flaw of Averages"– FoA just sneaks right up on you, doesn't it?

Using an average completion rate (Throughput) to project the completion date of multiple items in a backlog suffers from the same fatal flaw as the average commute time example from Chapter 2. That fatal flaw is trying to reduce uncertainty down to a single number. As with single items, there is more than one possible future outcome, so we must think probabilistically.

Probabilistic Thinking Redux

Let's revisit an example that I introduced in Chapter 1. Reconsider, if you will, the scenario where we roll two fair, six-sided dice and then add up the numbers that come up on the dice. There are certain things that we know about the possible outcomes:

- We know it is impossible to roll anything lower than two or higher than twelve.
- We know that possible outcomes could be any whole number between two and twelve (inclusive).
- We know that seven is the most likely outcome.

92   Chapter 5: How To Make A Forecast For Multiple Items

In Chapter 1 I said that the chance of getting exactly 7 is about 17% (remember the most like outcome is not very likely). But how did I come up with that answer? I could have chosen one of several options to calculate it.

The first method you might have tried would have been to simply guess. Certainly, WWIBD is often answered that way! If you have no other options available, who can blame you for guessing? But we can do better.

A second method is to enumerate all possible outcomes of dice rolls and then calculate probabilities. The following graphic is one such representation of that approach:

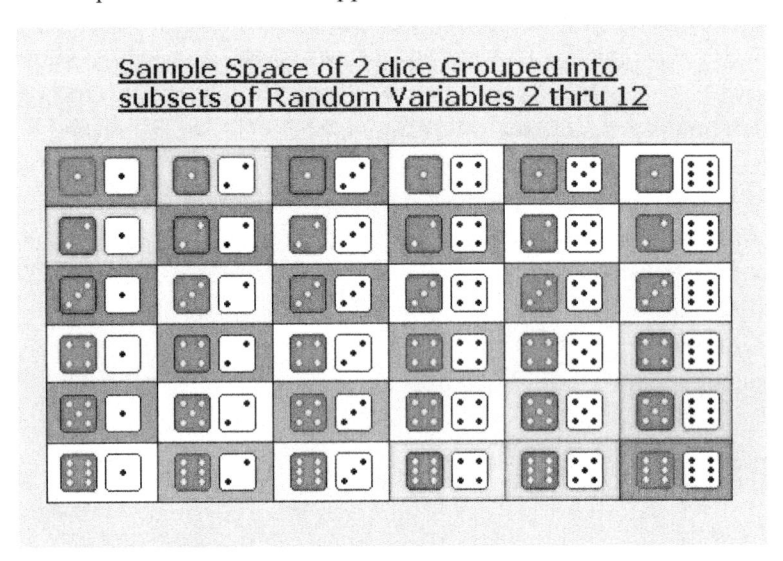

Figure 5.1 - All Combinations of Rolling Two Dice

From this picture (Figure 5.1), it is quite obvious that there are six different combinations for two dice to sum up to seven, while there is only one way for the dice to sum up to two. Therefore, if we know all the possible outcomes, and we know all the combinations for any of those outcomes, then we can calculate the probability of getting each one. We could easily rearrange Figure 5.1 to show you how we might do this calculation.

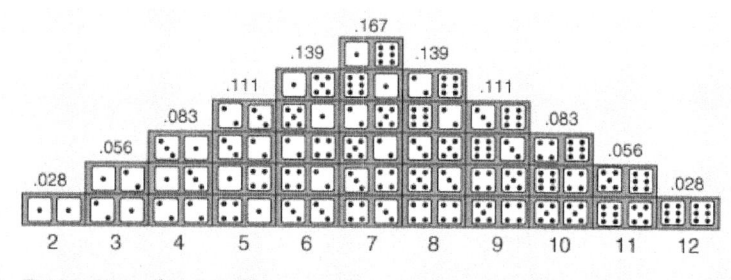

Figure 5.2 - All Combinations of Rolling Two Dice

Figure 5.2 shows us that of the 36 possible outcomes, there are six possible ways to get seven. Therefore the probability of rolling a seven on any particular throw is 6/36 or about 17%. The probability of rolling a two is 2/36 or about 3%, which is the same probability for rolling a twelve. As you have probably noticed, there are a couple of benefits to using this enumeration approach:

1. It is possible to determine the whole set of possible results. In the two dice example, we know there are exactly thirty-six ways to sum up two dice, and the range of those thirty-six results is two to twelve (inclusive).
2. Once we know our possible result set, then we can exactly calculate the probability of getting each outcome. Again, by enumerating, we know there are three ways to roll ten out of thirty-six possible results, therefore our probability of rolling a ten on any given roll is 8.3%.

Yet a third, very complicated method for solving this problem would be to come up with a formula that you could plug numbers into that would spit out an answer for the specific probabilities. This approach is sometimes referred to as the "applied probability" method and definitely could work in the dice example. Once such applied probability method we could use would be to employ a technique called "generating functions". As this is book is not meant to be a text on advanced probability, I won't go into too much detail about this procedure here. However, to give you a hint, figuring out the probability for a given outcome of rolling two dice using generating functions would mean to start with an expression that looked like this:

$$G(\eta) = 0\eta^0 + \frac{1}{6}\eta^1 + \frac{1}{6}\eta^2 + \frac{1}{6}\eta^3 + \frac{1}{6}\eta^4 + \frac{1}{6}\eta^5 + \frac{1}{6}\eta^6$$

Figure 5.3 - Generating Function

then square it, then use the resultant coefficients of each variable as the probabilities for each of the outcomes. Yikes!

Applied Probability could also help us to get a solution for the Operation Eagle Claw scenario mentioned above. Without going into too much detail, the applied probability equation to figure out the number of helicopters to send is:

$$P_m = \sum_{i=m}^{n} \binom{n}{i} P^i (1-P)^{n-i}$$

Figure 5.4 - Applied Probability Formula

Where:
P_m = the probability that at least m number of helicopters survive
m = the minimum number of helicopters needed for success
n = the total number of helicopters sent
P = probability of success of each individual helicopter

If you can calculate the above expression, then congratulations are in order. Most people's eyes will just glaze over if you show them something like that.

All of the above schemes for calculating probability are all very well and good, but what if you are faced with a problem where it is either

a. Impossible, too costly, or too lengthy to enumerate all the possible outcomes? Or,

b. Impossible to devise an applied probabilistic approach, or too difficult to compute even if you could?

Think about forecasting the probability that all the work items associated with your project will finish by a certain date. Could you enumerate all those possible outcomes? Considering all the variables, probably not. Could you come up with a formula to plug numbers into to calculate probability? Again, probably not. So what are we to do?

To understand the approach required, we need to take a page out of history and revisit the story of the development of the first atomic bomb, otherwise known as the Manhattan Project.

As you may know, the purpose of the Manhattan Project was to build the world's most powerful bomb by harnessing the energy created by splitting the nucleus of an atom. This process of nuclear splitting is called fission and, in the 1940's, not much was known about the mechanics of how to do it. What was known, however, was that to generate enough energy to create a bomb of any consequence several atoms needed to be split through a phenomenon known as "chain reaction". During a chain reaction, a free neutron hits the nucleus of an atom within some fissionable material (most typically an element with a large nucleus such as uranium or plutonium). The collision splits the nucleus, and that split gives off both a lot of energy and also one or more additional free neutrons. These new neutrons then potentially hit other nuclei, thus giving off more energy and more neutrons and so on and so on until the fissionable material is used up, or, rather, as much fissionable material as possible is used up. The key to creating the atom bomb, therefore, was to sustain a chain reaction at the right pace to create enough energy for a decent bomb—a chain reaction that was either over too quick or took too long to complete would not release enough energy to meet the definition of "bomb". Complicating matters further was the fact that just because a neutron hit a nucleus of another atom there was no guarantee that the contacted nucleus would actually split. There was a chance the neutron would simply be deflected, or pass through the nucleus, or be absorbed by the nucleus.

You can imagine that the math of a chain reaction is extremely complex due to the sheer number of neutrons and their interactions that must be tracked in order to determine the likelihood and speed of a chain reaction. There are so many variables involved that the task is all but impossible for a human to calculate. So instead of trying to brute force a calculation, the scientists at Los Alamos (where the Manhattan Project was based) simply ran simulations of several possible sample reactions. The tool they used to run these simulations was a machine known as FERMIAC.

FERMIAC is made mostly of brass and resembles a trolley car. In order to use it, several adjustable drums are set using pseudo-random numbers. One of these numbers represents the material being traversed. A random choice is made between fast and slow neutrons. A second digit is chosen to represent the direction of neutron travel, and a third number indicates the distance traveled to the next collision. Once these settings are dialed in, the device is physically driven across a 2-D scale drawing of the nuclear reactor or materials being tested. As it goes along, it plots the paths of neutrons through various materials by marking a line on the drawing. Whenever a material boundary is crossed, the appropriate drum is adjusted to represent a new pseudorandom digit. Figure 5.5 shows a picture of the FERMIAC and the result of a sample simulation.

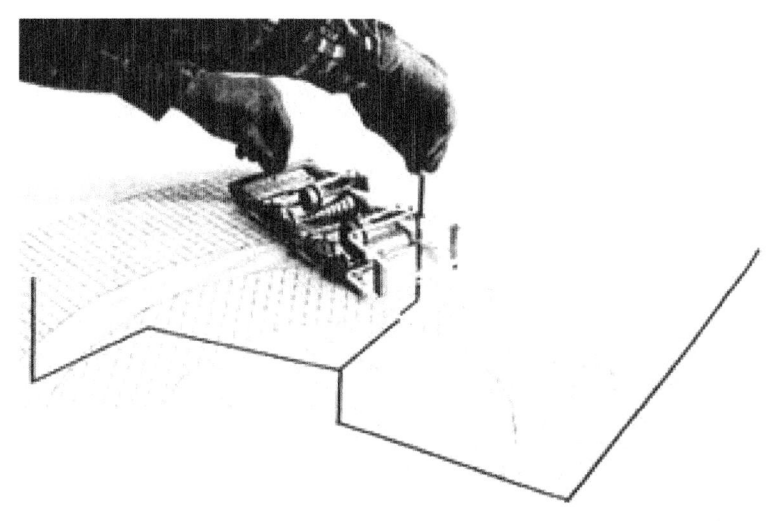

Figure 5.5 - FERMIAC

By studying these drawings, the Manhattan Project scientists were able to deduce all the probabilities associated with fission and chain reactions, and were able to successfully design and build the world's first atomic weapon. This method of using statistical sampling to determine probabilities came to be known as the Monte Carlo method.

In general terms, the Monte Carlo method can be used to describe any technique that approximates solutions to quantitative problems through statistical sampling. Monte Carlo Simulation (MCS) is one such implementation of the Monte Carlo method where a real world system is described using a probabilistic model. The model consists of uncertainties (probabilities) of inputs that get translated into uncertainties of outputs (results). Specifically, in MCS the model is run (i.e., the system is simulated) a large number of times. This results in a large number of separate and independent outcomes, each representing a possible "future" for the system. The results of the independent system realizations are assembled into probability distributions of possible outcomes.

The important thing to note is that the output of an MCS is not single values, but probability distributions that describe the uncertainty associated with future outcomes.

Let's illustrate MCS via our two dice example from before. The model for this MCS is very simple. We are just going to roll two dice over and over again and track the results of each throw. We will track the results of our experiments in a Histogram (for more information on Histograms, see Chapter 2). After a large number of throws, our Histogram will show an approximation of the probability distribution associated with the outcomes of this particular system. If all goes well, the probabilities in our MCS results Histogram should correlated strongly with the exactly calculated probabilities of our enumeration method.

After 100 rolls, our Histogram might look like this:

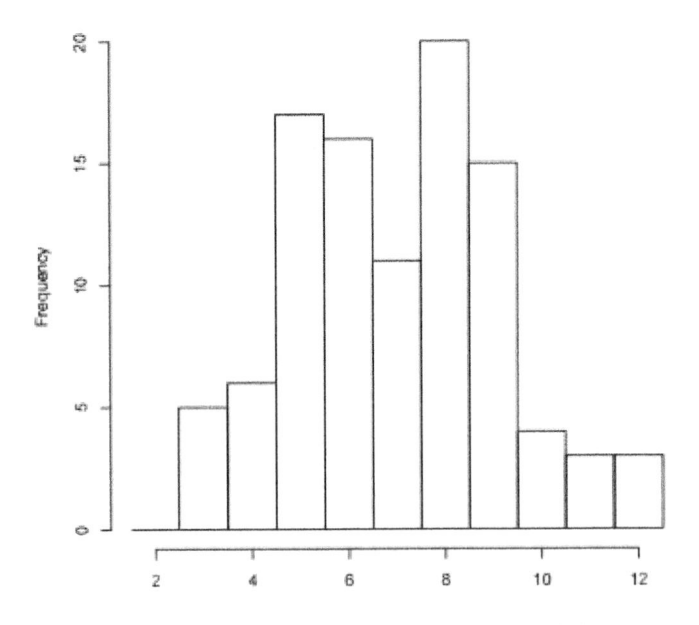

Figure 5.6 - Histogram of 100 Rolls of Two Six-Sided Dice

In Figure 5.6, you will see that we have enumerated all the possible results across the bottom (the x-axis), and, as always, we will be tracking the frequency of each outcome up the side (the y-axis).

We know from before that the most likely outcome of this experiment is 7. However, in Figure 5.6, 8 is the most likely outcome so far. This result should not be surprising since we have not run many trials yet, and our Results Histogram is only beginning to take shape. After 1000 trials, our Histogram looks like:

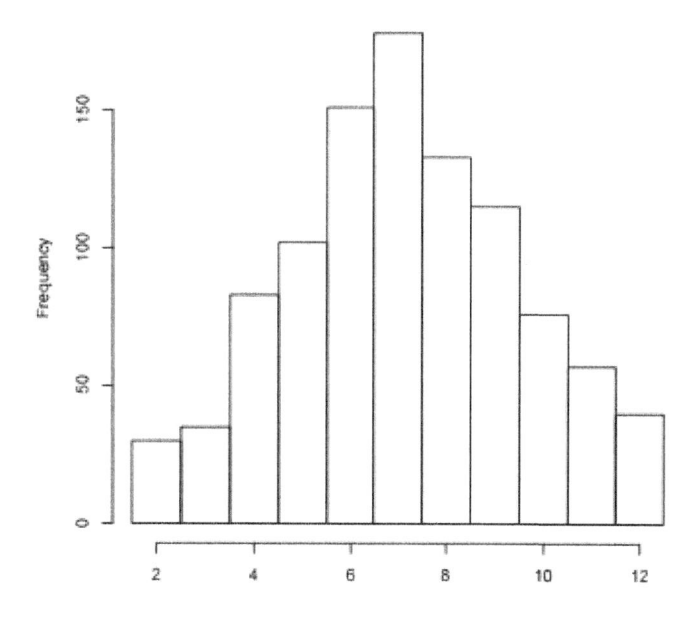

Figure 5.7 - Histogram of 1000 Rolls of Two Six-Sided Dice

Figure 5.7 is now starting to look more like Figure 5.2–which is what we expect to see. Continuing with our simulation, let's see what the Histogram looks like after ten thousand throws:

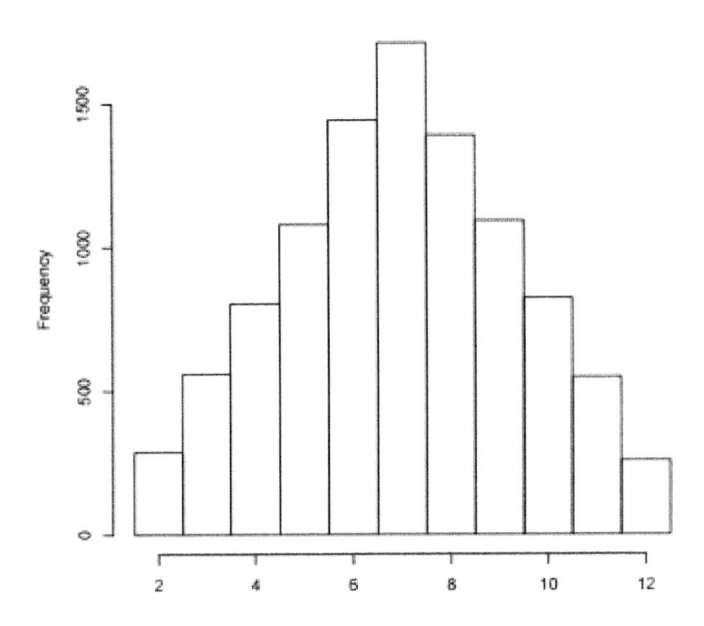

Figure 5.8 - **Histogram of 10000 Rolls of Two Six-Sided Dice**

Our Results Histogram in Figure 5.8 now agrees very well with what was predicted from our enumeration approach before. At this point running more trials will probably not do us any good.

You can see that as we run more and more simulations, the Results Histogram gets "sharper". To see that effect, let's put the three previous Histograms side by side:

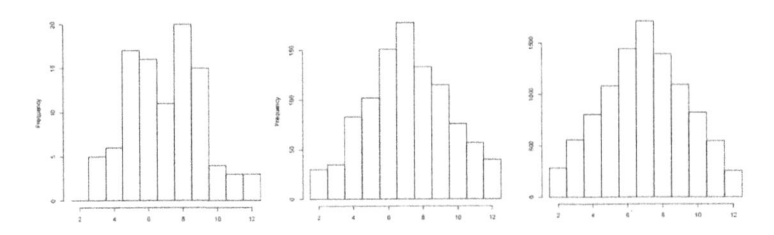

Figure 5.9 - **Histogram of 100, 1000, 10000, Respectively, Rolls of Two Six-Sided Dice**

More trials will improve your answer for a while. Eventually, though, you will reach a point of diminishing returns where your results stabilize. So how do we leverage this tool to answer the question at hand: WWIBD for multiple items?

Forecasts for Multiple Items

First we need to calculate the Throughput of our process. Once again, I have very good news: the data that we tracked to calculate Cycle Time is exactly the same data that we need to calculate Throughput. We do not need to do any special work to track any different data—we can use the exact same data we collected before!

> Use the same data you collected to calculate Cycle Time to calculate Throughput

Let's revisit the data that we previously used to calculate Cycle Time but let's add a few data points to make our Throughput calculation example a bit clearer:

Work Item Id	Arrived	Departed
1	01/01/2016	03/01/2016
2	01/02/2016	03/03/2016
3	02/02/2016	03/03/2016
4	01/02/2016	03/04/2016
5	03/02/2016	03/04/2016

Figure 5.10 - Sample Process Data

The calculation of Throughput from this data is almost as easy as the calculation for Cycle Time. For simplicity, I am going to show you how to calculate a daily Throughput. However, as I mentioned earlier, you can use any unit of time that you see fit for Throughput.

To calculate Throughput, begin by noting the earliest date that any item completed, and the latest date that any item completed. Then enumerate those dates. In our example, those dates in sequence are (again, please forgive the American-style dates!):

Completed Date
03/01/2016
03/02/2016
03/03/2016
03/04/2016

Figure 5.11 - Consecutive Calendar Days Between First and Last Finished Items

Now for each enumerated date, simply count the number of items that finished on that exact date. For our data, those counts look like this:

Completed Date	Throughput
03/01/2016	1
03/02/2016	0
03/03/2016	2
03/04/2016	2

Figure 5.12 - Calculated Throughput

From Figure 5.12 we can see that we had a Throughput of 1 item on 03/01/2016, 0 items the next day, 2 items the third day, and 2 items the last day. Note the Throughput of zero on 03/02/2016—nothing finished that day. Now we have a set of historical Throughput data from which to perform our forecast.

What is Past is Prologue

Monte Carlo methods vary, but in general, they tend to follow a typical pattern:

1. Define a probability distribution of possible inputs
2. Randomly select values from the input distribution and perform a computation on the selected inputs
3. Repeat steps 1-2 an arbitrary number of times and aggregate the results (usually by employing a Histogram)
4. Repeat steps 1-3 an arbitrary number of times until you have a clear picture of what the result set looks like.

The Monte Carlo Simulation of rolling two dice followed these steps. First, we defined our possible inputs—the sum of the numbers of two six-sided dice. Second, we rolled the dice. Third, we summed the numbers and tracked the result. Fourth, we re-ran the experiment repeatedly and aggregated the results in a Histogram. When finished, we were able to calculate probabilities of certain outcomes using the results histogram.

Let's take a minute and explore how we might apply this method to forecast the completion date of 100 work items.

Step 1: Define a probability distribution of possible inputs. Your candidate distribution is going to be your historical Throughput data that I just showed you how to calculate. However, as was the case when making forecasts for single items, the first thing you need to decide is which past data to include for the simulation. I mentioned before that the dirty little secret of all of the probabilistic forecasting methods is that the future that you predict is going to roughly look like the past that you have data for. Monte Carlo Simulation is no different. That means in order to make meaningful multiple item forecasts, you are going to have to choose a relevant set of historical data that you think will roughly mirror the future that you are trying to predict. Remember that this practice is more art than science and that you can refer to Chapter 11 for more information. Again, you are probably going to want to use a tool that allows you to easily select different sets of past data and to immediately show you the impact of those different selections.

Step 2: Randomly select values from the input distribution and perform a computation on the selected inputs. This is where the MCS rubber meets the road. To project out how long it will take 100 items to finish, we are going "simulate" how many items get done for each consecutive day into the future. The way that works is, say, for example, we are starting our simulation on January 1. For January, 1, then, we are going to select a random Throughput number from our historical (input) Throughput data. Let's say we randomly chose a 3. For the purposes of the simulation, that means that our process got 3 things done on January 1. We then subtract

3 from 100 to get 97 items left to complete. We then repeat the same calculation for the next day, January 2. Let's say we randomly choose a 5 for January 2. That means we got 5 things done this day so we subtract 5 from 97 to get 92. We do this over and over until we either get a 0 (or less than zero whichever comes first). We then note the date that we got to zero—let's say for this example it is February 28.

Just one last thing to note about Step 2 before we move on. The algorithm that we use here where we simply randomly select a historical Throughput input is just one such option for our simulation. There are many others. We will briefly touch on other options for selecting Throughputs in Chapter 12.

Step 3: Aggregate the results. For each "run" of the simulation, we are going to track the results in what we are going to call a Results Histogram. The Histogram is going to be built using dates across the bottom (the x-axis) and frequency up the side (the y-axis). For each date result we get from step #2, we will find that date on the x-axis and increment its frequency by 1 (so that the height of the histogram bar grows.

Step 4: Repeat steps 1-3 an arbitrary number of times until you have a clear picture of what the result set looks like. With each run of the simulation, the probability distribution as described by the Results Histogram will become clearer and clearer—exactly like what we saw with the rolling two dice example. You can use as many simulations as you like, but it has been my experience that you usually get a pretty good idea of what your distribution looks like after about 1000 runs, and the output has mostly stabilized by 10,000 runs. Once you have finished all of your runs you will get a results histogram that looks something like:

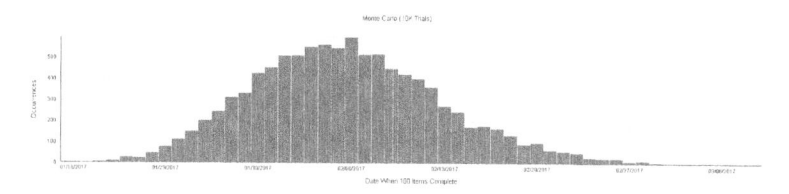

Figure 5.13 - Example Results Histogram

Note that unlike your Cycle Time data, your Results Histogram will indeed approximate a Normal Distribution. This is due to something in probability called the Central Limit Theorem (CLT). You need not worry yourself with the specifics of the CLT, only know that in general the Results Histogram will usually resemble a bell curve.

Congratulations! The simulation is complete. The only thing left now is to discuss how to interpret the results.

Percentile Lines on the Results Histogram

Just like we did on the Cycle Time Scatterplot and Histogram, we can draw percentile lines on our MCS Results Histogram to get a better idea of the chances of certain outcomes occurring. To do this, I must first point out an important principle Histogram that we just generated. And that is that if you sum the heights of all the bars together you will get the number of runs that made up the simulation. For example, if we ran 10000 runs in our simulation, then adding up the heights of the bars in the resultant chart would yield a value of 10000. We can leverage this property to draw our standard percentile lines on our Results Histogram.

Let's use the Results Histogram of Figure 5.14 to predict the date that 100 items will complete. To start, let's find the date that gives us a 50% chance of our project completing (the 50th percentile). Since 50% of 10,000 is 5000, and since we know that the height of all bars sum up to 10000, then, starting from the left of the chart, we can sum the height of each bar until the total reaches 5000. The date outcome associated with the bar that puts us at 5000 (or just over) is the 50th percentile of the results. We can now draw that 50th percentile line on our chart. Using Figure 5.13 as an example, taking this approach we would find that the 50% line occurs at date 02/05/2017. The same approach can be used to find the 85th percentile. Since 8500 is 85% of 10000, we want to find the bar at the date at which the sum of the heights all the bars to the right of that date equal 8500 (or as close to just over 8500 as possible). In Figure 5.14, the 85th percentile happens at date 02/13/2017. Drawing both of those line on the chart from 6.13, our Results Histogram now looks like:

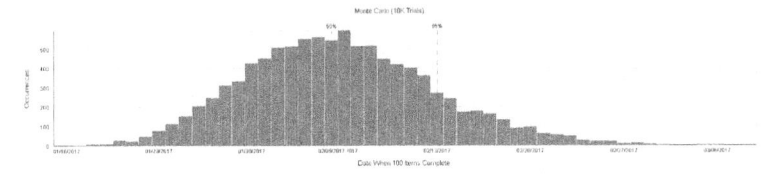

Figure 5.14 - Example Results Histogram

We can do the exact same thing for any percentile we wish.

Percentiles Are Forecasts

As was the case with Scatterplots, the percentile lines on your Results Histogram is your forecast. For example, in Figure 5.14 above, if you want to forecast to a confidence of 85%, then you will say that you will finish 100 items "on or before February 13, 2017 with an 85% confidence". The "on or before" part of the statement is very important. Remember that every bar to the left of the percentile you are interested in represents a set of results where the run of the simulation completed successfully. Therefore, you must include those outcomes as they are the "range" component of your forecast.

As was also the case with Scatterplots, you have to decide which percentile confidence is appropriate for your context. Again, this is more art than science. The placement of percentile lines helps you understand the risk associated with time to complete for a certain number of items to run through your process. We still have to deal with the tradeoff between higher confidence and a bigger date range. In Figure 5.14, the difference between 50% and 85% is 8 days. You still have to ask yourself the question "is the higher confidence worth the bigger range of possible completion dates?"

How Many Can I get Done?

We can use this same technique to answer a slightly different question: "How many items can I get done by a certain date?" The approach to this problem is similar to before, but there are a few nuances that you must be aware of.

First, you will still run a Throughput simulation for each day; however, instead of stopping the run when you get to having completed a certain number of items, now you will stop once you get to your target date.

Second, the possible outcomes that you will be tracking are not a set of dates, but a set of cumulative items completed. Therefore, the x-axis on your Results Histogram will be in units of items finished (not dates). The y-axis will be in units of frequency as always. By convention, the order of the items on the x-axis will be ordered from smallest to largest from left to right as shown in Figure 5.15:

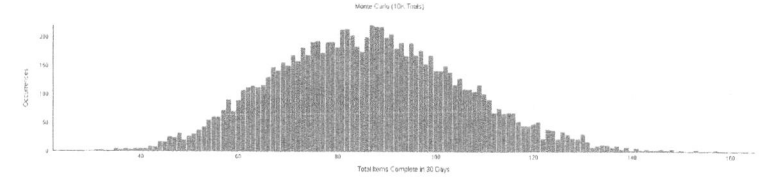

Figure 5.15 - Example Results Histogram

Third—and this is where it gets a bit tricky—the percentile lines on the Histogram will be drawn "backward". In the completed items scenario, we wanted to find out by what date a given number of items will finish. In that case, our chances of completing the items increased as the dates got further out. That is why in Figure 5.14, the 85th percentile date is further out to the right than the 50th percentile date. However, in the "how many items by a given date" scenario, we care about the *minimum* number of items that we can "commit" to completing with a certain percentage confidence, so our percentage chances actually *decrease* with the total number of items projected to complete. Think of it this way: it is much more likely that you will complete 1 item in the next 10 days than you will complete 100 items. Therefore, your chances of completing at least 1 item is probably pretty high (maybe somewhere around 99%) whereas your chances of completing at least 100 items is very low (probably somewhere much lower than 1%). Thus, drawing percentile lines on the Results Histogram in this case will look something like:

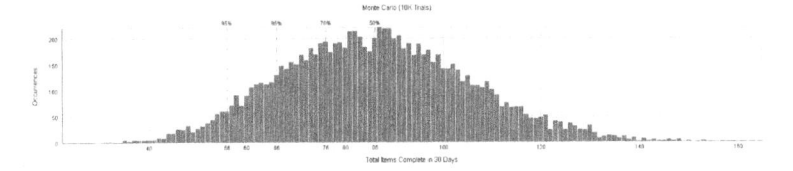

Figure 5.16 - Example Results Histogram

You will see in Figure 5.16 that you have an 85% chance of completing 66 items *or more* by a given date. You have a 50% chance of completing 86 items or more by the same given date. As expected, our chances go down with the more items forecasted to finish.

Conclusion

At its simplest, the Monte Carlo Simulation can be thought of as a set of experiments with random numbers. The method is normally applied to highly uncertain problems where direct computation is difficult, impractical, or impossible. It has proved a useful tool in many fields including nuclear physics, oil and gas exploration, finance, and insurance. Given the uncertainty in knowledge work it seems strange that our industry has been rather late to the Monte Carlo game. One might argue that it has taken the emergence of modern agile methods to get us to the point where we could even model the work that we do for simulation. Regardless, I firmly believe that the Monte Carlo Method is the future of forecasting in knowledge work.

Thus, in order to make an accurate forecast about the completion time of multiple items, you need to:

1. Run a MCS for your chosen scenario: either what date will you complete a given number of items or how many items can you complete by a given date.
2. Calculate Percentile Lines for the Results Histogram of your MCS
3. Decide how much "confidence" you need in your forecast
4. Communicate your forecast in terms of the range and probability of your required confidence.

You will almost certainly want to use a tool to do this for you, but more on that in Chapter 12.

Key Learnings and Takeaways

- Throughput is a measure of the number of work items completed per unit of time.
- Use the exact same data you tracked for Cycle Time to calculate Throughput.
- Throughput is the metric we use to make forecasts for multiple items.
- To make a forecast for multiple items run a Monte Carlo Simulation.
- Draw percentile lines the Results Histogram of your MCS.
- Communicate your forecast based on those percentiles.
- The Percentile Lines and the associated ranges and probabilities represent your forecast for multiple items.

Chapter 6: How To Improve Forecasts For Multiple Items – What To Do

As was the case with single item forecasts, forecasts for multiple items are a two-sided optimization. In this chapter, we will explore some things you should do. In the next, some things you should not.

Consistent Throughput

Let's consider two cases of a team that is working over a 30-day period. In the first case, a team closes exactly 30 items over the course of the thirty days. Their historical Throughput can be visualized like:

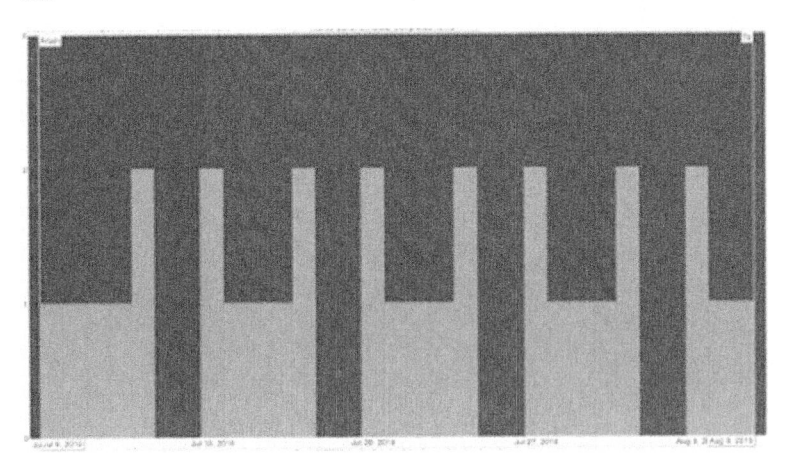

Figure 6.1 - Sample Historical Throughput

Figure 6.1 represents a historical Throughput bar chart. Note that this graph is not a Histogram! On this bar chart, we have a timeline across the bottom (x-axis) that, for this particular example, covers the 30-day period from July 6, 2015 to August 5, 2015. Up the side (y-axis) of the chart is the number of items completed for any given day. The way this chart is constructed is that for every single day of the timeline, the team's Throughput is plotted. The height of each bar, then, corresponds to the number of items that the team completed on that particular day. For example, you can see that on July 13, 2015 this team closed 2 items. On July 6, they closed 1 item. For every day that you see a blank space (no bar), the team closed 0 items.

As we just learned in the previous chapter, this is exactly the type of input data that we can use to run an MCS. So let's do that: let's simulate how many items this team can get done in the next 30 days given what they have done in the past 30 days. In this first case, after 10,000 simulations, the Results Histogram of our simulation might look like:

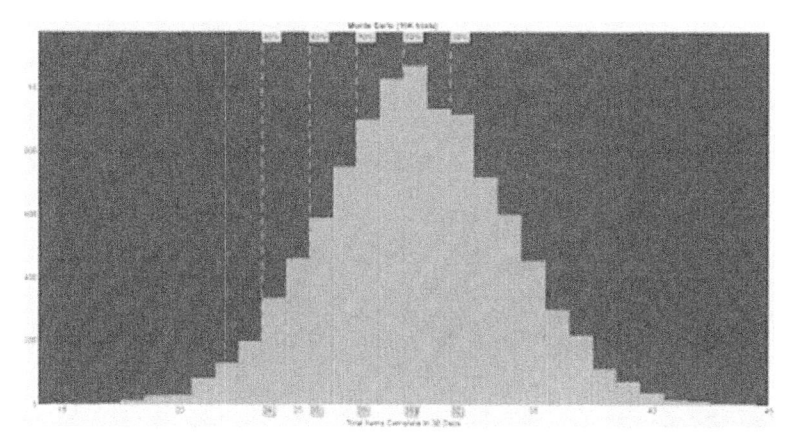

![Figure 6.2 histogram]

Figure 6.2 - Results Histogram

From Figure 6.2, you can see that the team has a 95% chance of getting 24 or more items done in the next 30 days, an 85% chance of getting 26 or more items done (remember that the percentile lines on the Results Histogram are "backward" for the "How Many" type of MCS).

But what if the team's historical Throughput looked different? In the second case I want you to consider, the same team gets the same exact 30 items done over the same 30-day time period. However, instead of their historical Throughput looking like Figure 6.2, it now looks like:

Chapter 6: How To Improve Forecasts For Multiple Items – What To Do

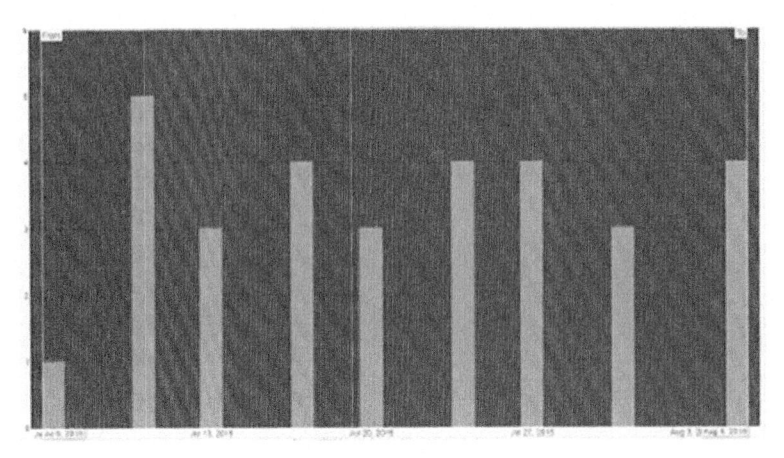

Figure 6.3 - Sample Historical Throughput

In this case, you can see the team had days with higher overall Throughputs than the first case, but they also had more days where they had zero Throughput. If we were to run an MCS on this new historical Throughput, then, after 10,000 runs, the Results Histogram might look like:

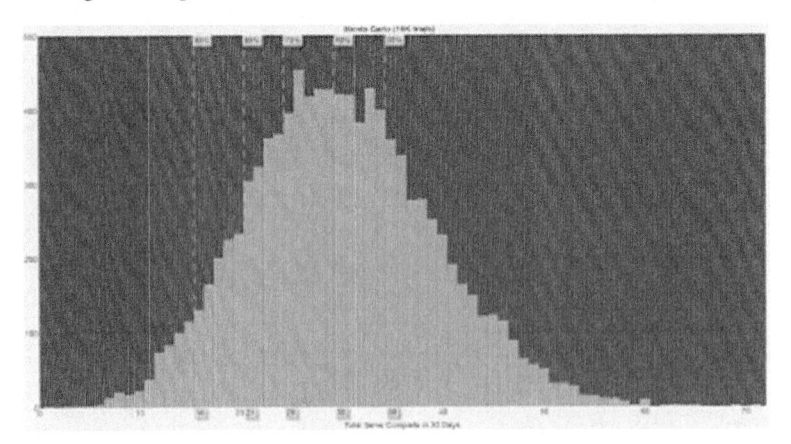

Figure 6.4 - Results Histogram

In this second case, the team has a 95% chance of getting 16 items or more done in the next 30 days. They have an 85% chance of getting 21 items or more done.

Let's take a look at these two results side by side:

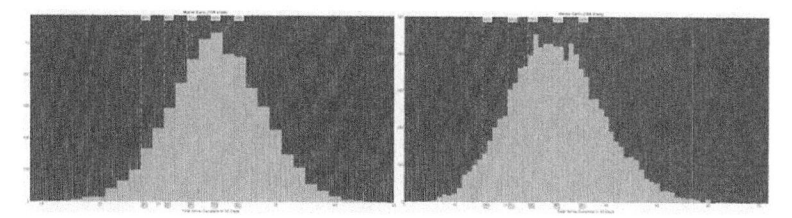

Figure 6.5 - Side by Side Comparison of Results Histograms

From our definition of a more accurate forecast from Chapter 3, you can see that the team in Case I is obviously much more predictable than the team in Case II, as Case I has far less possible outcomes per percentile. Interestingly enough, both cases have a 50% chance of getting 30 or more stories done in 30 days. However, Case II has many more possible outcomes both above and below that 50 percent line.

So what happened? Why the wildly different simulation results for the two situations where a team got exactly the same number of total items done over the same period of time?

The difference in possible outcomes is of course due to the variability of the inputted Throughput. To illustrate this, think about an extreme scenario for a second. Imagine that a team had a historical Throughput where they delivered one and only one item every day for 30 days. That is, they have zero days where they deliver zero items and they have zero days where they deliver more than one item. In other words, their Throughput is the model of consistency. Their historical Throughput chart would therefore look like:

Chapter 6: How To Improve Forecasts For Multiple Items – What To Do

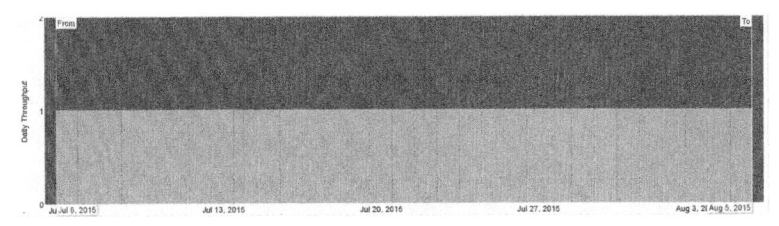

Figure 6.6 - **Sample Historical Throughput**

If we ran an MCS using this data, we would get a Results Histogram that looked like:

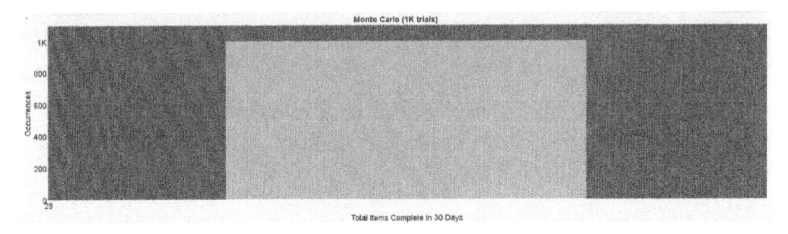

Figure 6.7 - **Results Histogram**

The results in Figure 6.7 are what we would expect: there is only one possible outcome for the next 30 days and that possible outcome is that we will get exactly 30 items done. No matter how many simulations we run, this will be the one and only outcome. In fact, in this scenario we need not even run an MCS—an average projection would be just fine (the dangers of projections based on average will be covered in the next chapter). We, however, live in the real world where there is variability in our process's Throughput–which is precisely why we need something like MCS.

Getting back to our original example, Case I clearly had a much more consistent Throughput than Case II. While the team in Case I did not deliver a many of items on any given day, on most days they did at least deliver something; i.e., they minimized the number of days with zero Throughput. In Case II, however, the team was much more variable in their daily Throughput. While they did indeed have days where they delivered a lot of items (e.g., a maximum of 5 items on July 10) they also had many more days where they delivered zero items. What that means is that when we run our MCS, for any given simulated day, we have a much higher chance of selecting a zero for our input Throughput. While it is true that, theoretically, in both cases, we could choose a zero for every single day of our 30-day simulation, the chance of that happening is much higher in Case II than in Case I. You can actually see this in the Results Histogram for Case II (Figure 6.4). In Figure 6.4, we had several outcomes of a low single-digit number of items being completed over the 30 days whereas in Case I (Figure 6.3), there were no results that were less than 15. The math proves out that processes with higher variability Throughput are less predictable, exactly as expected. At least now we can actually quantify that difference in predictability.

One last thing on variability I would like you to consider when dealing with very erratic Throughput. In this new case, our same team has one day where they have an extreme outlier in terms of the number items delivered on a single day of their historical Throughput. This case is shown in Figure 6.8:

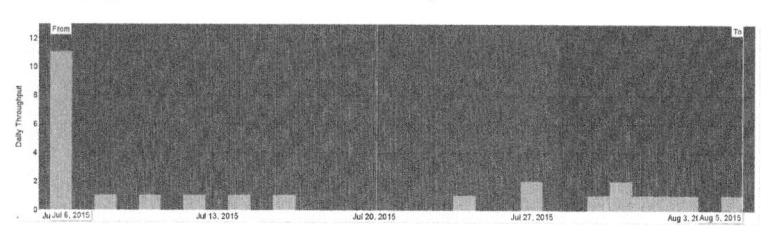

Figure 6.8 - Sample Historical Throughput

If we were to run an MCS on this data (this time I will do 1,000,000 runs so you can clearly see the shape of the results) we would get a Results Histogram that looks like:

Chapter 6: How To Improve Forecasts For Multiple Items – What To Do

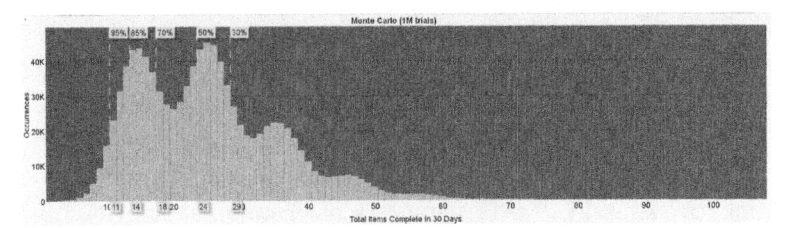

Figure 6.9 - Results Histogram

Notice anything interesting here? In the last chapter I said that your Results Histogram should approximate a Normal Distribution. However, Figure 6.9 looks nothing like a bell curve. It may sound self-evident, but whenever you see a "non-Normal"-looking distribution, then you know there is something not normal going on. Those multiple "humps" you see are due to the chances that the extreme Throughput outlier is selected one or more times for any particular outcome. I will refer you back to the last chapter when I said that—in general—when forecasting the number of items that can be completed by a certain date, chances of higher numbers are less than chances for lower numbers. The humps in Figure 6.9 are analytically strange because they make it look like there are some several higher number outcomes that are more likely than smaller number outcomes. This is due to the fact that whenever the extreme Throughput outlier is chosen as an input then it looks like we can get a lot of things done. However, the chance that the outlier is chosen is very small; even so, when chosen, you can see it has a profound impact on the outcome. Further, notice in Figure 6.9 how the long the tail to the right is for these results. There are many more possible outcomes here, again, because of the chance of selecting the outlier many times. All in all, this is not a very predictable process and you should be wary when you see a pattern like this emerge in your forecasts.

The moral of this story is that the more consistent (stable) Throughput you can get, then the more accurate your MCS forecasts are going to be. While, yes, we could just mine our Throughput data, run it through an MCS and simply accept the results that our simulation gives us, to me that kind of misses the point. Getting more accurate forecasts is more about the process improvements we can make than it is about how good our statistic skills are. Recognizing certain patterns that emerge from your simulations is going to help you to recognize (a) that a problem exists; and (b) what process interventions to make for improvement.

By the way, the basics of system stability and how to get more consistent Throughput will be covered in Chapter 8. You will want familiarize yourself with those concepts if you want to improve the overall accuracy of your forecasts for multiple items.

Reforecast Based on New Information

Just as with forecasts for single items, the most important thing you can do to produce an accurate forecast is to continually redo your MCS forecasts as you get updated data. We get new information about how our projects are progressing almost every day—just like the NHC continually gets new data on how hurricanes are progressing. How often do you reforecast based on this new information? If you do reforecast, do you use the probabilities associated with those new predictions to make meaningful interventions (again, like the NHC does)? Only a fool would ignore this new data in favor of a plan built on outdated information.

Professional poker players use this technique to great success—in fact, one might argue their whole livelihood depends on adjusting their game play to new information. Consider this Texas Hold 'Em example where you are dealt two Queens as your hole cards. A pair of Queens is actually a very good hand to stay in with—especially if you get to see the flop for cheap. However, if the flop comes and there is a King and/or Ace showing (and no Queen), and people start betting aggressively, it is probably a good time to fold. Why? Because the new information (visible cards, betting behavior) gives us a better idea of the probability that we have a winning hand. When we made our hole bet, we had imperfect information—that is, we only knew the two cards in our hand. Based on that information alone, it is a good strategy to stay in the game. However, when the flop comes we have much better information with which to formulate a new strategy. Clinging to the original plan of playing two Queens in this scenario will lose you a lot of money in the long run.

Let's consider a more project-based example. Meet Team A who had a historical Throughput that is characterized by Figure 6.10:

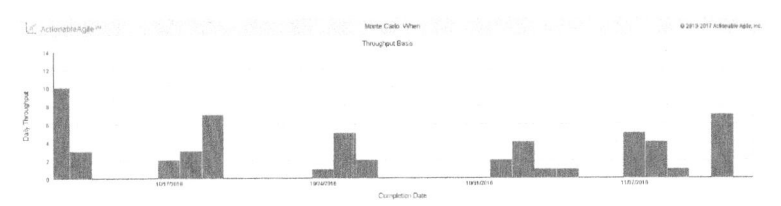

Figure 6.10 - Sample Historical Throughput

Let's say they have 100 items in their backlog to complete for this project. Using this historical Throughput they forecast how long it will take them to get these 100 items done. The Results Histogram for this forecast can be seen here:

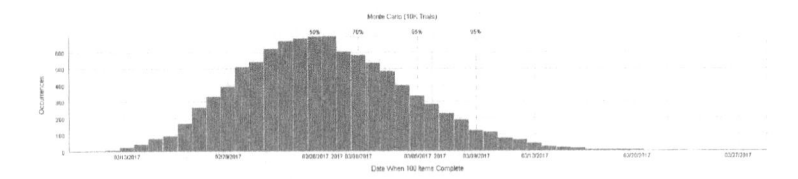

Figure 6.11 - Results Histogram

Figure 6.11 tells us that the team can get 100 items done on or before 03/05/2017 at 85% confidence. But a month into the project, some things have changed. The team's Throughput is less than the original input data, yet the team still thinks they have 100 items left to complete (due to missed or added scope). What are they to do?

I can tell you first what they definitely should not do: nothing. How many times during a release do you get new information (e.g., added scope, stolen resources, changed dates, etc.) and yet your team does nothing? (By the way, praying and crying do not count as doing something!) This new information should be embraced as an opportunity to improve the forecast. This, after all, is the essence of Agile: the ability to make progress with imperfect information coupled with the ability to adapt quickly when better information comes along.

> **The Essence of Agile**: the ability to make progress with imperfect information coupled with the ability to adapt quickly when better information comes along.

When this team re-runs their forecast based on the new information, the results are shown in Figure 6.12:

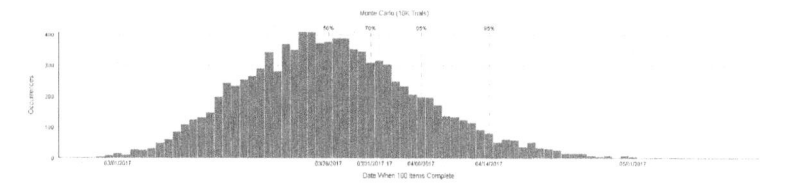

Figure 6.12 - Results Histogram

Plugging this new data into our model tells us the that team now has a 1% chance of hitting their original forecast date of 03/05/2017–down from 85%! Given the new forecast, now what actions should the team take? Some possible actions are:

- Remove scope
- Change the release date
- Add resources or work more hours
- Accept the lower confidence (but not be surprised if the project runs late)
- Any combination of the above

What option you choose will be completely dependent on your specific scenario, but now you have tools to help you decide. With

MCS, you can quickly run some "what if" scenarios, such as "What if we take 20 stories out of the backlog but keep the release date the same?", or "What would we have to change the release date to if we wanted to keep the number of stories in the backlog the same and still wanted an 85% chance of success?".

You have heard the old military maxim "a plan never survives engagement with the enemy." In knowledge work, we should expect things to go wrong with our plans and adapt our strategies when they do. Hope is not a strategy. Luck is not a strategy. Reforecasting is! The best forecasters in the world update their forecasts in the face of new information. You should too. A great example of how to do this is detailed in the Ultimate Software case study in Chapter 13.

Consider Different Selection Techniques for Inputs

In the last chapter, I outlined one strategy for how to select inputs for your MCS—the purely random approach. It turns out, there are many algorithms available to us on which to base a MC model. What follows is not an exhaustive list of some such selection techniques, but should give you an idea of some things you can play around with to increase the accuracy of your forecasts.

The first selection algorithm is what could reasonably be called the "day of the week" algorithm. For this method, we select an input based on what day of the week we are on at a given point in the simulation. For example, let's say we are running a simulation that is trying to simulate how many items we can get done between January 1, 2017 and February 1, 2017. We know from the previous chapter that to do this, we are going to have to select a random Throughput from some historical data for each day of the forecast time period. In the first approach, we simply randomly selected a number at random from all of our historical data. In this "day of the week" approach, though, we will only select inputs based on the day of the week we are forecasting. That is, let's say we are trying to choose a Throughput for January 3, 2013. In this algorithm, we know that January 3 is a Thursday, so we will only select a random Throughput for this day from all of the Thursday data we have in our input population. We will only select Mondays from Mondays, Tuesdays from Tuesdays, etc. This is not necessarily a better selection algorithm, but it might give more accurate results in your context.

A slight modification of the "day of the week" algorithm would be to select weekday inputs from weekday data and weekend inputs from weekend data. That is, if we are trying to simulate a Thursday—and since Thursday is a weekday—we would select any weekday's (Monday – Friday) data from our historical data. If we were trying to simulate a Saturday, we would select any Saturday or Sunday (i.e., any weekend day) from our historical data.

Yet something else you might play around with is Markov Chain Monte Carlo (MCMC). A full explanation of what MCMC is and how to use it is beyond the scope of this book, but for those of you looking for more advanced selection models, you might investigate the MCMC technique.

Again, I mention all of these not to suggest that any one algorithm is better than any other, but rather to give you some ideas of some experiments you might run in an attempt to make more accurate forecasts. Part of continuous improvement is continuous experimentation, and MCS makes it possible to try several different experiments and immediately validate results.

My guess is that more often than not the purely random approach is going to provide you with good enough forecasts—but, in the name of learning, there is certainly no harm in trying some of these other techniques.

Pay Attention to Your Model's Assumptions

There are implicit assumptions built into the historical Throughput you use as input into your MCS. For example, in the U.S. it would generally not be a good idea to choose historical Throughput data from the middle of November to the beginning of January to simulate how many items you can get done in February and March. That is because in the U.S. you have three major holidays in the November - December timeframe (Thanksgiving, Christmas, and New Year's) whereas you have none in the February – March timeframe. It stands to reason that the November – December Throughput is going to therefore be much lower and will provide poor predictive capability for what they can get done in the early part of the year.

Remember, the fundamental assumption that MCS is making is that the future that you are trying to predict looks roughly like the past that you have data for. If your historical data has a lot of holidays but your future does not, then you may want to try a different date range of historical inputs. If your historical data includes days where you had less people than normal—maybe you had team members stolen to help out with a different project—but the future that you are trying to predict assumes you will be at full team strength, then, again, maybe you should choose a different range of historical inputs.

The concepts in this section are more art than science but I am sure you are getting a feel for what I am trying to say. As always, leverage the power of MCS to quickly and easily try disparate historical data sets and assess the impacts of those choices. Once you experiment like that as well as incorporate all of the other concepts in this chapter, you will be well on your way to making much more accurate forecasts.

Conclusion

In this chapter, we have described several ways to improve multiple item forecasts. You have gained some insight into actions you should be taking in order to get more predictable. Next we will cover what you shouldn't do.

Key Learning and Takeaways

- One of the best ways to improve forecasts for multiple items is to improve the consistency of your Throughput.
- Consider reforecasting when you get new information: updated historical Throughput, a better understanding of the number of items to complete, etc.
- MCS allows you to run very quick "What If" scenarios to determine the best course of action based on new information received
- Consider using different input selection methods based on your specific context.
- Make sure the assumptions of your models match the future conditions that you are trying to forecast

Chapter 7: How to Improve Forecasts for Multiple Items – What Not to Do

When last we left Operation Eagle Claw (Chapter 5), the military was struggling to answer the question "how many helicopters do we send to rescue the hostages so that we ensure that at least six of the helicopters survive?" The answer to that question could not be "as many as you can!" because each added helicopter meant additional operational complexity, and, more importantly, more helicopters meant increased risk of early detection by the enemy. In addition to the lower limit (six), there was obviously also an upper limit to the number of airships they could send.

But how do you go about determining that upper limit? The first piece of information they needed was each helicopter's chance of survival during the mission. After detailed analysis, the planners determined that each helicopter would have a 75% chance of reaching Tehran in operational condition. At last the military had the real question they needed to answer: how many helicopters do you send if

(a) you know that you need a minimum of six working helicopters to ensure mission success; and ,

(b) you know that each helicopter has a 75% chance of survival?

It might seem obvious to you—and it certainly seemed obvious to the planners at the time—that the answer simply required a straightforward expected value calculation. In other words, the minimum number of helicopters needed equals the actual number of helicopters sent times the probability of each helicopter arriving successfully. Mathematically,

$$EV = X * P$$

Where the minimum number of helicopters expected to survive (EV) equals the required number of helicopters to send (X) multiplied by each helicopter's probability of success (P). We can then rearrange this equation to solve for what we are really looking for, X (the actual number of helicopters to send):

$$X = EV / P$$

For Operation Eagle Claw, we have EV = 6 and P = 0.75. Plugging numbers in, we get the solution that eight helicopters are required to ensure that six survive. In fact, it was reasoning much along these lines that convinced the military that eight was indeed the right answer and so eight helicopters were sent.

As you probably know, tragedy ensued almost immediately upon commencement of the operation. Of the eight helicopters that were originally sent, only six made it in operational condition to the *initial* staging area. Once at the staging area, one of the six surviving helicopters collided with a refueling plane. The collision resulted in an explosion that destroyed both aircraft and killed all on board. Down to only five helicopters, the Special Forces had no option but to abort the mission.

Was this disaster a failure of planning (risk management), a failure of execution, or a failure of both? Opinions are varied on the answer, but I'd like to look at this outcome from the "failure of risk management" perspective. Specifically, I'd like to challenge the reasoning that "if a minimum of six helicopters are required, and each helicopter has a 75% chance of survival, then sending eight helicopters will ensure the operations success". This type of reasoning is a classic example of the Flaw of Averages (in fact, much of the analysis of Operation Eagle Claw presented here is based on Dr. Savage's own supplemental material to his book and can be found here: http://probabilitymanagement.org/models.html). An expected value calculation is a classic example of a plan based on an average.

So, what should the military have done?

This brings us to the first point about what not do to when making forecasts for multiple items

Do Not Use Averages

The simple answer is that the military should not have used an average or expected value calculation, but rather should have used a more sophisticated (though not necessarily more complex) probabilistic method to gain better insight into overall operational risk. One such method is MCS.

Had the military run a simple MCS using their given data, they would have realized that sending eight helicopters would have resulted in only about a 68% chance of operational success—rather than the near certain chance of success assumed by the expected value calculation. If the operation's commanders knew they only had a 68% chance of success, don't you think they would have altered their plan? Don't you think they would have considered sending more helicopters, or considered sending a different type of helicopter with a higher chance of success, or considered scrapping the plan and coming up with a different one altogether?

In case you are wondering, if the military wanted to plan based on a 99% percent chance of success then they would have had to send no less than 12 helicopters. Would that have been a prudent approach?

But there are many other examples of planning based on average. Do you remember the very first multiple item forecast I asked you to make in Chapter 5? I asked you to forecast the completion of a project that had completed 10 items in two weeks and had 50 items left to do. The answer you probably came up with was 10 weeks. And you guessed it: this is yet another example of FoA.

Chapter 7: How to Improve Forecasts for Multiple Items – What Not to Do

Have you ever seen a Burn Up Chart that has a single projection line on it? An example might be:

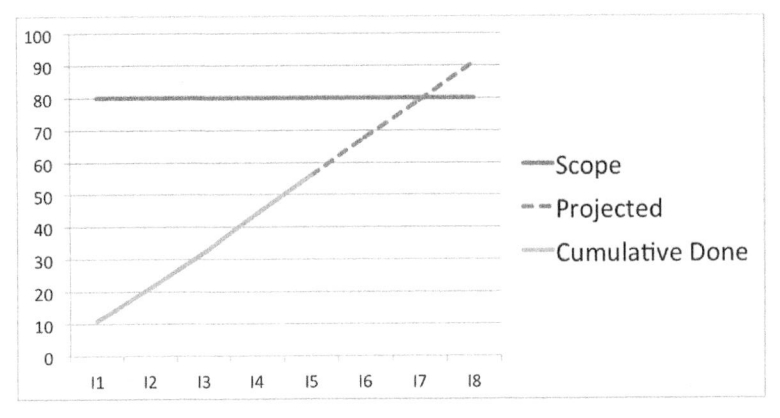

Figure 7.1 - BurnUp Chart

You will see from Figure 7.1 that there is a single backlog line at 80 that represents the number of stories that need to be completed. There is then a line that represents the number of stories (or, worse, Story Points) completed so far. Lastly, there is a dotted forecast line that is a dashed line off of the total completed line ultimately intersects with the backlog. In Figure 7.1, that intersection happens at Iteration 7 (not even a date!), so the implication is that this team will be done with all of their stories in the backlog some time during Iteration 7.

There are so many things wrong with this type of visualization that I am not sure where to begin. First, as I have just suggested, this is a classic example of FoA. Worse, it is FoA with a deterministic hack. While that dashed line projection may be the most likely option, remember that the most likely option is not very likely. The chances that the project will follow that pattern projected by the dashed line and intersect the backlog on the forecast date are minuscule.

Second, as I have said repeatedly, a forecast must include a range and a probability associated with that range. That straight-line projection gives us (a) no range, and (b) no probability. Depending on how our historical Throughput is distributed, it could be very dangerous to assume that the forecast line is around 50%. It might be much less; it might be much more—hence, the Flaw of Averages.

"No range?", some Burn Up proponents might say, "no problem! Here is a better chart" and then they will show you something like Figure 7.2:

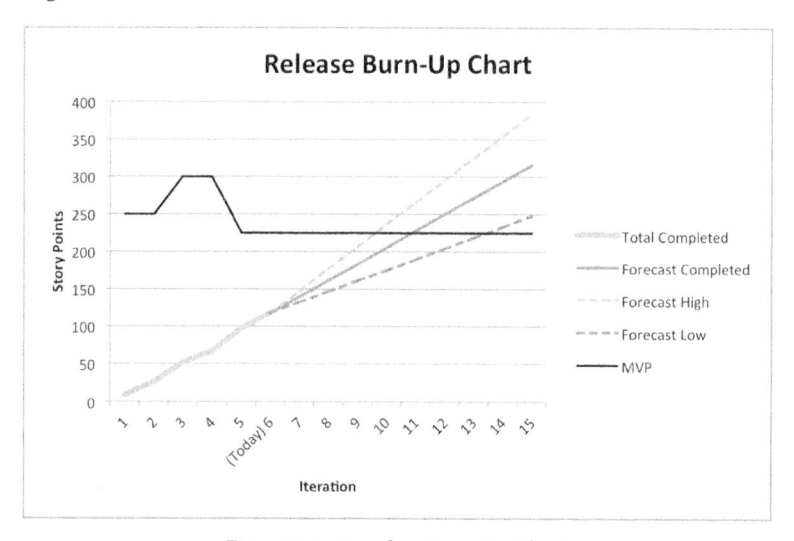

Figure 7.2 - Another Burn Up Chart

Figure 7.2 looks a lot like Figure 7.1 except now the chart has included "Forecast High" and "Forecast Low" dashed lines (this particular example uses Story Points, but the analogy holds for Throughput). This representation is better from the perspective that at least now there is an implicit acknowledgment of a probabilistic outcome; however, there is still no mention of the percentage probability of the future outcome falling between the two lines. You might assume that the high-low lines were drawn using the "mean plus and minus one standard deviation" algorithm discussed earlier (which is a dangerous assumption) and, therefore, the percentage range between the two lines is 68% (even more dangerous). Even if our historical Throughput was normally distributed, and the standard deviation range really was 68%, don't you think we can do better than a forecast with a 68% probability? Further, what if we wanted to know the probability of each discrete possible outcome? How would this chart visualize that? Therefore, we need to use MCS with its Results Histogram.

The last point I want to make about linear projection forecasts is that often they will give us a signal that something is wrong way too late. I discussed before that when a forecast communicates that a negative outcome is likely (e.g., we are going to miss our project completion date) that we need to take action. As mentioned in the previous chapter, some types of interventions that we can make are:

- Remove scope
- Change the date
- Add resources or work more hours
- Accept a higher risk of failure
- Any combination of above

How soon you know you are late will potentially dictate which of these options you choose. That is why we need a forecasting technique that will give us a warning signal as early as possible, thus leaving enough time to explore options and take action. In Chapter 14, I provide a real-world case study that details how a linear projection failed to warn a team soon enough and resulted in the late delivery of a project. In that case study, I also show how using MCS would have alerted the team much sooner in order to have affected a positive outcome.

Do Not Use Little's Law for Forecasting

I have not introduced you to Little's Law yet—you will have to wait for Chapter 8 for that. However no doubt that you have heard of Little's Law and that maybe you have even heard it as it pertains to forecasting. I will cover this in more detail in the upcoming chapter, but I would like to give you a "little" teaser now as to why using Little's Law to calculate a forecast is an incorrect application of the law.

As you will see, Little's Law is about examining what has happened in the past. It is not about making deterministic forecasts about the future. One of the reasons you cannot make deterministic forecasts with Little's Law is because it is impossible to predict which of the Law's assumptions will be violated in the future and how many times they will be violated. Each violation of an assumption invalidates the exactness of the law.

Even if you could use Little's Law for projections, you would not want to, because it is a relationship of averages (arithmetic means). This means any forecast made using Little's Law is susceptible to the Flaw of Averages. Further, Little's Law concerns itself with the probability distributions of the metrics associated with the underlying processes. If we do not know the distribution, then we cannot give a probability of where the average falls. If we do not know a probability, then we cannot make a forecast. It is that simple.

Alternatively, using Little's Law for a gut check validation of a forecast for a *qualitative* determination is perfectly acceptable. But, of course, you would not want to make any staffing, cost, or project commitments based on these back-of-the-envelope calculation type calculations.

Do Not Estimate

I do not want to repeat myself too much here so let me just say that all of the arguments that I made against estimation in Chapter 6 apply equally well here. Especially the observation that estimation usually only serves to make you less predictable, not more.

I have given you a technique, MCS, that provides more accurate answers with less effort. Use it.

Forget Curve Fitting

Not that I think about death a lot (usually only when I come across stupidity), but I have two leading candidates for epithets that will most likely appear on my tombstone:

1. "Here lies Daniel Vacanti, stolen from us in his youth because so-called process experts kept recommending Classes of Service for predictability"; or,
2. "Here lies Daniel Vacanti, stolen from us in his youth because so-called process experts kept recommending curve fitting for predictability".

(There are other epithet candidates that have to do with watching Rafael Nadal play tennis, playing games on the Xbox, driving in South Florida, and managing developers–but we can safely ignore those for now.)

Few things in this world make me angrier than when forecasting pundits advocate for fitting historical process data to well-known probability distributions. Maybe you have heard or read things like "your data fits a Weibull Curve with these shape parameters" or "your data is log-normally distributed with these parameters". This practice of mapping data to a specific probability model is called "curve-fitting". These "experts" will tell you to use those specific distributions as inputs to your MCS to make forecasts.

There are at least two problems with this advice. First, you almost need an advanced degree in mathematics or statistics to understand what they are talking about. And, more importantly, it does not matter!

Parameterized probability distributions (e.g., Weibull, Pareto, Gaussian, etc.) are generally data-analysis hacks that came about in an era when computations were done by hand. Computationally, it was much easier to assume that a set of data fit mathematical models with well know parameters and properties (think Normal distribution with mean, variance, standard deviation), than it was to have to manipulate thousands of numbers individually to come up with a forecast. Well-behaved, parameterized probability distributions gave mathematicians short cuts to deal with the ugliness of real-world, raw data. Those models had a time and a place. They still do—just not in the type of forecasting that we are talking about.

Donald J. Wheeler, an award-winning statistician (he is widely regarded as the world's foremost authority on Statistical Process Control), has this to say about curve fitting: "The first step in data analysis has nothing to do with what probability model is appropriate. Data are never generated by a probability model. Rather they are generated by a process or system that can change without warning." He goes on to say, "we will *never* have enough data to uniquely identify a specific probability model. Probability models are limiting functions for infinite sequences, and therefore, they can never be said to apply to any finite portion of that sequence. This is why any assumption of a probability model is just that–an unverifiable assumption."

Perhaps my favorite quote from Wheeler on this topic, however, is this one: "...even though you might find a probability model that provides a reasonable fit to your histogram, this does not mean that your data actually came from a single system. The erroneous idea that you can infer things from how well your data fit a particular probability model is known as the Quetelet Fallacy, after the Belgian astronomer who had this mistaken idea in 1840. Quetelet's Fallacy was exposed by Sir Francis Galton in an 1875 paper that proved to be the foundation of modern statistical analysis. In this paper Galton demonstrated that a collection of completely different processes, having different outcomes, could still yield a histogram that looked like a histogram produced by a single process having consistent outcomes. For the past 134 years statisticians have known better than to read too much into the shape of the histogram. Unfortunately, each generation of students of statistics has some individuals who follow in the footsteps of Quetelet. Some of them even write articles about their profoundly erroneous insights."

Whenever you see a published article that purports to show how to fit your process data to probability distribution, you should be skeptical. Very skeptical.

The reason that well-known statistical curves are irrelevant is because we have computers at our disposal now that can perform thousands of runs of an MCS almost instantaneously. I mean, can you imagine calculating the MCS algorithm that I explained in Chapter 6 by hand? Depending on the amount of data that you have and the number of days that you want to project out, it might take you days or weeks. If your dataset was large enough, there might not even be enough time left in the universe for you to finish your calculation.

Because we have computers that perform these simulations on raw data in the blink of an eye, there is no need to perform any mathematical shortcuts. Not only is using your raw data allowed but it will give you a much better answer anyway because, as Wheeler points out, probability distributions are at best an approximation of what is really going on in your process.

Probability distribution advocates will quickly point out that using raw process data fails in the case where you have no process data. This could be, for example, when putting together a brand-new team for a completely new type of project that you have never worked on before.

While I do not necessarily disagree that it is difficult to make forecasts based on past data when you have no data, I do have two things I would like to say in response. First, it is a very rare case where you actually have no data. There is usually some past project, some similar team, some kind of relevant data somewhere that is a close enough approximation that you can use to make a good enough first forecast. Even if not, then you certainly could use some type of probability distribution to generate your random inputs for you. And here's the kicker: which probability distribution you use does not necessarily matter that much because—as I mentioned in Chapter 1—you will want to reforecast using your own, real data once your new project has started and you have real data to use.

The accuracy of your forecast will ultimately come from the use of real project data and will have nothing to do with how good you were at choosing a probability model to begin with.

Therefore, to improve the accuracy of your models, do not do any kind of curve-fitting. At best, it is a mathematical boondoggle; at worst, it will lead you to make erroneous decisions. Repeat after me: "We have our data so let's use our data!".

Conclusion

In the past two chapters I have given you tips on what to do and what not to do when making forecasts for multiple items. Employing these tips for your process wil boost your overall predictability. I will come back to these topics in Chapter 11 when I give you some more ideas on how to put all of these forecasting techniques together.

Until then, however, we have yet to answer the most important question which faces us when making forecasts for single items or multiple items: "How do I know if I can even trust my forecasts?". How to answer that question requires a whole section of the book on its own, so we will go there next.

Key Learnings and Takeaways

- Estimation is a waste of time. Don't do it.
- Using an Expected Value calculation as a forecast is a plan based on an average. Don't do it.
- Using a Linear Projection as a forecast is a plan based on an average. Don't do it.
- Using Little's Law as a forecast is a plan based on an average. Don't do it.
- Curve fitting of historical data is a statistical hack. Don't do it.

Section IV: How To Know If You Can Trust Your Forecasts

> Much of the information presented in this section is restated material from my previous book, "Actionable Agile Metrics for Predictability". If you have recently read that book then this section can safely be skipped without loss of continuity.

Chapter 8: Process Stability As Defined by Little's Law

So far in this book I have discussed two basic metrics of flow:

1. Cycle Time (which we used to make forecasts for single items); and,
2. Throughput (which we used to make forecasts for multiple items).

But do you recall the most famous metric of all?

You probably have noticed that up until now I have ignored the most important of the three basic flow metrics: Work In Progress (WIP). Work In Progress is the most important metric for two reasons:

1. Both Cycle Time and Throughput are defined in terms of WIP (Cycle Time is the amount of elapsed time an item spends as WIP and Throughput is the amount of WIP completed per unit of time); and, more importantly,
2. WIP is the biggest influencer of both the other metrics

Point #2 is a result of what is probably the most famous equation in the flow-based world: Little's Law.

I will show you the exact equation that is Little's Law (LL) shortly, but I want to hold off for now because I do not want you focused on the math in the equation. As I will state in very strong terms below, the math of LL is not what is important (despite what you may have read until now). The reason that you must understand LL is because LL is what is going to define process stability. Having a process that is stable in terms of LL is the most important factor in knowing if we can trust the forecasts we are making using the techniques previously discussed. Making forecasts without some notion of system stability is little better than simply guessing. Worse, forecasting using the methods in the book but based on data from an unstable system will give you a false sense of accuracy and security. It could ultimately lead you to make poor decisions and leave you no better off than had you stuck with traditional Agile estimation practices.

As you will see, the beauty of the LL approach is that it will help you to improve the overall daily performance of your process. If you focus on that—as I have said many times before—the forecasting bits will take care of themselves.

But before I get any further, I should point out that a lot of what is presented in the rest of this chapter and the rest of this section is a repeat of information that I included in my first book, "Actionable Agile Metrics for Predictability" (especially chapters 3, 7, 8, and 9). If you are already familiar with those ideas, then you can safely skip on to Chapter 11. However, unless you read that book yesterday, I encourage you to continue to read on. A "little" refresher never hurt anyone, now, did it?

A Little's Law Refresher

In what may be one of the most miraculous results in the history of process analysis, the three metrics of flow are intrinsically linked by a very straightforward and very powerful relationship known as Little's Law:

$$AverageCycleTime = \frac{AverageWorkInProgress}{AverageThroughput}$$

When LL is introduced what is very often left out is the set of assumptions that must be in place for the law to work.

Understanding the assumptions behind the equation is the key to understanding the law itself.

> Understanding the assumptions behind the equation is the key to understanding the law itself, and therefore going to be the key to making accurate forecasts.

Once you understand the assumptions, then you can use those assumptions as a guide to some process policies that you can put in place to aid predictability.

The math of Little's Law is simple. But, strangely enough, this chapter is not about the math. What it is about—and I cannot stress this point enough if we want to gain a greater appreciation of the law's applicability to forecasting—is looking far beyond the elegance of the equation to get a deeper understanding of the background assumptions needed to make the law work. That is where things get more complicated, but it is also where we will find the greatest aid for forecast accuracy and process improvement. A thorough comprehension of why Little's Law works the way it does is going to be the basis for understanding how the basic metrics of flow can become predictably actionable.

We Need a Little Help

First, some background.

Dr. John Little spent much of his early career studying queuing systems like Figure 8.1:

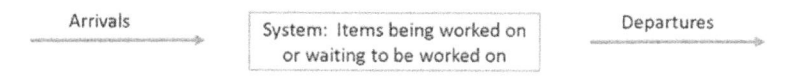

Arrivals → System: Items being worked on or waiting to be worked on → Departures

Figure 8.1 - Simple Queuing System

In fact, one of the best definitions of such a queuing system comes from Dr. Little himself: "A queuing system consists of discrete objects we shall call items, which arrive at some rate to the system. The items could be cars at a toll booth, people in a cafeteria line, aircraft on a production line, or instructions waiting to be executed inside a computer. The stream of arrivals enters the system, joins one or more queues and eventually receives service, and exits in a stream of departures. The service might be a taxi ride (travelers), a bowl of soup (lunch eaters), or auto repair (car owners). In most cases, service is the bottleneck that creates the queue, and so we usually have a service operation with a service time, but this is not required. In such a case, we assume there is nevertheless a waiting time. Sometimes a distinction is made between number in queue and total number in queue plus service, the latter being called number in system." The diversity of domains that he mentions here is extraordinary. While he does not specifically mention software development or knowledge work in general, I am going to suggest that these areas can also be readily modeled in this way.

In 1961, Dr. Little set out to prove what seemed to be a very general and very common result exhibited by all queuing systems. The result that he was researching was a connection between the average Arrival Rate of a queue, the average number of items in the queue, and the average amount of time an item spent in the queue (for the purpose of this chapter, when I say "average" I am really talking about "arithmetic mean"). Mathematically, the relationship between these three metrics looks like:

Equation (1): $L = \lambda^* W$

Where:

L = the average number of items in the queuing system.
λ = the average number of items arriving per unit time.
W = the average wait time in the system for an item.

Notice that Equation (1) is stated strictly in terms of a queuing system's Arrival Rate. This point is going to be of special interest a little later in this chapter.

Also notice that—if it is not obvious already—Little's Law is a relationship of averages. Most knowledge work applications and discussions of the law neglect this very important detail. The fact that Little's Law is based on averages is not necessarily good or bad. It is only bad when people to try to apply the law for uses that it was never intended (such as forecasting—which will be discussed a little later).

Dr. Little was the first to provide a rigorous proof for Equation (1), and this relationship has since been known as Little's Law. According to him, one of the reasons why the law is so important is the fact that (emphasis is mine): "L, λ, and W are three quite different and important measures of effectiveness of system performance, and Little's Law insists that they must obey the 'law.'... *Little's Law locks the three measures together in a unique and consistent way for any system in which it applies. Little's Law will not tell the managers how to handle trade-offs or provide innovations to improve their chosen measures, but it lays down a necessary relation.* As such, it provides structure for thinking about any operation that can be cast as a queue and suggests what data might be valuable to collect."

The great advantage of Little's Law is the overall simplicity of its calculation. Specifically, if one has any two of the above three statistics, then one can easily calculate the third. This result is extremely useful as there are many situations in many different domains where the measurement of all three metrics of interest is difficult, expensive, or even impossible. Little's Law shows us that if we can measure any two attributes, then we automatically get the third.

To illustrate this point, Dr. Little used the very simple example of a wine rack. Let's say you have a wine rack that, on average, always has 100 bottles in it. Let's further say that you replenish the rack at an average rate of two bottles per week. Knowing just these two numbers (and nothing else!) allows us to determine how long, on average, a given bottle spends sitting in the rack. By applying Equation (1), we have L equal to 100 and λ equal to 2. Plugging those numbers into the formula tells us that a given wine bottle spends, on average, 50 weeks in the rack.

Before we get much further, it is worth exploring what necessary contextual conditions are required for the law to hold. When stated in the form of Equation (1) the only assumption necessary is that the system under consideration has some guarantee of being in a steady state. That's it. Really, that's it. To illustrate the things we do not need, notice that we can arrive at the wine rack result without tracking the specific arrival or departure dates for each or any individual bottle. We also do not need to know the specific order that the bottles were placed in the rack, or the specific order that the bottles were taken off the rack. We do not need to understand anything fancy like the underlying probability distributions of the Arrival and Departure Rates. Interestingly, we do not even need to track the size of the bottles in the rack. We could have some small 20cl bottles or some large 2 litre bottles in addition to the more standard 750ml bottles. The variation in size has no impact on the basic result. (I mentioned in my previous book that I was in the process of verifying this result independently on my own. I want to be as thorough as possible in my experiment, so the validation is taking some time. Rest assured that I am still vigilant in my ongoing pursuit of the truth!)

As remarkable as all of this may be, the mathematics are not really what is important for our purposes here. What is important is that we acknowledge that the fundamental relationship exists. Understanding the inextricable link among these metrics is one of the most powerful tools at our disposal in terms of predictable process design.

But before we can get into how Little's Law can help us with predictability, it is probably helpful to first state the relationship in more familiar terms.

Little's Law from a Different Perspective

In the late 1980s (or early 1990s depending on whom you ask) Little's Law was usurped by the Operations Management (OM) community and was changed to emphasize OM's focus on Throughput. The OM crowd thus changed the terms in Little's Law to reflect their different perspective as shown by Equation (2):

$$AverageCycleTime = \frac{AverageWorkInProgress}{AverageThroughput}$$

Where: **Cycle Time (CT)** = the average amount of time it takes for an item to flow through the system. **Work In Progress (WIP)** = the average total inventory in the system. **Throughput (TH)** = the average Throughput of the system.

In the interest of completeness, it is ok to perform the algebra on Little's Law so that it takes the different, yet still valid, forms: Equation (3)

$$AverageThroughput = \frac{AverageWorkInProgress}{AverageCycleTime}$$

and Equation (4)

$$AverageWorkInProgress = AverageCycleTime * AverageThroughput$$

Because of its roots in Operations Management, the Lean, Agile, and Kanban communities have adopted this "Throughput" form of Little's Law as their own. If you have seen Little's Law before, you have almost certainly seen it in the form of Equation (2)—even though Equation (2) does not represent the law's original format.

The upshot of Little's Law is that, in general, the more things that you work on at any given time (on average) the longer it is going to take for each of those things to finish (on average). As a case in point, managers who are ignorant of this law panic when they see that their Cycle Times are too long and perform the exact opposite intervention of what they should do: they start more work. After all, they reason, if things take so long, then they need to start new items as soon as possible so that those items finish on time—regardless of what is currently in progress. The result is that items only take longer and longer to complete. Thus, managers feel more and more pressure to start things sooner and sooner. You can see how this vicious cycle gets started and perpetuates itself. After studying Little's Law, you should realize that if Cycle Times are too long then the first thing you should consider is lowering WIP. It feels uncomfortable, but it is true. In order to get stuff done faster, you need to work on less (again, on average).

What Dr. Little demonstrated is that the three flow metrics are all essentially three sides of the same coin (if a coin could have three sides). By changing one of them, you will almost certainly affect one or both of the other two. In other words, Little's Law reveals what levers that we can pull when undertaking process improvement. Further, as we are about to see, Little's Law will suggest the specific interventions that we should explore when our process is not performing the way we think it should.

At the risk of repeating myself, what I am talking about here is simple, incontrovertible mathematical fact. A change in one metric always results in a change in the others. Most companies that I talk to that complain of poor predictability are almost always ignorant of the negative implication of too much WIP on Cycle Time or Throughput. Ignore this correlation at your own peril.

It is all about the Assumptions

I said at the outset that Little's Law is deceptively simple. Here is where things get more complicated.

It is easy to see from a purely mathematical perspective that Equation (1) is logically equivalent to Equation (2). But it is more important to focus on the underlying difference between the two. As I mentioned earlier, Equation (1) is expressly stated in terms of the *Arrival Rate* to the system whereas Equation (2) is expressly stated in terms of the *Departure Rate* from the system. This emphasis on Throughput in Equation (2) probably seems more comfortable to us as it reflects the usual perspective of a knowledge work process. Typically, in our context, we care about the rate at which we are finishing our work (even though, as we shall soon see, we should care just as much about the rate at which we start work). What is nice to know is that Little's Law can morph to match either required perspective.

At first glance, this change may not otherwise seem all that significant. However, this transformation from the perspective of arrivals to the perspective of departures has a profound impact in terms of how we think about and apply the law. When we state Little's Law in terms of a system's Throughput then we must also immediately consider if any of the underlying assumptions must also change in order for the departure-oriented law to be valid.

Earlier when I first introduced Equation (1) I had stated that there was really only one assumption that needed to be in place for it to work. Well, in the interest of completeness, there were actually three. For Equation (1) we need:

1. A steady state (i.e., that the underlying stochastic processes are stationary)
2. An arbitrarily long period of time under observation (to guarantee the stationarity of the underlying stochastic processes)
3. That the calculation be performed using consistent units (e.g., if wait time is stated in days, then Arrival Rate must also be stated in terms of days).

Do not worry if you do not know what "stochastic" or "stationary" means. You do not need to. As I have just said, I mention these things for completeness only.

When we shift perspective to look at Little's Law from the perspective of Throughput rather than from the perspective of

Arrival Rate, however, we also need to change the underlying assumptions necessary for the law to be valid. This point is so important, I want to place it in its own callout:

> Looking at Little's Law from the perspective of Throughput rather than from the perspective of Arrival Rate necessitates a change in the assumptions required for the law to be valid.

When applying the Throughput form of Little's Law (Equation (2)), there are two basic cases to consider. And each case is going to require its own assumption to be valid.

The first case to consider is if you ever operate a process where the total WIP of the system is ever allowed to go to zero. If so, then Little's Law is exact between any two time instances where the total process WIP is zero (and, yes, I did say exact). Further, only one additional assumption is needed for this case. All we require is that everything that enters the system eventually exits. That's it. Reflect on this result for a second and see if you can think of any circumstance where you start a time period with zero WIP and end the time period with zero WIP. Two examples immediately come to my mind. An ideal software "project" would start with zero WIP and end with zero WIP. If that is the case, then at the end of the project, using Little's Law we could exactly determine the average of any of the three basic metrics of flow assuming we collected data on the other two. Another good example would be any Scrum sprint. If you are doing canonical Scrum, then, by definition you start each sprint with zero WIP and you end each sprint with zero WIP (remember, we are talking textbook Scrum here—I know practice usually falls far short of prescription). If so, then just as in the previous example, you could use Little's Law to calculate an average of any of the three basic metrics of flow assuming that you have collected the data for the other two.

Unfortunately, though, most of us do not live in a world where we ever run out of WIP. We work on multiple projects simultaneously, or there is never a clean break between when one project starts and another finishes, or we are forced to do maintenance requests and production support in addition to regular project work, or we never finish all the work that we had started at the beginning of sprints, etc.

Which brings us to the second case we need to consider for LL: when process WIP never goes to zero. In this case, we have to be much more careful about the assumptions that are required for a valid application of Little's Law. When WIP never goes to zero, then the assumptions that are necessary to make Little's Law (in the form of Equation (2)) work are:

1. The average input or Arrival Rate (λ) should equal the average output or Departure Rate (Throughput).
2. All work that is started will eventually be completed and exit the system.
3. The amount of WIP should be roughly the same at the beginning and at the end of the time interval chosen for the calculation.
4. The average age of the WIP is neither increasing nor decreasing.
5. Cycle Time, WIP, and Throughput must all be measured using consistent units.

The first two assumptions (#1 and #2) comprise a notion known as Conservation of Flow and the second two assumptions (#3 and #4) speak to the notion of system stability.

The last assumption (#5) is necessary for the math (and any corresponding analysis) to come out correctly (you will notice this is the same assumption necessary when stating the law in terms of arrivals). The necessity for using consistent units when performing a Little's Law calculation should be intuitively obvious, but it is fairly easy to get tripped up over this. When we say "consistent" units what we are really saying is, for example, if we are measuring average Cycle Time using the unit of time "day", then the average Throughput must be in the form of the number of items per that same unit of time (day), and the average WIP must be the average amount of items for one unit of time (day). As another example, if you want to measure average Throughput in terms of items per week (i.e., the unit of time here is "week"), then average Cycle Time must be stated in terms of weeks, and average WIP must be the average for each week. You might think I am wasting your time by mentioning this, but you would be surprised how many teams miss this point (one is immediately reminded of when NASA slammed an orbiter into the side of Mars because one team used metric units while another used English units—moral of the story: do not do that). For example, I saw one Scrum team who was measuring their velocity in terms of story points per sprint (as Scrum teams are wont to do). For their Little's Law calculation, they proceeded to plug in their velocity number for Throughput, their WIP number as total number of user stories (actual stories—not story points) completed in the sprint, and expected to get a Cycle Time number in days. You can imagine their surprise when the numbers did not come out quite the way that they expected (but why they were plugging numbers into LL to begin with I will never understand).

Assumptions as Process Policies

Understanding these foundational assumptions is of monumental importance. Despite what many people will tell you, the true power of Little's Law is *not* in performing the mathematical calculation. Even though I have spent so much time on it already, I want you to forget about the arithmetic. In truth, most of us will never need to compute Little's Law. The collection of the data to calculate the three flow metrics is so easy that you should never have to compute one of them from the other two—just go look at the data!

Rather, the true power of Little's Law lies in understanding the assumptions necessary for the law to work in the first place. If there are three things that I want you to have taken away from this conversation about Little's Law they are:

1. It is all about the assumptions.

2. It is all about the assumptions.
3. It is all about the assumptions.

Every time you violate an assumption of Little's Law your process becomes less predictable. Every time. This increased unpredictability may manifest itself as longer Cycle Times or more process variability or both. Or, worse still, these violations may not even immediately show up in your data. The whole time you are violating Little's Law your data may be showing you a rosier picture of the world than is really occurring. The danger here is that you may be basing some forecast on this overly optimistic view—only to find that things are much worse than they seemed.

Of course, we live in the real world and there are going to be times when violating these assumptions is going to be unavoidable or even necessary. But that is exactly why it is all the more important to understand the implications when these violations occur. There are always going to be things that happen to us that are outside of our control. However, the last thing we want to do is compound those uncontrollable events by allowing bad things to happen that were in our control and could have easily prevented. Control what you can control and then try to eliminate or mitigate the things you cannot.

The above principles (especially the first four) are going to help us do just that. We can use these assumptions as the basis for some simple policies that will govern the operation of our process. These policies will serve to control the things that we can control. These policies will serve to make our process more predictable.

Based on the assumptions above, some process policies might include (but certainly would not be limited to):

- We will only start new work at about the same rate that we finish old work.
- We will make every reasonable effort to finish all work that is started and minimize wasted effort due to discarded work items (this will necessitate some notion of late-binding "commitment").

- If work becomes blocked, we will do everything we can do unblock that work as expeditiously as possible.
- We will closely monitor our policies around the order in which we pull items through our system so that some work items do not sit and age unnecessarily.

The design of your process is really just the sum of all the policies you have in place. How well your system performs or does not perform is directly attributable to those policies and to how well you adhere or do not adhere to them. When I talk about designing for predictability, what I am talking about is giving you some clues—some insights—into appropriate policies that you can build into the day to day operation of your process. These policies will serve to normalize and stabilize your system in order to give your process the predictability that you are looking for. It is only from this stable base that we can even hope to implement real, long-lasting process improvement.

As my friend and colleague Frank Vega so often likes to say, "your policies shape your data and your data shape your policies". The policies that I have mentioned here will in no small way influence the data that you collect from your process. That is a good thing, by the way. It is a good thing because that data in and of itself is potentially going to further suggest where our process policies are deficient. It is this virtuous cycle that I am talking about when I say "actionable metrics for predictability".

Kanban Systems

From a WIP perspective, it may seem that running a Kanban system guarantees Little's Law's assumptions are taken care of. There are several reasons why that may not be the case:

1. It is possible that changing WIP limits may have no effect on total average WIP (e.g., decreasing or increasing a WIP limit after a clear systemic bottleneck). This may be one reason you

do not get the "forecasted" behavior you might expect from Little's Law.
2. Setting a WIP limit is not necessarily the same as limiting Work In Progress. I cannot tell you how many teams I come across that set WIP Limits but then routinely violate them. And violate them egregiously and with (self) management impunity.
3. Average WIP over a time period is highly dependent on pull policies in place. E.g., are as many items as possible pulled in order to satisfy WIP limits at all times? Are pull policies in place that are in direct violation of the law (e.g. Classes of Service)?

The point here is that if you are using a Kanban system, you cannot just simply add up all the WIP Limits on your board and think that you have calculated WIP for your process (as discussed previously in Chapter 2). You are going to have actually track physical WIP. Fortunately, I am going to show you a very easy way to do that in the next chapter!

Lastly, most people think that Little's Law is the single greatest reason to implement a Kanban-style Agile process. While I would not strictly disagree with that statement, I would offer a better way of stating it. I would say that Little's Law is the single greatest reason to move to a more WIP-limited, pull-based, continuous flow process. The thing is, once we do that, we can then start to use Little's Law as our guide for process predictability.

Size Does Not Matter

I have one last topic I want to cover before wrapping up. Notice how in the assumptions for Little's Law I made no mention a requirement for all work items to be of the same size. That is because no such requirement exists. Most people assume that an application of Little's Law specifically—and limiting WIP in general—necessitates that all work items be of the same size. That is simply not true. The precise reasons why would fill up a chapter in its own right, so I am going to limit my comments to two brief points.

First, work items size does not matter because for Little's Law we are dealing with relationships among averages. We do not necessarily care about each item individually, we care about what all items look like on average.

Second, and more importantly, the variability in work item size is probably not the variability that is killing your predictability. Your bigger predictability problems are usually too much WIP, the frequency with which you violate Little's Law's assumptions, etc. Generally, those are easier problems to fix than trying to arbitrarily make all work items the same size. Even if you were in a context where size did matter, it would be more about right-sizing your work and not same-sizing your work.

Forecasting

As this is a book about forecasting, my guess is that you were expecting me to say that once you understand Little's Law all you need to do is to plug in the numbers and out will pop the forecasting result that you are looking for (à la Newton's F = ma or Einstein's $E=mc^2$). However, nothing could be further from the truth.

The first thing that you need to know about Little's Law is that it is concerned with looking backward over a time period that has completed. It is not about looking forward; that is, is not meant to be used to make *deterministic* predictions. As Dr. Little himself says about the law, "This is not all bad. It just says that we are in the measurement business, not the forecasting business".

Little's Law should not be used to make forecasts!

This point requires a little more discussion as it is usually where people get hung up. The "law" part of Little's Law specifies an exact relationship between average WIP, average Cycle Time, and average Throughput, and this "law" part only applies only when you are looking back over historical data. The law is not about—and was never designed for—making deterministic forecasts about the future. For example, let's assume a team that historically has had an average WIP of 20 work items, an average Cycle Time of 5 days, and an average Throughput of 4 items per day. You cannot say that you are going to increase average WIP to 40, keep average Cycle Time constant at 5 days and magically Throughput will increase to 8 items per day—even if you add staff to the keep the WIP to staff ratio the same in the two instances. You cannot assume that Little's Law will make that prediction. It will not. All Little's Law will say is that an increase in average WIP will result in a change to one or both of average Cycle Time and average Throughput. It will further say that those changes will manifest themselves in ways such that the relationship among all three metrics will still obey that law. But what it does not say is that you can deterministically predict what those changes will be. You have to wait until the end of the time interval you are interested in and look back to apply the law.

But that restriction is not fatal. The proper application of Little's Law in our world is to understand the assumptions of the law and to develop process policies that match those assumptions. If the process we operate conforms—or mostly conforms—to all of the assumptions of the law then we get to a world where we can start to trust the data that we are collecting from our system. It is at this point that our process is probabilistically predictable. Once there we can start to use something like Monte Carlo simulation (Chapter 5) on our historical data to make forecasts and, more importantly, we can have some confidence in the results we get by using that method.

There are other, more fundamental reasons why you do not want to use Little's Law to make forecasts. For one thing, I have hopefully by now beaten home the point that Little's Law is a relationship of averages. I mention this again because even if you could use Little's Law as a forecasting tool (which you cannot), you would not want to as you would be producing a forecast based on averages. This gets us back to the Flaw of Averages which I have already belabored in this book.

Having said all that, though, there is no reason why you cannot use the law for quick, back-of-the-envelope type estimations about the future. Of course you can do that. I would not, however, make any commitments, staff hiring or firing decisions, or project cost calculations based on this type of calculation alone. I would further say that it is negligent for someone to even suggest to do so (as so many Lean-Agile pundits do). But this simple computation might be useful as a quick gut-check to decide if something like a project is worth any further exploration.

Remember that being predictable is not completely about making forecasts. The bigger part of predictability is operating a system that behaves in a way that we expect it to. By designing and operating a system that follows the assumptions set forth by the Little's Law, we will get just that: a process that behaves the way we expect it to. That means we will have controlled the things that we can control and that the interventions that we take to make things better will result in outcomes more closely aligned with our expectations.

Conclusion

I know I have said it before, but I need to say it again: Little's Law is not about understanding the mathematics of queuing theory. It is about understanding the assumptions that need to be in place in order for the law to work. We can use those assumptions as a guide, or blueprint, or model for our own process policies. Whenever your process policies are in violation of the assumptions of Little's Law then you know that you have at least diminished—or possibly eliminated—your chance of being predictable.

As you operate your process think about the times and reasons why work flows in at a faster rate than work flows out. Think about why items age unnecessarily due to blockages or poor pull policies. Think about why work is abandoned when only partially complete (and how you account for that abandonment). Think about how these occurrences are violating the assumptions Little's Law and how they are ultimately affecting your ability to be predictable. But more importantly, think about how your understanding of Little's Law should result in behavior changes for you and your team. When violations of Little's Law occur, it is usually because of something you did or chose (intentionally or not) not to do. Remember, you have much more control over your process than you think you do.

Now that we have an understanding of Little's Law and the basic metrics of flow, it is time to turn our attention to how these concepts are visualized through the use of flow analytics. As we are about to see, it is the quantitative and qualitative interpretation of these unique analytics that will make our process truly predictable, and will make the flow metrics truly actionable.

Key Learnings and Takeaways

- Little's Law relates the basic metrics of flow in an elegant, fundamental equation.
- Little's Law is a relationship of averages.
- Do not get distracted with the math of Little's Law—the significance of the law does not necessarily come from plugging numbers into the equation.
- When stating it in terms of Equation #2, for contexts with continuous WIP, there are five assumptions necessary for Little's Law to work, they are:
    - The average input or Arrival Rate (λ) should equal the average Throughput (Departure Rate).
    - All work that is started will eventually be completed and exit the system.
    - The amount of WIP should be roughly the same at the beginning and at the end of the time interval chosen for the calculation.

- The average age of the WIP is neither increasing nor decreasing.
        - Cycle Time, WIP, and Throughput must all be measured using consistent units.
- Use these assumptions as a guide for your process policies. The more you violate these assumptions, the less chance you have of being predictable.
- Even if the assumptions do not hold for the entire time period under consideration, Little's Law can still be used as an estimation. However, the "goodness" of the estimation depends on how badly the assumptions have been violated.
- Little's Law is not for forecasting. To do forecasting we will need other tools. If someone tells you that you can forecast with Little's Law or shows you an example of how to do it, you have my permission to slap them (I put that in to see if you were still reading).

Chapter 9: How to Visualize System Stability

Luckily for us (even though we do not believe in luck) there is a chart available that simultaneously shows the interactions of all three basic metrics of flow. In short, this one chart is Little's Law in action. Its name is a Cumulative Flow Diagram (CFD).

What makes a CFD a CFD?

The very first thing to know about Cumulative Flow Diagrams is that they are all about arrivals and departures. In fact, when researching this book, the very first reference that I could find to a CFD appeared in the 1960s and that article actually labeled the chart as a "Cumulative Arrival and Departures Diagram". I am not entirely sure when the name got changed to Cumulative Flow Diagram. However, the concepts of arrivals and departures are central to the idea of flow, so the name change makes perfect sense.

As its name suggests, therefore, a Cumulative Flow Diagram is an excellent way to visualize the flow of work through a process. CFDs are among the least known, and therefore one of the least understood charts in all of Agile analytics; yet, they represent one of the most powerful process performance gauges available to us. They are a powerful tool for a couple of reasons. First, these charts offer a concise, coherent visualization of the three metrics of flow. Second, they offer massive amounts of information at just a glance, or by just doing some very simple calculations. Visualizing flow via a CFD gives us both quantitative and qualitative insight into problems—or potential problems—in our process. Gaining an understanding of actual process performance is one of the necessary first steps for introducing overall system predictability.

In order to gain this insight, however, we have to be very precise in terms how we define exactly what a CFD is, and—more importantly—how to construct one. In a point that I will hammer over and over, an improperly constructed CFD can lead to improper conclusions about process problems. Worse, improperly constructed CFDs can lead to team or management apathy amid claims that the charts are just not very useful.

So, without any further ado, let's get to it. If you have never seen a Cumulative Flow Diagram before, then here is your chance:

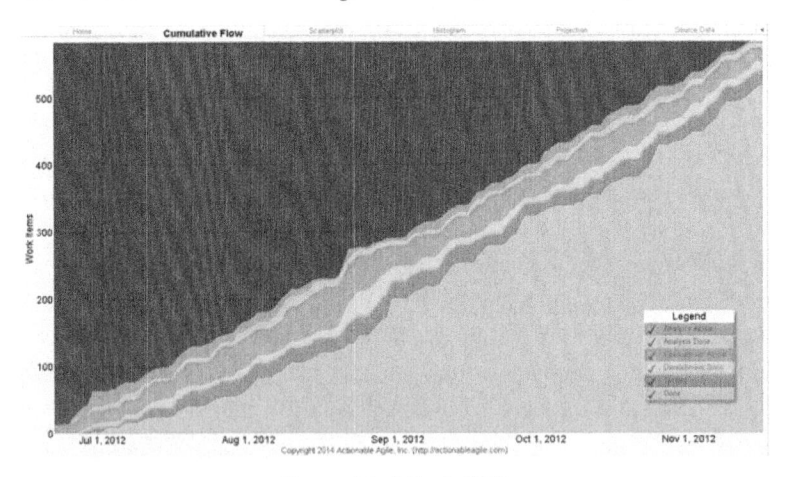

Figure 9.1: A Basic CFD

It may not look like much to you right now, but as I just mentioned this chart is actually communicating a lot of information.

To get you oriented with what you are looking at, I first want to spend some time going over the anatomy of a CFD. Once you have got that under your belt, then we can move on to what this graph is actually telling us.

The first thing to note about a CFD is that across the bottom (the X-axis) is some representation of a progression of time (usually calendar time). It could be said that the X-axis represents a timeline for our process. The tick marks on the X-axis represents our choice of labels for that timeline. When labeling the X-axis, you can choose whatever frequency of labels you want. In this particular CFD, we have chosen to label every month. However you can choose whatever label is best for your specific needs. You can choose to label every two weeks, every month, every day, etc.

A very important point here is that these labels can be very different than the reporting interval that you choose to build your CFD. The reporting interval is the frequency that you choose to add data to your chart. Just as with the labels, your reporting interval is up to you. You can choose to report on your process data every day, every week, every month, etc. Just note that whatever reporting interval that you choose will change the shape of your diagram (choosing a different reporting interval may certainly be the tweak you want to make in order to get a clearer picture of what's going on in the CFD). Further note that the reporting interval and the labels need not be of the same frequency. On the above graph, the reporting interval is every day, yet you can see that we have only labeled the timeline at every month.

Lastly, I should point out that in Figure 9.1 I have chosen to show the timeline progression from left to right. This is not a requirement, it is only a preference. I could have easily shown time progression from right to left. The vast majority of CFDs that you will come across (unless your name is Frank), however, will show the progression of time from left to right. Thus, for the rest of this chapter (and this book), I will show all CFD time progressions from left to right. Further, know that all properties of CFDs that I am about to describe assume a CFD with a time progression from left to right.

If across the bottom is a progression of time, then up the side (the Y-axis) is a cumulative count of items in the process. To build our CFD, at each reporting interval we are going to calculate the total number of items at each step in our process and plot them on our graph (how to properly "count" items will be explained a little later in this chapter). Just as with labels and reporting intervals, you can choose whatever scale you want for the work item axis. Choosing different scales will cause the picture to change, but, again, that may just be the adjustment you need in order to "sharpen" your chart's picture.

As you plot items at each reporting interval, then over time "bands" will emerge on your chart. Those bands will correspond to each of the workflow steps in your process, as in in Figure 9.2.

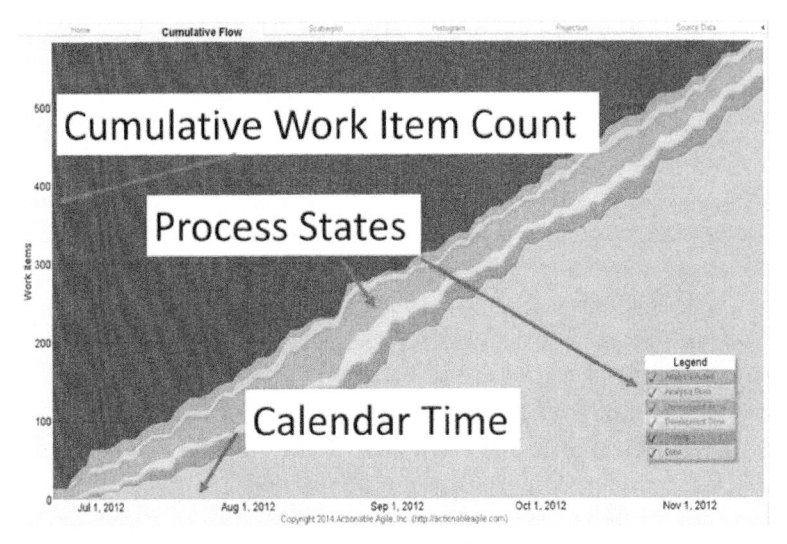

Figure 9.2: Anatomy of a CFD

A quick note about what I mean by "bands" on a CFD versus what I mean by "lines" on a CFD. By "band" I mean each different colored section on the graph. By "line" I mean the demarcation boundary of any band. Any band on a CFD is always going to be bounded by two lines: a top line and a bottom line. The bottom line of a given band will be the same as the top line of the succeeding band—should such a subsequent band exist. The chart in Figure 9.2, for example, has six bands corresponding to each of the process states and it has seven lines that mark the boundaries. For clarification, technically, the bottom line of the "Done" band in Figure 9.2 is the line that runs along the bottom of the chart at the

X-axis. For the purposes of CFD definition, though, this line can be ignored.

Note: unless otherwise specified, when I say "top line of a CFD" I mean the top line of the top-most band. When I say "bottom line of a CFD" I mean the top line of the bottom-most band. This is illustrated in Figure 9.3:

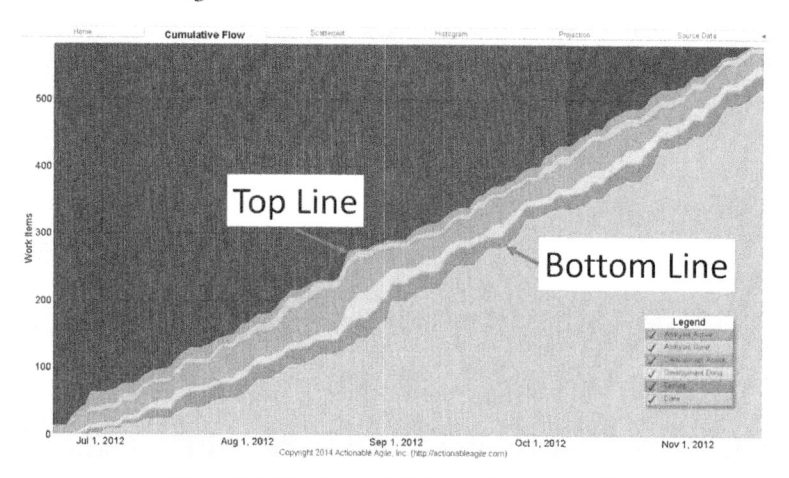

Figure 9.3: The Top and Bottom Line on a CFD

I began this section by pointing out that the most important thing to remember about CFDs is that they are fundamentally about process arrivals and departures. Any chart that does not model or graph these arrivals and departures properly or any chart that includes extraneous information not considered an arrival or departure cannot be properly called a Cumulative Flow Diagram. This brings us to the first of several fundamental properties of CFDs:

> CFD Property #1: The top line of a Cumulative Flow Diagram *always* represents the cumulative arrivals to a process. The bottom line on a CFD *always* represents the cumulative departures from a process.

When I say "always" I mean "always". Any chart that contains additional outside lines that do not represent process arrivals and departures is not a CFD. Also note the use of the word "cumulative" (this is a *Cumulative Flow Diagram*, after all). Any chart that does not account for cumulative arrivals and departures properly is not a CFD (more on this later). It is important to remember that the definition of the boundaries of your process is essentially up to you. However, once chosen, those boundaries will be represented by the lines on your chart as defined above. You can have as many bands that represent as many workflow steps as you want in between your two boundaries. It can be very advantageous and strongly recommended—but by no means necessary—to represent those additional states on your diagram. If you choose to include those additional states, then the top and bottom line of the band at each workflow step represents that state's arrivals and departures, respectively.

For example, let's say I have a process that looks like:

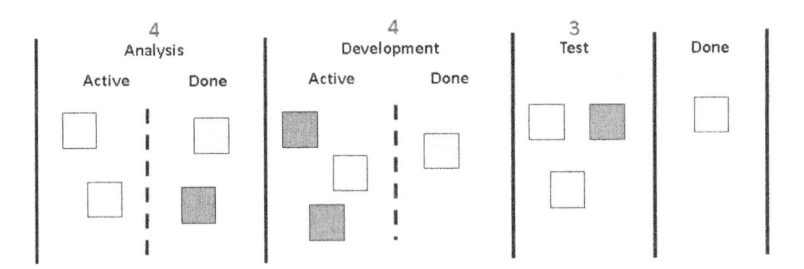

Figure 9.4: Example Process

Those of you familiar with Kanban may recognize this as a Kanban board, but the following discussion is equally applicable to a more Scrum or XP style of process that has columns as simple as "To Do", "Doing", and "Done" (how Kanban can be used to model a Scrum or XP process is well beyond the scope of this book; however, the principles discussed here apply regardless of the particular methodology that has been chosen).

In this example, arrivals to the process are denoted by the "Analysis Active" column, and departures from the process are denoted by the "Done" column. A simple CFD that models *only* the overall cumulative arrivals and departures in this process might look like:

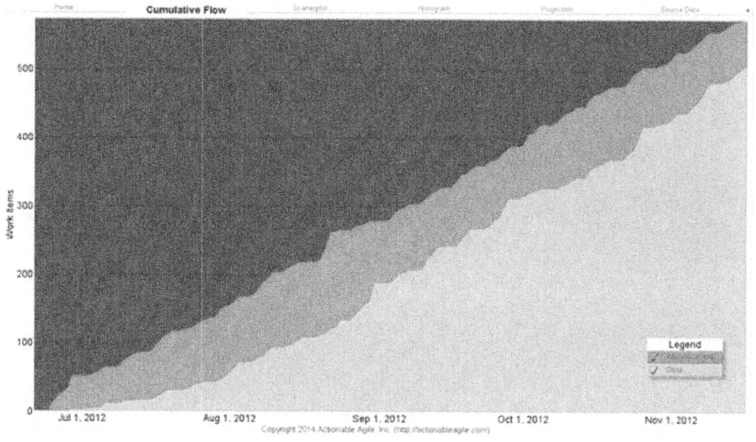

Figure 9.5: Total Process Arrivals and Departures Only on a CFD

Notice that there are only two bands on this diagram. As always, the top line of the top band represents the cumulative arrivals to the "Analysis" column and the top line of the bottom band represents the cumulative departures to the "Done" column. Figure 9.5 is a perfectly valid CFD for the process shown in Figure 9.4. One question that you may want to keep in the back of your mind as you go through this discussion is: what do you think the advantages or disadvantages of visualizing your flow as only two lines and bands as shown in Figure 9.5?

If we wanted a little more detail about our process, we could easily include in the above diagram the cumulative arrivals and departures for each of the intermediate workflow steps between "Analysis Active" and "Done". If we were interested in doing so, then our CFD would morph into the diagram depicted in Figure 9.6:

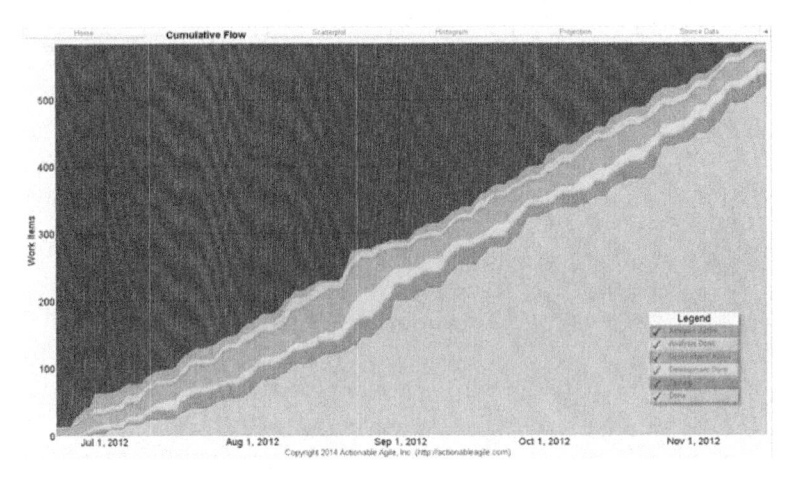

Figure 9.6: A Basic CFD

The several lines in Figure 9.6 now correspond to the cumulative arrivals and departures at each step in the workflow.

One quick thing before I proceed: you will notice that in this picture I have shown the queuing states or "Done" columns for Analysis and Development rather than just showing the Analysis and Development steps each as their own layer on the CFD. I have become a big fan of this approach as I believe this has the potential to give us greater insight into flow problems. For example, in the above chart we will potentially want to pay particular attention to the bands that represent the "Analysis Done" and "Development Done" columns. A widening of these layers could hint at something going wrong in our process—but I am getting a little ahead of myself here.

Lastly, properly constructed CFDs are intrinsically linked with Little's Law. In fact, Dr. Little has used CFDs in several of his publications when explaining his eponymous law. I spent so much time in the last chapter discussing Little's Law's assumptions because many times a violation of one or more of those assumptions will clearly show up on a CFD. That is the good news. The bad news is that many times an assumption violation will not clearly reveal itself on a CFD. This is why it is so important to know the assumptions behind the law and be able to map them to the context in which the data was collected. If you understand the assumptions, then you will be able to make the necessary process adjustments for improved predictability.

Constructing a CFD

The next step in learning how a CFD can help us is to understand how to construct one. To start, most people will tell you that to create a CFD, all you need to do is physically count all work items in progress at each step of your process and then just plot those counts on your chart at regular reporting intervals. I call this approach "building a chart based on counts". Not to put too fine a point on it, but building a chart just by counting items in progress almost always wrong. I go into great detail in my previous book as to why this approach fails, but long story short, simply counting items will normally not account for arrivals and departures properly. This bad accounting leads to an incorrectly structured diagram which normally manifests itself as lines that decrease (go down). Which leads us to the second property of a CFD:

> CFD Property #2: Due to its cumulative nature, no line on a CFD can ever decrease (go down).

You can immediately spot that a CFD has not been constructed properly if you see lines on the chart that go down. A properly constructed CFD always has lines that are either increasing (going up) or are flat. Not to belabor the point, but this non-decreasing effect is precisely why these charts are called *Cumulative* Flow Diagrams.

The only way to guarantee that arrivals and departures have been accounted for properly is to track a timestamp that an item enters and leaves the process. Sound familiar? It should. The exact same data that we capture to calculate Cycle Time and Throughput is the exact same data that we will use to construct an CFD. I cannot stress this particular point enough: by collecting data in this way, not only are we assured of being able to build a correct CFD, but we also get all the data we need to build an array of other very useful charts—i.e., the analytics we need to help us along the path toward predictability.

If you want to do any more serious analysis of your flow, then, in addition to capturing start times and end times for items, it may be beneficial to capture timestamps for when items enter each stage of your process.

Another thing that you have probably noticed by now is that none of the CFD examples that I have shown have a line labelled "backlog". There are some very good reasons for that. For example, why cannot I have a picture that looks like Figure 9.7:

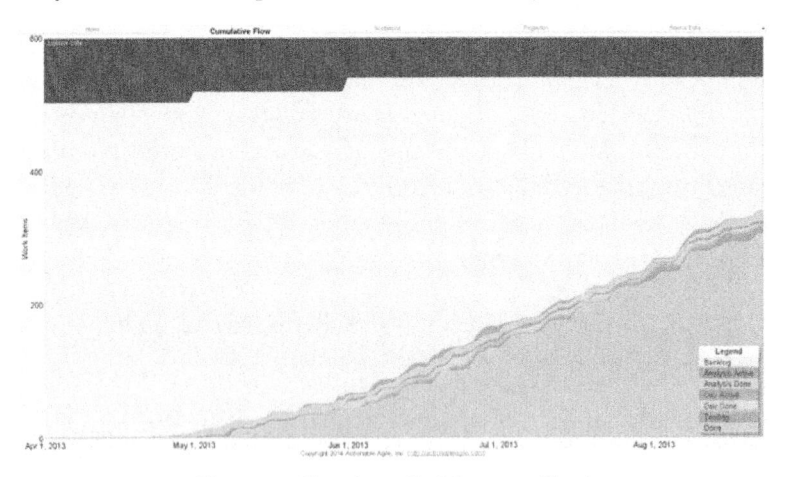

Figure 9.7: Showing a Backlog on a Chart

For the most part, any diagram that shows a backlog is not a CFD. To explain why, I would first like to describe my problem with the word "backlog" itself.

I am not trying to denigrate any particular process here, but, unfortunately, the word backlog is so prevalent nowadays that its use carries with it connotations that are counter-productive. Whether or not those connotations are correct is a different debate;

the point here is to just acknowledge that they exist.

It has been my experience that people immediately assume two things when using the term backlog:

1. That items placed in a backlog are somehow committed to (or that they otherwise inherently have value), and,
2. That items placed in a backlog are somehow prioritized.

A backlog, therefore, is merely a convenient container for these candidate ideas. Commitment does not happen until a team actually has capacity, and prioritization does not happen until at the time of commitment (see Chapter 8 for how just-in-time commitment and prioritization work).

To be clear, you could definitely have a CFD that looks like Figure 9.8, but then it would be subject to all the properties of a CFD that I have outlined in this chapter. If you do not want to signal that items in your backlog have been committed to, then do not include a backlog band on your chart. If you do want communicate that backlog items have been committed to, then, by all means, display the backlog. That decision, as you already know, could have serious ramifications for your Cycle Time calculation.

I am not saying that a chart that shows a backlog is not useful—far from it. However, for the most part, a diagram that has a backlog on it is not a CFD. But, you may ask, "How then are we to do projections of when we will be done?" As we have already discussed, if you are truly serious about forecasts, then what you really should be doing is some type of probabilistic modeling like Monte-Carlo simulation—and not doing projected lines off of a CFD.

The reason I have been so pedantic about how to build CFDs is because only with a properly constructed CFD can we accurately perform the analysis techniques that we need for predictability. Those techniques are precisely what I plan to present in this chapter. We begin our discussion with some quantitative analysis.

Work In Progress

Since the top line of a CFD represents the cumulative arrivals of items to our process, and the bottom line of a CFD represents the cumulative departures of items from our system, then the vertical difference between those two lines at any reporting interval represents the total Work In Progress in the system. As you have probably figured out, this principle can easily be extended such that we can measure the Work In Progress between any two points in the system at any point in time. That is to say, we can quickly measure the Work In Progress in the Analysis Active step, in the Development Done step, or the total Work In Progress between Analysis Done and Test (just to name a few examples). Thus, our next fundamental principle of CFDs is:

> CFD Property #3: The vertical distance between any two lines on a CFD is the total amount of work that is in progress between the two workflow steps represented by the two chosen lines.

Figure 9.8 shows the total WIP as 90 work items on September 1:

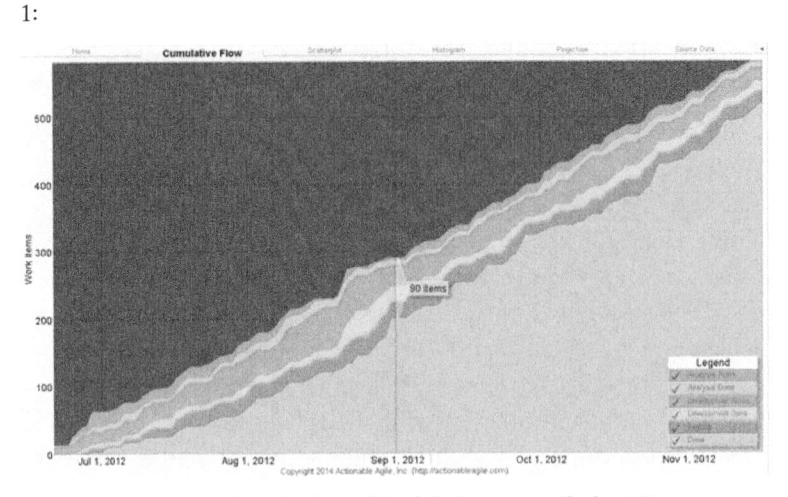

Figure 9.8: Reading Total Work In Progress off of a CFD

In this example, we got to the number 90 by subtracting the number of work items (or y-value) of the bottom line of the CFD on September 1 from the number of work items of the top line on September 1. Specifically, the bottom line on the chart shows a value of 200 work items on September 1. The top line shows a value of 290 work items on September 1. Subtracting the bottom line number of work items from the top line number of work items (290 – 200) gives us a total WIP of 90 work items.

Reading WIP off of each step in the workflow is accomplished in much the same way as shown in Figure 9.9:

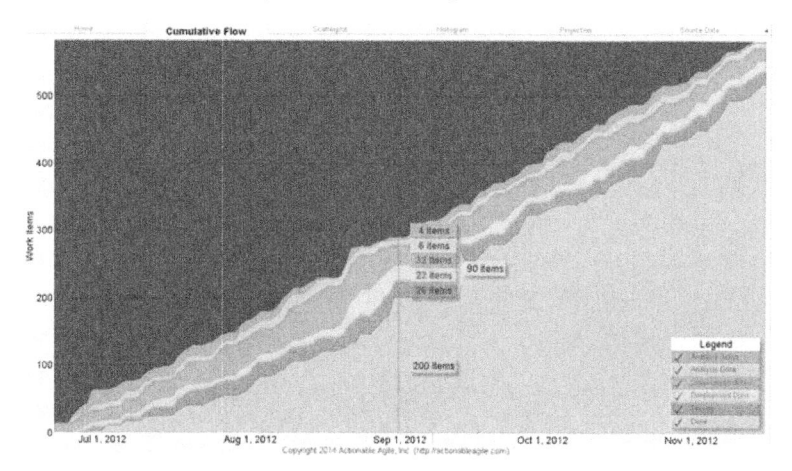

Figure 9.9: Reading WIP at Each Step of the Workflow

The calculation of these numbers was performed in exactly the same way as the total WIP calculation; i.e., by subtracting the y-value of the bottom line of a given band from the y-value of the top line of a given band.

Approximate Average Cycle Time

Continuing the same example, the horizontal difference between the top line of a CFD and bottom line of a CFD at any point along the graph is your process's *Approximate Average Cycle Time*. To approximately calculate how long—on average—it took for items to complete at a particular reporting interval, we choose the point on the bottom line of the CFD that corresponds with the date that we are interested in, and then we draw a horizontal line backward until it intersects the top line of the CFD. We then look to see what date corresponds with that top line intersection and subtract it from the date we just got from the bottom line. This subtraction will give you the Approximate Average Cycle Time for the items that finished on the bottom line date of interest.

This leads us to the next fundamental property of CFDs:

> CFD Property #4: The horizontal distance between any two lines on a CFD represents the Approximate Average Cycle Time for items that finished between the two workflow steps represented by the chosen two lines.

Continuing on from the previous example, let's say we want to know what the Approximate Average Cycle Time was for items that finished on September 1st. In this case our calculation would look like Figure 9.10:

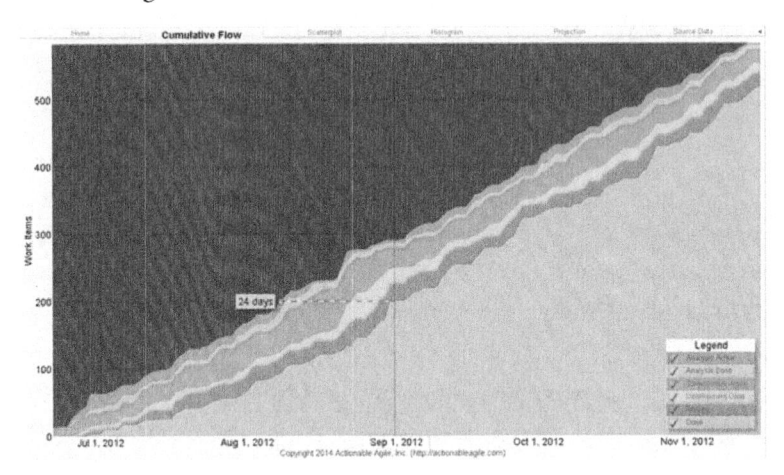

Figure 9.10: Overall Process Approximate Average Cycle Time Calculation

In this example, to calculate the Approximate Average Cycle

Time for stories that finished on September 1 (which is this example is 24 days), you perform the following steps. (Please note that in this case the reporting interval is days. These steps would be the same for whatever time unit you choose to report your data; e.g., weeks, months, etc.):

1. Start with date you are interested in on the bottom line of the graph. In this case, that date is September 1.
2. Draw a horizontal line backward from that point on the bottom line until the line intersects a point on the top line of the CFD.
3. Read the date value of the top line of the CFD at that intersection point. In this case that date is August 9.
4. Subtract top line date from the bottom line date. In this case, September 1 minus August 9 is 23 days.
5. Add 1 to the result. In this case, 23 plus 1 is 24 days.

Why add one day in Step #5? I always advise the addition of one "time unit" (in this case that time unit is days) because I would argue the shortest amount of time that an item can take to complete is one unit. For example, if a given work item starts and completes on the same day (e.g., September 1), what is its Cycle Time? If we were just to subtract September 1 from September 1 we would get a Cycle Time of zero days. I think that result is misleading. After all, zero days suggests that no time whatsoever was spent completing that item. That is not reflective of reality which is why one day needs to be added. Further, the addition of one day makes the calculation more inclusive. For example, if a work item starts on September 1 and finishes on September 2, what is its Cycle Time? If all we did is subtract those two dates, we would get a Cycle Time of one day. But I would suggest that since time was spent on that item on both September 1 *and* September 2 that the more representative Cycle Time is two days. Which means that we would again need to add one day to our calculation. You might disagree with this advice for your own particular situation. And that is ok (as long as you are consistent in your calculations). You will just want to note, though, that all Cycle Time calculations in this book follow the "addition of one time unit" rule.

Getting back to our original discussion, the fact that you can draw a horizontal line on a CFD and subtract two dates to come up with an Approximate Average Cycle time should be amazing to you for a couple of reasons. The first is that to normally calculate an average you simply add up a whole bunch of values and then divide by the total number of values that you have added up. However, in this case all we are doing is subtracting two dates to come up with an average. Seems strange that that would work, but it does.

The second reason that this result is remarkable, is that the items that started in the Analysis Active column (the first column on the board) are not necessarily the stories that have finished in the Done column (the last column on the board), yet this calculation will still yield an Approximate Average Cycle Time. Interestingly enough, how good an approximation this calculation is will depend on how well we are adhering to the assumptions that make Little's Law work.

As with the Work In Progress calculation, this property can also be extended to handle the calculation between any two arbitrary points on your chart. That means we can draw horizontal lines to calculate the Approximate Average Cycle Time through Analysis Active, or through Test, or the Approximate Average Cycle Time from Analysis Done through Development Done (again, to name a few examples). Pictorially, some of these examples would look like Figure 9.11:

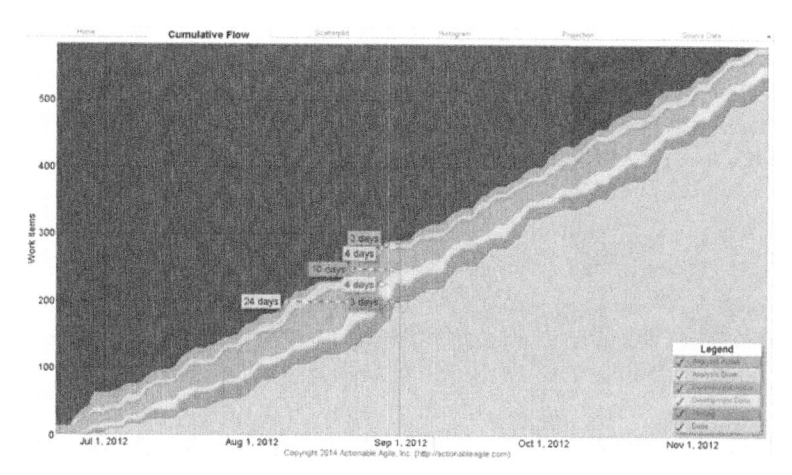

Figure 9.11: Approximate Average Cycle Times at Each Step in the Workflow

Note that this calculation is only valid for items that have finished. That is to say, this horizontal line that you draw to make this calculation must begin at the top line of the bottom band at the reporting interval that you are interested in and be drawn "backward" until it intersects the top line. Starting at the top line and drawing a line "forward" could cause you to never intersect the top line of the bottom-most band. The implication here is that CFDs are only good at exploring what already has happened in your process. This point is so important that I am going to call it out as its own property of CFDs:

> CFD Property #5: The data displayed on a CFD depicts only what *has* happened for a given process. Any chart that shows any type of projection is not a CFD.

Again, I am not saying here that projections are not important—far from it. All I am saying is that projections forward about what will or could happen in your process will require a completely different approach (like Monte Carlo Simulation). Just know that we cannot use CFDs for that forecasting purpose or that, if you do, you cannot call the resulting projection graph a CFD.

As you have probably noticed, I have gone through great pains to stress the fact that this horizontal line calculation only gives us an Approximate Average Cycle Time. I am being so pedantic about this because there is a lot of misinformation or disinformation about CFDs out there. If you were to go out and do some research on Cumulative Flow Diagrams, you will probably find that many people will tell you that doing this horizontal line calculation will give you an exact Cycle Time. It does not. The reason is because the items that start on the top line of your Cumulative Flow Diagram (at the beginning of your horizontal line) are not necessarily the items that finish at the bottom line of your Cumulative Flow Diagram (at the end of your horizontal line). Therefore, it would be impossible to calculate an exact Cycle Time for those items using just the diagram alone. Further, some people will tell you that this horizontal line calculation will lead to an exact *average* Cycle Time. This statement is also potentially incorrect. Unless we go in and look at the data that was used to generate the chart, or we have an understanding of some of the policies that have been put in place to generate the diagram the best we can say is that this horizontal calculation will lead to an Approximate Average Cycle Time. However, this approximation can be very good.

There is another great (potentially most important) reason to understand why this horizontal line represents only an Approximate Average Cycle Time. It turns out the comparison of the Approximate Average Cycle Time off of your CFD with the exact average Cycle Time from your real data can give you tremendous insight as to the health of your process.

Average Throughput

If the bottom line of your CFD represents the departures from your process, then the slope of that line between any two points (reporting intervals) is your *exact* average Throughput between those two points. This slope calculation is the very same "rise over run" calculation that you may remember from your previous mathematics training. Just to be clear, this is indeed an exact average Throughput calculation, not an approximate average as in the Cycle Time calculation above.

Likewise, if the slope of the bottom line of the CFD is your average Throughput, then the slope of the top-most line is your average arrival rate. The slope of that top line represents how fast work is coming into our system, while the slope of the bottom line represents how fast work leaving our system.

This leads to the last of our fundamental properties of Cumulative Flow Diagrams:

> CFD Property #6: The slope of any line between any two reporting intervals on a CFD represents the exact Average Arrival Rate of the process state represented by the succeeding band.**

As you have probably already guessed, Property #6 is a direct result of Property #1, but it is so important that I wanted to call it out on its own. One important corollary to this property is that the slope of any line also represents the exact average Throughput (or Departure Rate or Completion Rate) for the preceding workflow step.

To visualize this result, let's continue to look at the same example that we used in the WIP and Cycle Time sections. To calculate the Throughput of the overall process, we simply compute the slope of the bottom line of the CFD. Likewise, to calculate the arrival rate we use the same slope calculation for Analysis Active line. Both situations are shown in Figure 9.12:

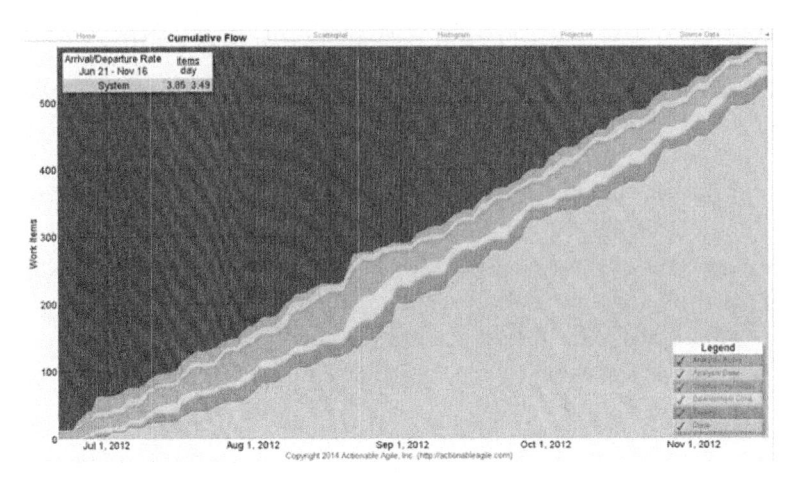

Figure 9.12: Arrival Rate and Departure Rate on a CFD

To calculate Average Throughput, you will first need to ascertain the date range you are interested in. In this example that date range is June 21 – November 16. The number of days in that range is our "run", or, in this case, November 16 minus June 21 equals 148 days. Second, we need to figure the "rise" of our bottom line work item data over that date range. The number of items on the bottom line at June 21 is zero and the number of items on the bottom line at Nov 16 is 517. Subtracting those two numbers gives us our "rise", or in this case 517 – 0 = 517. To calculate Average Throughput, then, you simply divide the rise by the run. In this case, our Average Throughput is 517 divided by 148 which equals 3.49 items per day. You can perform the exact same calculation for Average Arrival rate by substituting the data for the top line of the CFD into your rise over run formula.

Just as with WIP and Cycle Time, we can perform the slope calculations to get the Average Arrival or Average Departure rate for any step of the workflow as shown in Figure 9.13:

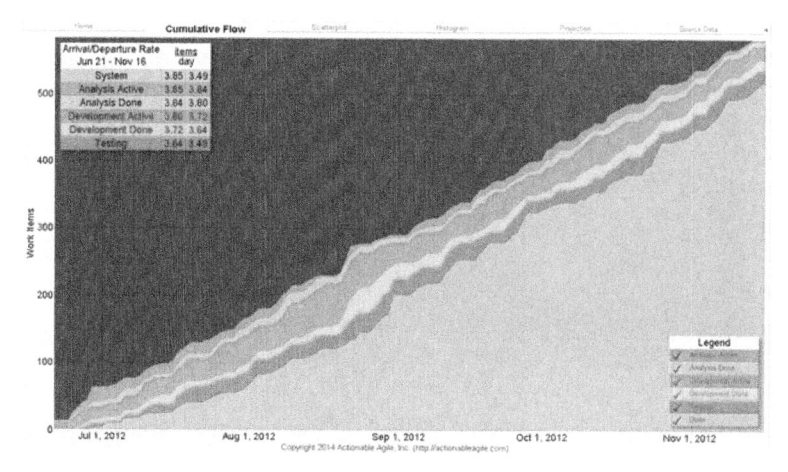

Figure 9.13: Arrival/Departure Rates for Each Step of the Workflow

Conclusion

Mapping cumulative arrivals and departures to a process over time is one of the best tools you have at your disposal to visualize flow. Observing flow in this way allows us to discern an impressive amount of useful information regarding the health of our process.

To suitably construct a CFD, therefore, we must account for arrivals and departures appropriately. One of the best ways to ensure that arrivals and departures are displayed correctly is to make sure that we capture the date that items enter each step of our workflow. Those dates can then easily and accurately be converted into the data we need to build a proper CFD.

One of the things that makes CFDs so powerful is that you can easily visualize and/or compute all of the basic, most important metrics of flow off of just one diagram. Putting it all together pictorially is shown in Figure 9.14:

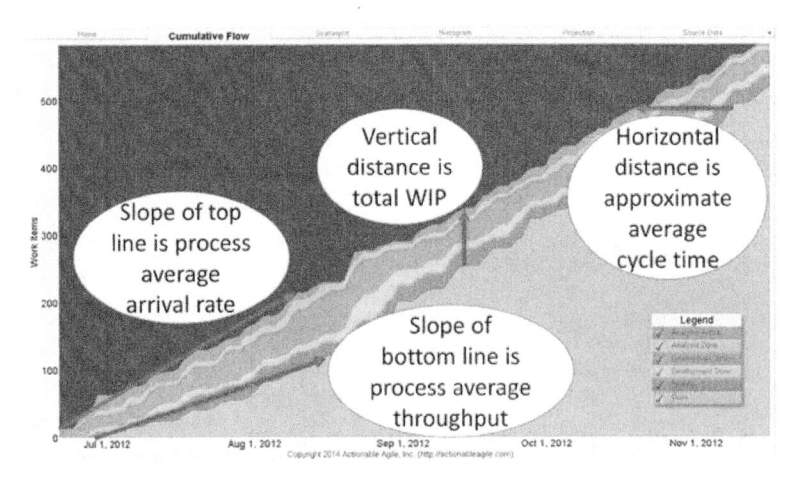

Figure 9.15: The Three Basic Metrics of Flow on a CFD

Numerically, these calculations look like Figure 9.15:

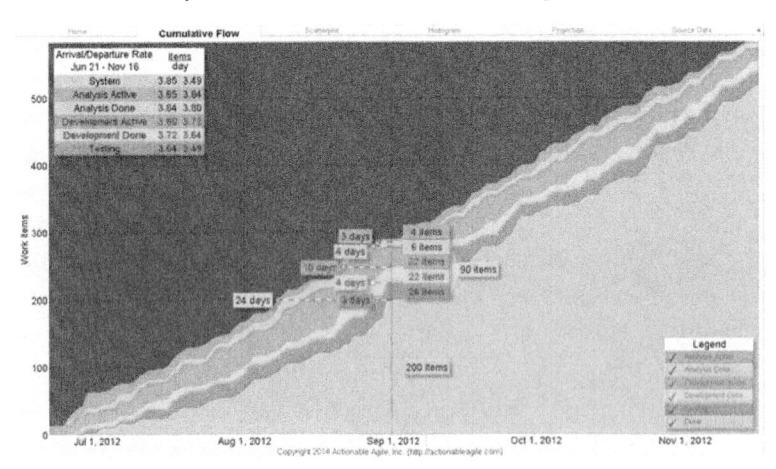

Figure 9.16: Numerical Representations of the Metrics of Flow

As I mentioned in Chapter 8, it is possible to segment WIP into several constituent types. CFDs are no different. As you may have guessed by now, when we collect our flow data, we can either look at that dataset as a whole in a CFD, or we can construct a CFD based on only one or more of the subtypes. For example, we can look at a single CFD that shows just the data for the user story type, or we can build a CFD based on just defects, or we can generate a CFD that combines both user stories and maintenance—to just name a few. This property of CFDs will open up all kinds of avenues of analysis for you. For example, at the portfolio level, you may want to look at data combined across all teams, or you may just want to filter based on an individual team. Or maybe you want to filter by release. At the team level, you might want to filter by some other custom field that is particularly relevant to your context (as in the "bad data" example from above). All of these activities are perfectly ok and I would challenge you to think about what data attributes you might want to collect and then filter on when analyzing your CFDs.

CFDs offer a concise way to simultaneously visualize the three basic metrics of flow: WIP, Cycle Time, and Throughput (albeit sometimes in the form of averages or approximate averages). You can only be guaranteed to calculate these metrics, however, if your graph obeys all six properties of a CFD:

CFD Property #1 is that the top line of a Cumulative Flow Diagram always represents the cumulative arrivals to a process. The bottom line on a CFD always represents the cumulative departures from a process.

CFD Property #2 is that due to its cumulative nature, no line on a CFD can ever decrease (go down).

CFD Property #3 is that the vertical distance between any two lines on a CFD is the total amount of work that is in progress between the two workflow steps represented by the two chosen lines.

CFD Property #4 is that the horizontal distance between any two lines on a CFD represents the Approximate Average Cycle Time for items that finished between the two workflow steps represented by the chosen two lines

CFD Property #5 is that the data displayed on a CFD depicts only what has happened for a given process. Any chart that shows any type of projection is not a CFD.

CFD Property #6 is that the slope of any line between any two reporting intervals on a CFD represents the exact Average Arrival Rate of the process state represented by the succeeding band.

Now that you know what CFDs are all about and how to construct them, it is time to discuss how use them to improve overall system stability for better forecasting.

Key Learnings and Takeaways

- CFDs demonstrate the cumulative arrivals and departures to a process over time, and, as such, are one of the best tools available for visualizing flow.
- This type of visualization communicates a lot of quantitative and qualitative information at a glance.
- The X-axis of a CFD represents the process timeline.
- The Y-axis of a CFD represents the cumulative count of items in the process at each reporting interval.
- The labels and reporting intervals on the chart are at the sole discretion of the graph's creator.
- Understanding the correct way to construct a CFD is essential to knowing how to interpret it.
- CFD Property #1 is that the top line of a Cumulative Flow Diagram *always* represents the cumulative arrivals to a process. The bottom line on a CFD *always* represents the cumulative departures from a process.
- CFD Property #2 is that due to its cumulative nature, no line on a CFD can ever decrease (go down).
- The best way to capture data for a CFD is to track the date at which an item enters each step of your process workflow. You are going to need those data points for other analysis anyway, so you might as well collect those from the start.
- Three easy ways to spot if a CFD has not been constructed properly:

- If any line on the chart slopes downward on any part of the graph.
- If something that sounds like a "backlog" has been graphed (remember, a visualized backlog may not necessarily be bad—but it usually is!).
- If some type of projection has been plotted.
- CFD Property #3: The vertical distance between any two lines on a CFD is the total amount of work that is in progress between the two workflow steps represented by the two chosen lines.
- CFD Property #4: The horizontal distance between any two lines on a CFD represents the Approximate Average Cycle Time for items that finished between the two workflow steps represented by the chosen two lines.
- CFD Property #5: The data displayed on a CFD depicts only what *has* happened for a given process. Any chart that shows any type of projection is not a CFD.
- CFD Property #6: The slope of any line between any two reporting intervals on a CFD represents the exact Average Arrival Rate of the process state represented by the succeeding band.
- A CFD is only a CFD if it obeys all six properties because only by following all of these properties can you be guaranteed to derive the correct quantitative metrics of flow off of your graph.
- Consider building CFDs that show both "Active" and "Done" states within workflow steps. For example, if your "Development" workflow step if further segmented into "Active" and "Done", then think about showing both of those sub columns on your CFD.
- Some common myths about CFDs:
    - It is always correct to build a CFD from work item count data at each reporting interval.
    - A horizontal line represents an exact Cycle Time or an exact average Cycle Time.

- It is always ok to represent a traditional backlog on a CFD.

Chapter 10 - Improving System Stability

Now that we have defined the basics of system stability, it is time to look at what we can do to improve overall stability for better, more accurate forecasts.

Matching Arrivals to Departures

> Little's Law Assumption #1: The average input or Arrival Rate of a process should equal the average output or Departure Rate.

Stated in more layman's terms, Little's Law demands that we only start work at about the same rate at which we finish old work (on average). Assumption #1 constitutes the first part of a principle known of the Conservation of Flow (CoF). Any time that flow is not conserved, predictability suffers.

You can easily see the relationship of arrivals and departures on a Cumulative Flow Diagram. For example, let's suppose we are running a Kanban board that looks like the one in Figure 10.1:

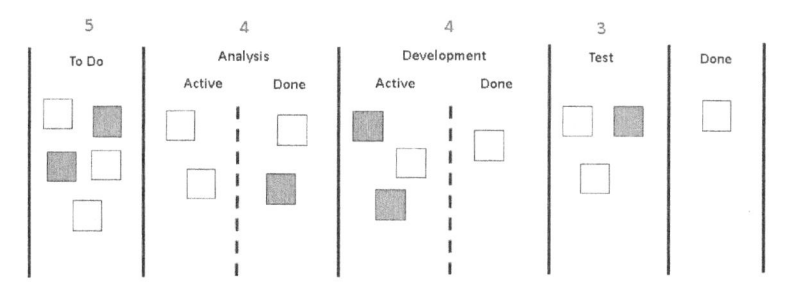

Figure 10.1: Example Kanban Board

Note that this particular team has chosen to name their arrivals column "Input", and that they have limited that column to five work items in progress at a time. Note also that the team has chosen to display the departures column and that they have labelled that column "Done". This departures column is WIP unlimited and the implication is that they have put in place explicit policies for what it means for items to be moved from "Test" to "Done".

So what might a CFD look like for a board like this? It might look like the one shown in Figure 10.2:

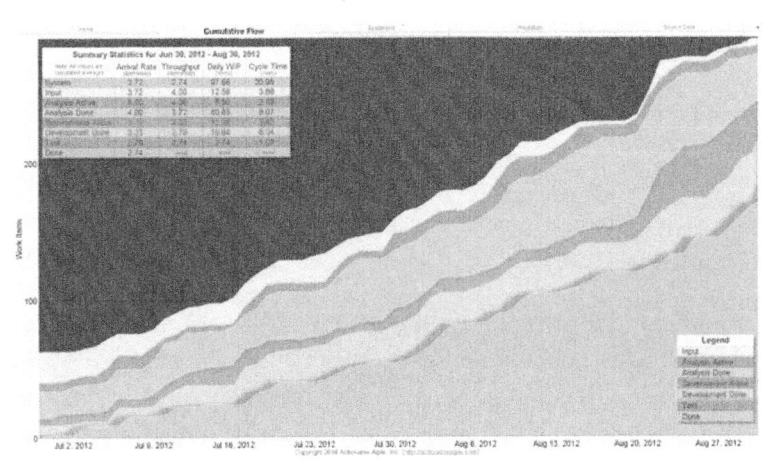

Figure 10.2: An Example CFD

From the last chapter, we know that each layer of this CFD represents a step in the workflow of the Kanban board shown in Figure 10.1. We also know that the slope of the top line of the topmost layer represents the Arrival Rate of the process and the slope of the top line of the bottommost band represents the Departure Rate (or Throughput). You can see from Figure 10.2 that those rates have been calculated to be 3.72 items per day and 2.74 items per day for the Arrival and Departure Rates, respectively. This calculation tells us that items are arriving to the process faster than items are leaving the process at about the rate of one item per day. What might the implications of this situation be?

The nice thing about CFDs, however, is that we need not necessarily perform this quantitative analysis to see that something is going wrong with our system. CFDs are such a powerful visualization technique that we can quite quickly do a qualitative assessment of the health of our system.

For example, imagine you had CFD that looked like the one in Figure 10.3:

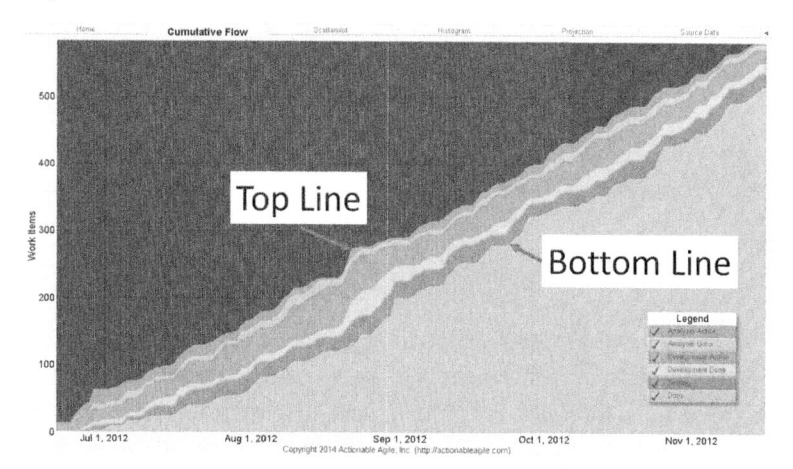

Figure 10.3: Quick Qualitative Assessment of CFD

It would not take you long to figure out that there was something wrong with your process. In this picture it is quite obvious—without doing any quantitative analysis—that work is arriving into your system at a much faster rate than work is departing from you system. A few paragraphs ago I asked you to think about the implication of this particular situation. To answer that question we need to reexamine how WIP and Cycle Time are visualized on CFDs. From Chapter 9, we know that WIP is the vertical distance between arrivals and departures and that Approximate Average Cycle Time is the horizontal distance between arrivals and departures. These properties are summed up in Figure 10.4:

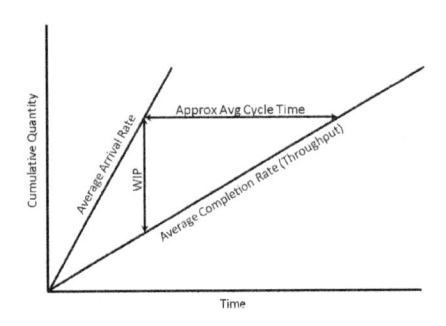

Figure 10.4: Flow Metrics on a CFD

But look what was going on earlier on in this diagram. When the Arrival Rate and Departure Rate lines were much closer together, you can see that WIP was much smaller and Approximate Average Cycle Times were much shorter. As arrivals continued to outpace departures—as the arrival line diverged from the departure line—the amount of WIP in the system got larger and larger and the Approximate Average Cycle Times got longer and longer (as shown in Figure 10.5).

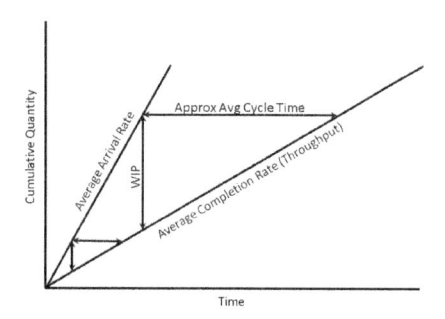

Figure 10.5: The Implication of Arrivals faster than Departures

In a situation like this, you have almost no chance at predictability. The actionable intervention suggested by a CFD that looks like Figure 10.5 is that we must get arrivals to match departures.

So how exactly do we get arrivals to match departures? The first thing we would do is to calculate the average Throughput off of the diagram. Let's say, for argument's sake, that we deploy items off our process at a cadence of once per week. Let's additionally say that the average Departure Rate of those deployed items comes out to five items per week (note here that we are choosing "week" as our unit of time). That number, five, gives us a clue as to what the WIP limit should be on our arrivals column. Since we are finishing five old items per week, that means we only want to start five new items per week. The implication here being that we would want to set a WIP Limit of five on the arrivals column (depending on the variability of our system, we might want to make that WIP Limit a little larger—say six or so—to make sure that our system is never starved for work). An important subtlety here is that the WIP Limit of five on the arrivals column assumes that you are replenishing the arrivals column at the same cadence as which you are deploying; i.e., once per week. But remember from before, that this need not be the case. If you wanted to replenish the input column once a day, then you would need to divide the original Arrival Rate number, five, by the number of times per week that you would do the replenishment (in this case five). Since five divided by five is one, then your new WIP limit on the arrivals column would be one.

Properly setting the WIP limit on the arrivals column will allow you to match the average Arrival Rate of items into your system with the average Departure Rate of items out of your system. When we do this, we will get a CFD that looks something like Figure 10.6:

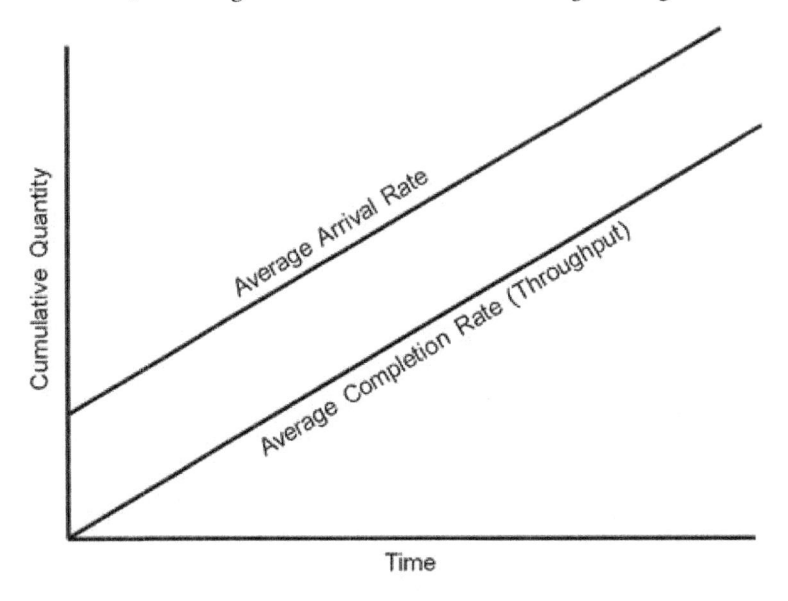

Figure 10.6: Average Arrival Rate equals Average Departure Rate

It should be immediately obvious from looking at the CFD in Figure 10.6 that the situation here is much better than that illustrated in Figure 10.5. As we will see in a subsequent chapter, having a pretty CFD is not a guarantee of a healthy system, but it is certainly a pretty decent start.

By the way, any time you expressly limit WIP throughout your workflow, and, more importantly, any time you honor the WIP limit(s) you have set, you will get a picture that looks like Figure 10.6. What I am saying is that you must operate a constant WIP style of pull system. Setting a WIP limit on the arrivals column is a necessary—but not sufficient—means to balancing arrivals and departures. For example, imagine that we have no explicit limit on our Test column but that we do have a WIP limit on the arrivals column. As work gets pulled (pushed, really) into Test because of the lack of a WIP limit, then that action will ultimately cause a pull of work from the arrivals column. Work getting pulled from the arrivals column will signal to the world that there is capacity to start new work and thus the arrivals column will be replenished even though no work has been completed. I hope it is easy to see that in this scenario how we can have items that arrive to our system faster than items that depart our system. So do not think your work is done by just limiting WIP at the front of your process. You must make sure that a constant amount of WIP (on average) is maintained throughout the whole process. Remember, the further you stray away from this principle, the less predictable you will be.

Limiting WIP on the arrivals column in the manner described here is one way to ensure that not too much work is started and just queuing at the beginning of your process. I have said it before, and I will say it again: delay is the enemy of flow. This approach will ensure a proper balance between having enough work to start such that your process is not starved and not having too much work such that work begins but just sits.

By the way, once we get a picture that looks like Figure 10.6, we will have taken the first—and probably most important—step to balance the demand on your system against the supply that your team can offer. We are now very far down the path to true process predictability.

Most Kanban boards have an explicit arrivals column at the front of the process, but this is by no means a requirement. It is completely reasonable that your particular work context allows your team to pull new work items in an immediate, ad hoc manner. That is to say, you need no coordination with any external stakeholder to prioritize items or you have a proxy for those stakeholders embedded with your team. In this case the arrivals column (e.g., the

"To Do" or "Input" or "Ready" column) may be superfluous. This situation is perfectly ok. As I just mentioned, the way to match arrivals to departures in this context would be to make sure that a constant amount of WIP is maintained through the process at all times. Constant WIP could be maintained either by expressly limiting Work In Progress at each step of your work flow or by setting one global limit for the whole process (or some mixture of both). The point I am making here is that it does not really matter how you limit WIP throughout the whole system just as long as you do.

It should be said, though, that even in this particular situation a team could benefit from an arrivals column for many of reasons. Just know that an explicit arrivals column is neither prescribed nor required for predictable process design.

One Way or Another, Finish All Work That is Started

> Little's Law Assumption #2: All work that is started will eventually be completed and exit (depart) the system.

Whether you realized it or not before now, every time you started a piece of work (be it a project, a feature, or story) but then later abandoned it you violated the principle of Conservation of Flow and thus impaired your predictability. If work flows only part way through the system and gets kicked out or discarded—for whatever reason—then any effort that was expended on the eliminated item immediately becomes waste. Taken to its logical conclusion, you can understand why a team might want to conserve flow as much as possible. If work is constantly started but never finished, if this partially completed work is constantly discarded in favor of starting new work, then the Cycle Time metrics are going be skewed, and the system you are operating becomes infinitely unpredictable.

Of course, we live in the real world and these things are going to happen. Some might argue—and I certainly would not debate them if they did—that it is even more waste to continue to work on an item once we have gained information that the item is no longer necessary. Maybe we have gained some knowledge that makes continuing to work on these particular items unnecessary, duplicative, or otherwise wasteful. Well, obviously, in those circumstances it makes perfect sense to abandon that work. When this happens, though, we should challenge ourselves with the following questions: "Why did that happen?" "Was there something that we could have done further upstream in our process to help avoid this situation?"

But, potentially more importantly, when these exceptions occur it is absolutely necessary to account for them properly in your data. Instead of just removing (or deleting) an item from your process never to track it again, it is probably best to mark that item as "finished" (whatever that means in your context), mark the date it was done, and then tag it with some attribute like "abandoned" or "discarded".

Annotating an item in this way gives us several options when we go to generate our analytics later. You can imagine that we may want to generate several different views of all of our analytics for our exception cases. We may want to see all of our process data together, we may want to only see items that have finished normally, or we may want to just see those items that were abandoned. Further, by accounting for these abandoned work items in this way, not only have we not violated the principle of the CoF, but we can also guarantee that we will be able to generate a valid CFD for all of those views.

A violation of the principle of conservation of flow should be treated as an opportunity for learning. Hopefully, your new-found understanding of this principle helps you to more readily recognize these learning opportunities and is yet another tool for you in your toolbox of continuous process improvement for predictability

The idea of matching the arrival rate of your system to its departure rate, and the idea of making sure that flow is conserved for all items that enter your system go a long way to stabilize what would otherwise be considered an unstable system. When we have taken these steps we can now start to have some confidence that the metrics we are collecting off of our system are more reflective of a team's true capability. However, doing these two things alone still does not guarantee that our system is completely stable. It is this underlying sense of system stability that we need in order to reach one of our ultimate goals—a goal that I keep harping on throughout this text: predictability.

Do Not Let Items Age Unnecessarily

> Little's Law Assumption #4: For the time period under consideration, the average age of WIP should neither be increasing nor decreasing.

The Approximate Average Cycle Time as predicted by the CFD can be compared to the exact Average Cycle Time as calculated from the very data used to build the CFD to begin with. The comparison of these two numbers will tell us if we can expect our exact Average Cycle Time to grow, decline, or stay the same over time. If our exact Average Cycle Time is either growing or declining then we have a violation of Little's Law assumption #4 which means that our predictability is in jeopardy.

So what are the scenarios we need to consider when comparing Approximate Average Cycle Time to exact Average Cycle Time? It turns out there are three. Those scenarios are:

1. The Approximate Average Cycle Time is *greater than* your actual Average Cycle Time.

2. The Approximate Average Cycle Time is *less than* your actual Average Cycle Time.
3. The Approximate Average Cycle Time is *roughly equal to* your actual Cycle Time.

It may sound trite, but an easy way to remember which of these is best is "scenario three is where you want to be." But it is because both scenarios one and two put predictability at risk that we will begin our discussion with those.

Approximate Average Greater Than Actual Average

If the Approximate Average Cycle Time is greater than the exact Average Cycle Time, then you can conclude that your process is incurring what I would call "Flow Debt".

> **Flow Debt** is when Cycle Time is artificially reduced for some items of Work In Progress by "borrowing" Cycle Time from other items of work in progress.

To explain, a smaller exact Average Cycle Time calculation when compared to the approximate average would tell you that you have (either explicitly or implicitly) favored the faster completion of some work items over the regular completion of others. You were not able to conjure that shortened Cycle Time out of thin air (we are not like the Fed who can just print money). This new ability to complete some items faster than they normally would have finished must have come from somewhere. What you did—whether you knew it or not—was to borrow Cycle Time from other work items that were already in progress. What you did was to create Flow Debt. This debt was used to pay for the expedited completion of the preferential work.

One great example of a process taking on Flow Debt is when a system has been designed with an expedite lane. A simple example

198   Chapter 10 - Improving System Stability

of what an expedite lane looks like on a Kanban board is shown in Figure 10.7:

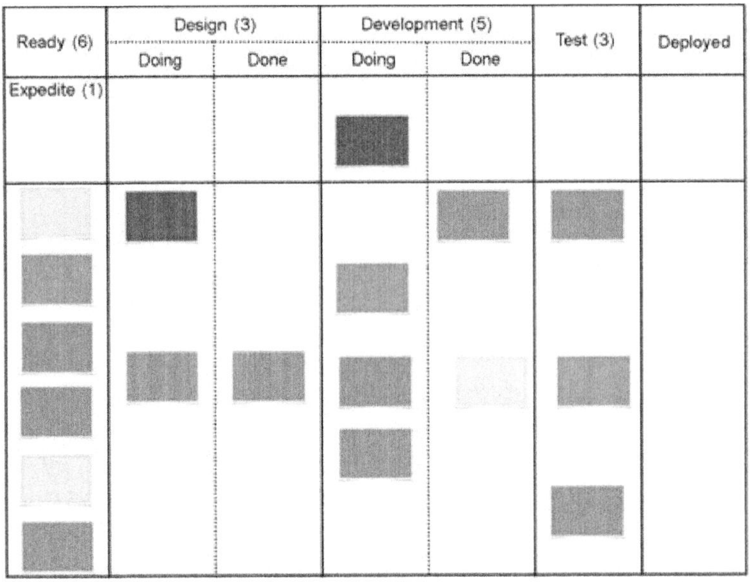

Ready (6)	Design (3)		Development (5)		Test (3)	Deployed
	Doing	Done	Doing	Done		
Expedite (1)						

Figure 10.7: Expedite Lane Example

When used, most expedite lanes have an extremely low WIP limit on them (often set to one). Policies are also usually put in place such that items in expedite lanes can violate WIP limits at each step in the workflow. Further, most systems are designed such that when an expedite item is introduced, it is pulled immediately for work—it is allowed to "jump the queue" ahead of other work that is also ready to be pulled. If no resources are available to immediately pull the expedited entity, then many teams will block other items to free up team members to go act on the expedited work. Given these normal policies, you can see why it is so important to be extremely conservative when setting the WIP limit on an expedite lane (more information about expedited items, pull policies, and their effect on predictability, please see Chapter 13 from AAMFP).

Looking at Figure 10.7, you will notice that the WIP Limit for the expedite lane is indeed set to one. This means that only one work item can be in progress in that whole lane at any given time (but that work item can be anywhere in the lane: Ready, Design, Development, or Test). As you can also see, the expedite WIP limit has been adhered to and that the expedite item is in the Development column. Let's assume for a minute that no developers were available when this item was pulled into the Development step. What might happen is that the team would choose to block one (or more) of those other three items in progress in order to free up resources to go work on the expedited ticket. The team has chosen to take the time that was to be allocated for work that was already in progress and apply that time to the expedited item. What has happened is that the team has chosen to artificially age one item (or more) in order to shorten the Cycle Time of another. This is a classic example of the creation of Flow Debt.

The problem is that this debt must be repaid (think the Mafia here and not the U.S. Government). The payment of this debt will come in one of two ways:

1. The work items that were "passed over" in deference to the expedited items will eventually themselves complete (in accordance with the principle of Conservation of Flow). When they do complete their Cycle Times will be much longer than they normally would have been because they were forced to artificially age. Thus, debt repayment comes in the form of longer Cycle Times for items already in progress. The resulting consequence is that you can have no confidence in the "average" Cycle Time you thought you were capable of because the metrics you had collected did not include this debt. You can have no confidence in this average because the accumulation of debt has made it invalid; or,
2. The work items that were "passed over" will be eventually kicked out of the system because they are no longer considered valuable (in violation of Conservation of Flow); i.e., the window of time to realize their value has passed. When

these items are thrown out of your process, any effort or time that has been spent on progressing them through the system immediately becomes waste. Thus, the payment of Flow Debt is the wasted effort that could have been spent in realizing the value of the discarded work item or in the form of wasted effort that could have been spent realizing the value of something else.

Either way, Flow Debt is repaid in the form of less predictability for your process.

I do not want you to conclude that all Flow Debt is bad. What you need to do is simply recognize that your system is incurring debt. The challenge for you, then, is to think about how you might categorize your borrowing into one of Minski's types: Hedge, Speculative, or Ponzi.

To classify what type of debtor you might be, ask yourself the following questions:

1. Hedge: Are expedites in your process more the exception than the rule (that is to say, does your board not have expedites significantly more often that it does have expedites)? When you do have expedited requests, do you truly only ever have one item (or some WIP limited amount of expedited items) in your process at a time? Does this time with no expedited items give you an opportunity to finish work that was otherwise blocked for previously expedited items? When you get an expedited item, are you allowed to finish existing work before the expedite is picked up? If the answers to these questions is yes, then you are probably running a properly "hedged" system.
2. Speculative: Is there always at least one item in your process and never a time when you are not working on expedited work of some kind? Do you routinely violate your expedited item WIP limit? If the answers to these questions is yes, then you are probably running a speculative system and you might

want to explore some options to apply more rigor to your expedite process.

3. Ponzi. Is all the work you do considered an expedite? Do expedited items take up all of your available capacity such that you never get a chance to work on more "normal" items? Are your pull criteria based not on explicit policies but on whomever is screaming the loudest? If the answer to these questions is yes, then what you are really running is a process Ponzi scheme. You will never be able to repay the debt you have accumulated and any notion of total process predictability is gone. You are fooling yourself if you continue to start "normal" work in addition to expedited work in this world. That normal work will almost never complete, or it will swapped out for other work, or it will finish far too late for anyone to care. In my mind, this is the antithesis of flow.

I want to make sure that you know that I am not advocating that you spend a lot of time on this classification nor that you become an expert in economic theory. What I do want you to ask yourself is are you able to repay the debt that you are taking out? How much debt is reasonable in your context? I guarantee that there are going to be some very good reasons to take on "Hedge" Flow Debt from time to time (a great analogy to this in the real world is when prospective homeowners take out a mortgage—assuming they can be repaid, most mortgages are considered good debt). The question for you becomes: are you able to service the Flow Debt that you have taken out?

By the way, I have picked on expedite work items here, but it should be noted that an explicit expedite lane is not the only way to incur Flow Debt.

Extending the scenario from above, let's say that you have an item in the "Design Done" column. And let's say that that item just sits there and never gets pulled into "Development Doing" because you care constantly choosing to pull other items in preference to it. If so, then congratulations, you have Flow Debt.

This particular scenario is depicted in the following diagram (Figure 10.8):

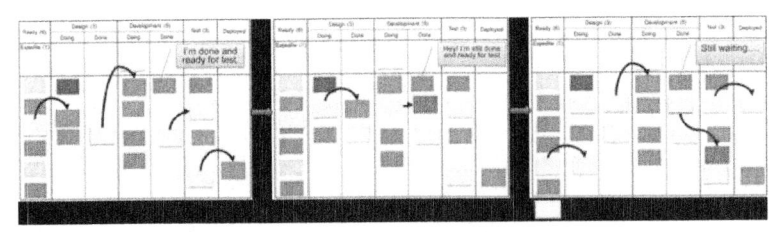

Figure 10.8: Ignoring an Item While it is Queuing

Another example of the creation of Flow Debt might be if you have blocked items that you ignore or do not actively work to get unblocked and moving again as quickly as possible (Figure 10.9):

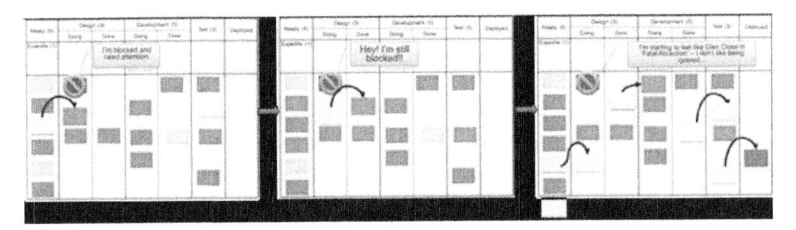

Figure 10.9: Ignoring a Blocked Item

I am sure there are other examples, but I will leave it as an exercise for the reader to identify the types of Flow Debt in your context.

By the way, the concepts in this chapter can be applied to any type of debt that you may incur in your process (e.g., technical debt). The trick is to recognize that you are creating debt and have a constructive conversation about how that debt is going to be repaid.

Approximate Average is Less Than Actual Average

This scenario is a bit less interesting than the last one. If in the above situation we were talking about accumulating Flow Debt, then the case where the Approximate Average Cycle Time on your CFD is less than your actual Average Cycle Time means that you are paying off Flow Debt (again, for the time interval under consideration).

A larger actual Average Cycle Time means that those items that have—for whatever reason—languished in progress are now finally completing. The actual average has become inflated because as the artificially aged items complete they make the actual average calculation come out "larger" than it otherwise would have been under normal circumstances.

However, paying off Flow Debt also hampers predictability. Items that finish with large amounts of Flow Debt attached to them skew Cycle Time numbers. An increased variability in Cycle Time means that we must communicate a larger range for the SLA of our process (see the discussion in Section II). A good analogy of why this might be dangerous is that of a restaurant who has customers waiting to be seated. Imagine that the true wait time for customers is fifteen minutes, but because of variability in their seating process, the restaurant has to communicate a two hour wait time to arriving patrons. What do you think those customers will do? The same thing will happen in your own process. The more your system is unpredictable, the more your customers will begin to look elsewhere for service.

Remember that these conclusions can only be drawn assuming we are running an otherwise stable system (i.e., nothing about the underlying system design has changed materially).

Approximate Average Roughly Equal to Actual Average

This case is where you want to be most of the time. If your Approximate Average Cycle Time is approximately equal to your actual Average Cycle Time, then your process is probably performing in a fairly orderly, predictable manner. You are not overloaded with expedite requests, you are not allowing items to stay blocked indefinitely, and you are not allowing items to queue arbitrarily.

In other words, you are neither accumulating nor repaying Flow Debt.

That is not to suggest that there are not any other areas of your process that are unhealthy. And if you do find yourself in this situation, do not pat yourself on the back too quickly. A more stable system such as the one that you have just engineered requires constant vigilance against the multitude of destabilizing forces that present themselves every day.

Key Learnings and Takeaways

- Design your process such that you match arrivals to departures.
- Make sure all items that enter your process exit properly—potentially accounting for those that were cancelled or abandoned.
- Take action every day to make sure that items do not age arbitrarily.

Section V: Putting It All Together

Chapter 11: How to Get Started

Disclaimer: Some of the information here is a copy of some of the guidelines I gave in AAMFP. Much of it, however, is presented in a different format so as to be more useful for you.

A Recipe for Getting Started

Probably the best way to outline how to get started is to provide you with a quick checklist of things to consider as you roll these practices out:

- Define the boundaries of your process.
- If necessary, define steps in between start and finish.
- Track the timestamp that an item enters each step of the workflow.
- Extract your data into a proper format.
- Generate flow analytics.
- Validate that you can trust your forecasts.
- Choose confidence level.
- Make your first forecasts.
- Experiment.
- Improve.
- Scale.

Allow me now to give you some hints and things to watch out for as you implement some of the things listed here.

Define the boundaries of your process. All metrics are measurements and all measurements imply a start point and an end point. If we are going to make meaningful, accurate forecasts, then we must understand what it means for a work item to be started what it means for a work item to be finished. Ask yourself if you have those boundaries clearly defined for your process. If not, that is step number one. By the way, you will find much more information on how do this in AAMFP.

If necessary, define steps in between start and finish. When starting out, it is perfectly valid to simply to have two steps in your workflow: "Doing" and "Done". In fact, there are many people who would recommend starting out that simply. However, to gain greater insight into where problems are in your process, you will probably have to add additional steps. Be careful when adding steps as less is usually more in this case. Adding extra steps is an easy way to implicitly increase WIP, so you are going to want to add with caution. Once you have the steps in your process defined, then consider subdividing each of those columns (except the last one) into "Active" and "Done". Having these columns will, most importantly, help you to detect problems with flow more quickly, but will also allow you to perform other metrics calculations later (e.g. Flow Efficiency).

Track the timestamp that an item enters each step of the workflow. This is both easier and harder than it sounds. To answer why, we must consider two cases.

The first case we need to consider is if you are tracking data manually (i.e., independent of any other Agile tooling). In this case, you need to physically record the date that each work item enters each step of your workflow. For example, let's say your workflow is Analysis Active, Analysis Done, Development Active, Development Done, Test, Done. In this process, you would need to document the day that each item entered each state. An excerpt of what that data might look like is shown in Figure 11.1:

Story_ID	Analysis Active	Analysis Done	Development Active	Development Done	Testing	Done
1	06/25/2012	06/25/2012	06/26/2012	06/28/2012	06/29/2012	06/29/2012
2	06/25/2012	06/25/2012	06/27/2012	06/29/2012	06/29/2012	06/29/2012
3	06/21/2012	06/21/2012	06/21/2012	06/27/2012	06/27/2012	07/02/2012
4	06/21/2012	06/21/2012	06/21/2012	06/27/2012	06/27/2012	07/02/2012
5	06/21/2012	06/21/2012	06/21/2012	06/28/2012	07/02/2012	07/02/2012
6	06/21/2012	06/22/2012	06/22/2012	06/28/2012	06/28/2012	07/02/2012
7	06/25/2012	06/25/2012	06/25/2012	06/26/2012	06/29/2012	07/02/2012
8	06/25/2012	06/25/2012	06/25/2012	06/26/2012	06/29/2012	07/02/2012
9	06/21/2012	06/22/2012	06/22/2012	06/28/2012	06/28/2012	07/03/2012
10	06/25/2012	07/02/2012	07/02/2012	07/05/2012	07/06/2012	07/06/2012

Figure 11.1: Example Collected Data

You may want to further augment your data with certain item attributes. For example, you may want to capture which team worked on an item, what type it was (e.g., user story, defect, etc.), if it finished normally—to name just a few. The attributes you choose to decorate your data are completely up to you. The reason you will want to do this, however, is those attributes will serve as filter points later. For example, maybe we only want to see data from Team A. Maybe we only want to see data for defects. Maybe we want to see all the items that got canceled while in progress. Tagging data with appropriate attributes is a powerful practice that will enhance your understanding of overall process performance.

The second case to consider is if you are using some other type of electronic tooling (Jira, Trello, etc.). In this case, the tooling is probably tracking timestamps for you automatically as you move your item through your workflow. The assumption here, of course, is that you are updating the tool in real time, but more on that in a minute.

Extract your data into a proper format. If you are using an electronic Agile tool, you will need to mine the data out of that tool so that it looks something like Figure 11.1. That is easier said than done. The problem is that most Agile tools do not track data in this way. That is not necessarily the fault of the tool—they were not designed with a flow metrics approach in mind. However, it does mean that it will require some work on your part to get your data in the format as shown in Figure 11.1. Luckily for us, most electronic tools offer an API (or direct access via SQL) to get to the data.

The algorithm needed is going to be tool-specific and is beyond the scope of this book, so I will not be going into any detail here. Keep in mind, though, that you are still going to have to handle the special cases of work flowing backward, work skipping steps, work being cancelled versus closed, etc. Also, remember that you will want to mine the same item metadata that I just mentioned (type, team, etc.) to allow us to filter the data later.

Another word of caution that I need to mention is that your data is only as good as your use of your Agile tracking tool—whether that tool be an electronic system or a physical board. If work items are not updated in a timely manner, or blockers not captured properly, or items are moved back and forth randomly, then that lack of attention to process policies will be reflected in your data (this is classic "Garbage In Garbage Out" problem). You will then be forced to make the awkward decision to either try to fix the data or discard it altogether. It is a much better strategy to make sure all team members use your Agile tracking tool in an agreed upon matter so that you can have confidence in any subsequently collected data.

If using a physical board, enter all dates from the cards in a spreadsheet according to the format in Figure 11.1. Make sure to extract relevant attribute data, too: e.g., work item type, team, release number, etc. Refer to AAMFP for tips on how to handle items that move backward, are canceled, or that otherwise drop out of the process abnormally.

Lastly, I am always skeptical of extreme outliers or masses amounts of items that finish in one day. An extreme outlier is due to someone forgetting to "close" and item as like as not. And many items that finish in one day are usually due to people forgetting to properly "open" an item when they start it. They will usually notice their mistake when they go to close it and will therefore open and close the item on the same day—thus giving the item a Cycle Time of one. Your data will only be as good as your diligence in using your Agile tool.

Generate flow analytics. Once you have all of your data in the correct format, you are now ready to put that data in all of the analytics mentioned in this book. You do not necessarily have to use a tool to do this—there is no reason why you cannot build these analytics yourself. In that case, I want you to think of AAMFP as a "specification" for the Cumulative Flow Diagram and the Cycle Time Scatterplot. Additionally, this book gives you a specification for the Aging Chart (Chapter 3) and some example Monte Carlo charts (Section III). If you want to build these analytics yourself, then make sure you adhere to the rules outlined in those references.

If you do want to use a tool, then—if you will please forgive the shameless plug—allow me to recommend the ActionableAgileTM Analytics tool (https://www.actionableagile.com). At the time of this writing, it is the only tool on the market that I know of that generates all flow analytics correctly. More on the dangers of incorrectly constructed charts and how to spot them below.

Validate that you can trust your forecasts. If you have an intrinsically unstable process, then that process might not be a great candidate for Monte Carlo Simulation. For example, one indication that your process data might not be suitable for Monte Carlo simulation is if you have a CFD where arrivals far outpace your departures (Chapter 9). Ever increasing Cycle Times mean that any selection of data from a past timeframe is a poor indication of what might happen in a future timeframe. This problem is mostly eliminated if you operate a process where arrivals match departures.

However, getting to a process that produces a CFD where average arrivals match average departures is not necessarily good enough. Another "smell" that our data might not be suitable for Monte Carlo Simulation is if we have a triangle-shaped Scatterplot. A triangle pattern on a Scatterplot is also the result of an inherently unstable process. Recall that even if you have a CFD where average arrivals match average departures, you still can have a Scatterplot that looks like a triangle. The culprit in that scenario is Flow Debt. Large accumulations of Flow Debt destabilize a process and make it imminently unpredictable. Could you unstable Cycle Time data into a Monte Carlo Simulation? Yes. Would the resulting forecast be reasonable? Probably not.

If you are at a point where you cannot trust y our forecasts, then determine what assumptions of Little's Law you are violating and correct them. Do your average arrivals not match your average departures? Do you allow items to age arbitrarily and/or unnecessarily? Do you abandon work before it is completed but not account for it properly? There are any number of policies you can change to make your process perform better. Make the changes and reforecast.

Choose confidence levels. Choose a confidence level that works for your context for both single item and multiple item forecasts. When starting out, most teams that I work with choose something around the 85th percentile. There are a couple of reasons for this.

Make your first forecasts. As discussed at great length before, for single items, calculate percentiles off of the Cycle Time Scatterplot (Chapter 2). For multiple items read percentiles off of the Results Histogram (Chapter 5).

Experiment. Play around with different historical date ranges for inputs. Filter on different attributes. Determine what works best for your context. When experimenting, you will be tempted to use metrics and analytics to compare individuals against one another, or teams against one another. Do not do it.

Improve. Monitor your work item aging daily—potentially tweak your standups to accomplish this. Look at Scatterplots and CFDs in retrospectives. Let Flow Efficiency be your guide as to where to look for improvement. Change process policies (WIP limits, definitions of done, blocker policies, pull policies, etc.) to increase overall process performance. Again, consider which assumptions of Little's Law you are violating if predictability starts to suffer.

Scale. I have talked to my good friend Klaus Leopold many times about what it means to "scale" an Agile process. Our take on the matter is probably different than other scaling definitions that you may have come across previously. It seems to me that most definitions of scale speak only to rolling out Agile across multiple teams. We believe this definition to be deficient as it misses several other critical dimensions of running an Agile process at scale. Those dimensions are:

1. "Multiplying" a process or framework across many teams (the "traditional" definition of scaling)
2. "Inflating" a process to different levels of the organization (what Klaus calls "flight levels")
3. "Expanding" a process both up and down the whole organizational value stream
4. "Deepening" a process implementation by having better understanding of flow principles

So, in addition to rolling this out to additional teams, consider expanding the scope of your predictability implementation either upstream or downstream of current process boundaries. Implement these things at different levels: team, project, portfolio, other. Increase your understanding by learning more about flow and flow principles.

Some Other Things to Consider When Getting Started

How Much Data?

"How much data do I need?" is one of the most common questions I get when introducing these methods to my clients. Most people assume you need copious amounts of data in order to glean any useful information. That is not necessarily correct. While more data is generally better, the truth is that less (often much less) data can be good enough.

For example, Douglas Hubbard (whose book "How to Measure Anything" is listed in the Bibliography) advises his clients on his "Rule of Five":

Rule of Five – There is a 93.75% chance that the median of a population is between the smallest and largest values in any random sample of five from that population.

Recall from Chapter 2 that the median is the 50th percentile line on our Scatterplot. The Rule of Five seems remarkable but it is true (please see Hubbard's book for a detailed proof as to why this rule works). If you think of your process as a random Cycle Time number generator, then you will have a very good idea of where the median of your Cycle Time data is after only five items complete.

While powerful, the Rule of Five only gets us to the median of our population—which is actually not a bad place to start. But how much more data do we need to have confidence in the overall bounds of our process's Cycle Time? To answer that, let's consider a dataset that is uniformly distributed. A uniform distribution assumes that all samples from its population are equally probable. The textbook example of a uniform distribution is rolling a fair, six-sided die. All numbers on the die have an equal chance of coming up on each throw. If you were to plot the results of several rolls, what would emerge over time is a histogram with equal-height bars for each number on the die. Uniform distributions are interesting to study as they have several useful properties. For example, let's say we have eleven samples from a uniformly distributed population. The fact that we know we have a uniform distribution means that there is a 90% probability that the next sample (i.e., the 12th sample) will be between the min and the max of the previous eleven samples. That means that we have a fairly good understanding of the range of our uniform distribution after having collected only eleven data points. Our Cycle Times for our processes are not going to be uniformly distributed (please see Chapter 2 for more info), so we are going to need more than eleven samples to gain insight to our world, but not much more.

I mention the Rule of Five and Uniform Distributions to give you a feel for the greatly increased knowledge that can be gained after observing only a few data points. Do not think you need to collect hundreds or thousands of samples over several months to have any confidence in what your data is telling you. Probability is on your side here. Trust that you are getting very valuable feedback with even a very small data set.

Yes, You Can Do All of This in a Spreadsheet, But...

While Excel may be a great tool to use when just starting out, you will no doubt quickly run into some limitations with that particular software package. First and foremost, Excel offers only a static view of your data. It does not allow you to readily interact with your analytics such as dynamically zooming in on a particular part of the graph, easily filtering out different types of work items, doing on-the-fly metrics calculations, and so forth. Secondly, Excel can become a bit unwieldy if managing thousands or tens of thousands of rows of data spread across multiple teams or departments. Still, Excel is not a bad option when starting out to make some quick progress.

Other Pitfalls

You should also know that most major Agile tools vendors include some basic form of the analytics presented in this book. You might be asking yourself why you cannot just use the analytics included with your favorite tool. There are several answers to this question. And each answer must be considered carefully.

I mentioned earlier that chances are the CFD you are looking at has probably not been generated properly. The telltale sign of this is if any line on the chart goes down. You will recall CFD Property #2 from Chapter 9:

> CFD Property #2: Due to its cumulative nature, no line on a CFD can ever decrease (go down).

Any time you see a CFD that has one or more lines go down, then you can immediately tell that whoever constructed that CFD did not account for arrivals and/or departures correctly. Not accounting for arrivals and departures properly invalidates any resultant analysis of your chart.

To illustrate the point a little better, if you are currently using an electronic tool for reporting, have it generate its CFD for you. If you do not see any lines on the chart that go down, that is a good sign. However, as a test, try to "turn off" some of the latter workflow steps (if you can) starting from the bottom up. Do you see any of the remaining lines go down now? If so, it is a safe bet that the overall CFD has not been built according to all of the required CFD principles.

The second telltale sign that a CFD is suspect is if it contains a state called "Backlog". Strictly speaking, there is nothing wrong with displaying a backlog on a CFD, but the question remains how is the tool calculating the overall process approximate average Cycle Time (does it even call this calculation an approximate average Cycle Time or does it lead you to believe it is an exact Cycle Time)? Again, I refer you to CFD Property #1 from Chapter 9:

> CFD Property #1: The top line of a Cumulative Flow Diagram *always* represents the cumulative arrivals to a process. The bottom line on a CFD *always* represents the cumulative departures from a process.

This property demands that overall process approximate average Cycle Time always be calculated from the top line of a CFD through to the bottom line of a CFD. If your chart includes a backlog and your tool's computed Cycle Time does not include the time spent in the backlog, then, again, you should be skeptical about whether the tool is calculating flow metrics properly.

Another pitfall to watch out for is how your Scatterplot is generated—assuming your tool even generates a Scatterplot. Your tool may call its Scatterplot a "Control Chart"—which it most certainly is not. As I mentioned in Chapter 2, why Control Charts (at least Control Charts in the Shewhart and Deming tradition) are probably not applicable to knowledge work is beyond the scope of this book. The thing you need to watch out for, though, is that if your tool takes a "Control Chart" approach, it is almost certainly assuming that your data is normally distributed. When looking at your Agile tool's Control Chart, look to see if displays lines that say something like "mean plus one standard deviation" or "$\mu + \sigma$". It might also give you an associated percentage akin to the standard percentages that I demonstrated in Section II and Section III. In this case, that percentage is going to be based on an assumption that your data is normally distributed—which I can guarantee it is not. How do I know it is not? Look at your Histogram. You may remember from your statistics training that the shape of a normal distribution is a bell curve. When you look at your Histogram you will see that your data does not follow a bell curve pattern.

Using the mean plus a standard deviation (or the mean plus any number of standard deviations) approach and then associating the result with percentiles is dangerous given that your data is not normally distributed. You will get calculation errors that are not insignificant and you will potentially make poor decisions based on bad data.

The moral of this story is that when you are starting out with this type of analysis, do not necessarily trust the data or charts that your Agile tool displays for you. Do not trust its associated calculations. It may seem tedious, but I would encourage you to initially track some sample data yourself and then compare it to what your electronic tool generates for you. You may be surprised at how different those results can be. And when those results are different, which method will you trust more?

Conclusion

There are at least four reasons why the forecasting practices in this book are better than others you have used:

- They are easier than you think
- Take less time that you think
- Give better (more accurate) answers than you think
- Require less data than you think

Key Learnings And Takeaways

- It is very easy to get started with the forecasting methods described in the book. As a start, follow the recipe described at the beginning of this chapter.
- You do not need much data to get started.
- Consider starting out with a spreadsheet. Then "graduate" to more advanced tooling as you get more comfortable.
- Do not necessarily trust the flow analytics that are packaged with your chosen Agile tooling. Try calculating some of your metrics manually yourself and see how they compare.
- Experiment with your own metrics and analysis once you have mastered the techniques mentioned here.

Chapter 12: Putting It All Together

In recent years, I have gotten a reputation of being an "Agile Metrics Guy". To set the record straight, I am not really a "Metrics Guy" I am a "Predictability Guy". Yes, metrics are a large part of predictability—but only just a part. And not even the most important part. The more important part is the actions that you need to take every day in order to get the process predictability that you are looking for. Take the right action at the right time, and the metrics and forecasting will take care of themselves. Unfortunately, it is these actions that are normally overlooked when talking about forecasting even though they have a much bigger impact than any statistical, estimation, or planning approach. This chapter will help fix that.

Standups for Predictability

Quite possibly the most important team meeting for any Agile process is the standup. I am on the record as preferring flow-based standups over Scrum-style standups. The reason is a flow-based standup focuses on the work and what the team collectively is doing to get work done as opposed to a Scrum-style standup where the focus is on the individual and what she/he is doing to get work done. Either way, from a predictability perspective, there is one practice that all standups should incorporate. In Chapter 3, I discussed the Aging Chart and how it should be used on a regular basis as an aid to predictability. In order to deliver on accurate forecasts, team must monitor the age of items in progress and do whatever they can to make sure those items are completing in a timely manner. The standup is one of the best places to do that, and the Aging Chart is one of the best tools to enable that discussion.

Retrospectives for Predictability

Traditionally Agile teams run retrospectives to facilitate learning, development, and improvement. Most teams experiment multiple different formats to get the right outcomes. Even so, the retrospective remains of the more enigmatic Agile meetings. No matter what teams try, these meetings seem to devolve into lack of participation, finger pointing, irrelevant topics, and lack of prioritization of issues. It is not long before these problems derail the whole purpose of the retrospective. I would argue that the root cause of these problems lies with the subjectivity of the meeting.

Subjective Retrospectives

The most common type of retrospective employed is the subjective form. Subjective retrospectives take many shapes but usually consist of the collecting and listing of ideas/topics, prioritization (either by a moderator or by the participants via voting), discussion, and, finally, the extraction and assignment of action items. Based on what you have read so far, do you think the subjective form of the retrospective really achieves its intended outcome—especially from a predictability perspective?

Objective Retrospectives

My answer is probably not. When forecasting, we must decouple subjective feeling from objective fact. We must move beyond statements like "stories take too long to complete" to "stories this month took 12 days or less to complete at the 85th percentile where last month they took 8 days or less to complete at the 85th percentile". We must move beyond statements like our Sprint forecasts are unpredictable to "Are our arrivals matching departures? Are we accumulating flow debt?" To have conversations like this is going to require you to bring up all of the analytics that I have discussed in this book.

Once the conversation becomes rooted in observable fact, the dynamic of the meeting changes. Instead of opinionated argument, the team can have direct discussion about what is wrong and what can be done to improve. The guidelines presented in this book, then, become a clear recipe for action items to be completed before the next retrospective

To be fair, objective retrospectives do have the side-effect of the team trying to game the system to make the numbers look good. That, in my opinion, is not necessarily a bad thing—as long as you are looking at the right metrics. Let's say a team tries to game Cycle Time by breaking up Stories into arbitrarily smaller pieces. If I were going to have them game that metric, then that is exactly the first thing I would recommend. Assuming you have your customer define your acceptance criteria, and assuming your customer has to sign off on that criteria before the story is closed, then you will see right away if breaking stories up is gaining you anything. However, if you are trying to game a different metric, velocity for example, the all the team needs to do is "over-point" stories—the customer has no way of knowing whether that estimation has been done correctly or not.

In your retrospectives, look at your Cycle Time Scatterplot, look at your CFD, look at your Flow Efficiency. Use these metrics and analytics as a guide for process improvement. Your predictability will thank you.

How to Do Release Planning

First and foremost, my preference would be that you do not do big batch releases. I would much rather see you do some type of Continuous Delivery/Continuous Deployment. Having said that, I understand that this is not always possible in certain contexts (yet!)

and that there are still teams that must do some type of release planning.

How long does it take you to do release planning now? Hours, days, weeks? Using the methods in this book, I hope you have seen how you can get your release planning down to just minutes. A release plan is a forecast for how long it will take you to get many items finished. We know that a multiple item forecast will require something like Monte Carlo Simulation. By applying something like MCS, you can have an almost immediate idea of either (a) how many items you can have completed by a certain date, or (2) how long it will take you to get multiple items done. Not only do you have the instant gratification that MCS brings but you also have a risk profile associated with all possible outcomes. This risk profile could help you shape what you are "committing to" in your release.

However, remember that release planning is not done only at the beginning of a release. You must continually update your forecasts based on new information as the release progresses. You might also wonder why you would care about things like Cycle Time if all your company cares about is getting big bang releases out the door. Your objection might be something like "Why does it matter how long individual items take if I have to get them all done by a specific date anyway?". There are two answers to this. First, by Little's Law you should understand that Cycle Time and Throughput are inextricably related. Ignore Cycle Time for long enough and your Throughput will start to suffer. Second, in almost every release I have been in, there have been particular items that must be completed before the release goes out. This might be for contractual, regulatory, or technical reasons. If you have specific items that must be completed, now we are back in the world of single items forecasts. As you recall, single item forecasts require Cycle Time as their basis.

Some Other Ideas

I want to reiterate that the ideas presented in this book work regardless of the level of organization that you are talking about. I have tried as much as possible to use the generic term "work item" as the proxy for the concept of customer value because customer value could take the form of Stories at the team level; they could take the form of Features at the project level; or they could take the form of Projects or Initiatives at the portfolio level. They could even take the form of Tasks at the personal level. To put these ideas into practice, you will want to read up on Klaus Leopold's thoughts on how to apply flow principles at different parts of the organization. These aptly-called "Flight Levels" will give you tremendous insight on how to drive better improvement, efficiency, and predictability across the whole organization.

Segmenting WIP

I have alluded to this several times before, but it is worth calling out again that it is possible to segment your WIP into several different types. For example, it might be useful to think of your WIP not as just generic work items, but categorize it into types like "User Stories", "Production Defects", "Maintenance Request", etc. This is a perfectly valid approach and actually may be desirable in many circumstances. The good news is that if you choose to segment your WIP in such a manner then your forecasts will apply to both the overall WIP in the system as well as to each type or groups of types.

For example, we might want to come with a forecast for all work flowing through our process, or we may want to come up with a forecast based just on work item type "User Story". We might want to investigate how badly our Production Defects are violating the assumptions of the law. Or maybe it is our maintenance requests grouped together with defects that are the culprit. In most cases this type of segmentation is very useful and could provide a more sophisticated approach to analyzing process performance. Lastly, as discussed in Section III, we may want to compare forecasts that include all work versus a forecast that excludes all cancelled or abandoned work.

The point here is you can slice and dice your work items however you see fit, and I encourage you to play around with different segmentations as an aid to forecasting.

Other Forecasting Techniques

There are no doubt other statistical techniques that you can use to achieve the same goals other than the ones I have provided here. I have a bias toward these methods because they are:

- Easy to explain and understand
- Easy to implement
- Do not require much data

In other words, even though we are talking about probabilities here, you do not need an advanced statistics degree to understand what is going right or wrong in y our process. Nor do you need to have been running your process for several years to have enough data for meaningful analysis.

Further, if the estimation scheme you have in place is working for you, then I do not necessarily recommend that you change. I would recommend that you at least experiment with some of these approaches as you will find they will give more accurate forecasts with less effort—but I will leave it up to you to prove me right or wrong on that.

My point here is that if you have other preferred forecasting methods that you would like to use, then, by all means, use them. I do not profess to have the monopoly on good ideas for forecasting. For most organizations, however, these practices will be good enough. Give them a shot and let me know what you think!

But What If I Don't Care About Predictability?

I get this question all the time at client sites and in the workshops I give. I have to say that I am always surprised by it. I have never met a customer or manager who does not care about the answer to WWIBD. That is usually the *only* thing they care about. However, I am willing to accept that there are certain contexts where predictability is not king. Even so, the very same practices outlined here for better predictability will also enable you to run a much more efficient, effective process. In fact, I would argue that better overall process efficiency is the goal anyway. Most of the tips that I will share are going to be centered more around running a more efficient process. Get your efficiency up and you essentially get predictability for free.

Whether predictability is a part of the equation or not, I am sure all of your stakeholders will care running your process as efficiently as possible (after all, somebody somewhere is paying your paycheck).

Key Learnings and Takeaways

- You still have to think, experiment, and evolve
- Emphasize it is the little things you do every day that have the greatest impact on predictability: pay attention to WIP Aging, pull policies, etc.

Section VI: Case Studies

Chapter 13: Case Study - Ultimate Software

The following case study was written mostly by Prateek Singh with contributions from Stephen Reid. In the interest of full disclosure, I would like to point out that it has been previously published on two separate occasions. One version appeared on the InfoQ website and the other on the Agile Alliance website. The version included here represents a more detailed and more thorough discussion of the evolution of the use of flow metrics at Ultimate Software than has been previously available. It can act as a guide to implementing and evolving agile processes using flow metrics whether at scale or for a small team. It demonstrates how teams and organizations can identify inefficiencies in their processes and eliminate waste to run a leaner, more predictable and more profitable organization. The study will not just talk about what Ultimate Software learned, but also how Ultimate learned. The methods explored here can be applied in the context of most development organizations.

Ultimate Software

Ultimate Software is a leading provider of Global HR and Payroll software. As of 2016, Ultimate had been on "Fortune's 25 Best Companies to Work For" list for the past 5 years and was named "#1 Best Company to Work For in Tech" that year. The development organization at Ultimate spans 25 teams with over 350 developers. All 25 of the development teams at Ultimate follow agile principles in order to provide greater predictability and productivity. The development teams at Ultimate have to be especially agile and nimble for two major reasons. First being the competitive market space which Ultimate Software finds itself in. Second is the need to react to federal, state and local laws concerning payroll, taxation and human resources, which don't have a regular cadence of going into effect.

These were the major factors due to which the development organization started experimenting with agile principles in 2005. Ultimate has had a few major waves of agile progression since then. Every adoption and progression of Agile methods at Ultimate has been at scale. A couple of the waves have started from one or two teams, but have quickly spread across the organization and implemented at the scale of the entire department. Agile transformation at Ultimate Software has been an 11 year journey. There was a slightly bumpy but org wide adoption of Scrum that promised a lot of agility, flexibility, predictability and productivity to the teams. While this helped Ultimate "walk" with Agile, it was the transition to Kanban that helped Ultimate "run". The transition has been a steady but bumpy ride where Ultimate has learned from the missteps they have taken and continued to experiment with Agile techniques.

Starting With Scrum

In 2005 Ultimate Software's development management realized that certain problems plagued the way teams were developing and deploying software. The traditional Waterfall system was not producing the results that Ultimate knew its development team was capable of producing. Ultimate had also embarked on a new version of its flagship product and began to realize that most of the projects were falling prey to being 80% done for long periods of time. This would often lead to cutting down of testing effort as the deadline for release came closer. Business analysts, engineers and testers were often working on separate, consecutive releases and there was a constant need for context switching as the defects discovered were often in the codebase for the previous release. The estimation for how long any task would take was extremely unreliable as the developers had no historical data to base their estimates on. While testing was one release behind, automation of these tests could be even further behind and there could be a lag of a year or more between the writing of new code and creation of automated tests for the same code.

As Ultimate embarked on new projects, the organization sought to alleviate these problems by implementing Scrum across the development teams. The teams were trained in how to organize their work and accomplish the project goals using Scrum. The new Scrum Masters were also trained as Certified Scrum Masters. This put Ultimate firmly on the track of experimenting with Agile techniques. All development activities were accomplished within the scope of two week iterations. The feedback loop within the team shortened from months (sometimes years) to days. Scrum allowed the teams to plan and attempt to stick to the plan with some consistency. Teams were able to deliver value with every iteration and the progress was measurable. The shorter feedback loops also allowed product owners to prioritize items into sprints and know well in advance when the project dates were slipping.

Ultimate used a Scrum of scrums every day to bubble up issues from the team to the department level. This was the scaling method that Ultimate adopted and has stuck with for the past 11 years. The Scrum of Scrums has evolved over time and become increasingly effective, but has been the main scaling method used at Ultimate. As new scaling frameworks have appeared on the horizon, Ultimate has evaluated them. They have usually been bulkier than the simple "Scrum of Scrums" method that Ultimate started with.

Scrum also brought with it a renewed focus on quality. Instead of being the last piece that was forced to fit into a tight window at the end of the release, testing became an activity that was consistently happening throughout the release. Most teams were working as mini-waterfalls, with the first couple of days dedicated to estimation, planning and analysis, a week of development work and the remaining time allocated to manual testing and automation. While this did not force direct collaboration between different roles on the team, it made the roles explicitly aware of the issues faced by other roles on the team. This helped improve quality of the artifacts that were provided by each step to the next one.

Despite the benefits that the adoption of Scrum brought to the organization, the hyper-productivity that was initially promised by agile methods never materialized. The mini-waterfalls within sprints also were a clear anti-pattern. In order to reinforce some of the Scrum principles and to achieve the productivity the teams were capable of, Ultimate embarked on a second wave of Scrum adoption. Ultimate retrained the leads, many of whom were new and had not been trained before. Extreme Programming principles of unit testing, pairing and code reviews were also brought in, as a supplement to the Scrum principles teams were already following. Test driven development and test first development were both experimented with to varying degree of success.

This second wave of Scrum adoption helped the teams become more balanced in approach as the engineers started taking more responsibility for quality assurance through unit tests. Testers started learning how to automate their test cases and the technical vs manual tester separation ceased to exist. Teams became tighter units producing value regularly. There were still some problems that were unsolved and new ones that became evident as a result of the Scrum adoption.

Problems With Scrum Adoption

While Scrum had helped Ultimate come a long way from the waterfall days, there were issues they were facing that Scrum was not able to resolve. After having used Scrum for four years, the hyper productivity that Ultimate was looking for had not emerged. Teams still had not been able to fully remove the mini-waterfall system that had become the prevalent style of operation. There were a few other problems with the implementation of v itself that started to become increasingly evident.

The first major issue was that estimation and planning meetings took a long time. These activities often took half a day out of a two week sprint. The loss of half a day per team would still be time well spent if the benefit of the planning offset the costs. Despite multiple sprints of experience in estimating, the teams still often under or over-estimated the complexity of a task. The estimates done in story points were not providing much value in terms of predictability. Teams also found it hard to stick to the plan for the sprint. This was mostly due to the interrupt driven nature of requirements and priorities. A new regulatory taxation law that was just signed into effect would often take precedence over feature work planned for the sprint. The same was the case for any issues reported from the 3000+ client base that effected running and reporting of payroll or critical HR projects. Based on the estimates that the team had provided, the product owners liked to plan up to 6 months of sprints out and the interrupts would very often change those plans. The issue here was that very often the plans would have already been communicated out to the stakeholders.

In order to avoid communicating plans that would most likely be changed, product and development management only committed to 50% of the team's capacity. This was both due to instability in prioritization and the team's inability to estimate work with a high degree of accuracy. The Features the team worked on were split between committed and desired. The teams were often pushed hard to finish the committed features. This meant some of the desired features were left unfinished. These features would sometimes be dropped from the next release due to higher priority items coming in. This lead to large amounts of wasted time and effort from the development teams.

The small size (8-10 members) Scrum teams also led to a major coordination problem. It often required 2 to 3 teams working on the same feature to get the feature released successfully. With the committed/desired model, it was often possible that the one of the product owners could not commit to a feature that was committed by two other teams. In essence, even though two teams could get their pieces of a feature done, the third team would not be able to commit to the feature, even when on paper they had the capacity to fit the feature in the release.

Progression to Kanban

In 2009 Ultimate started experimenting with Kanban on one of the teams in the development organization. This was an infrastructure team which provided the other development teams with their development environments. The team was plagued with the problem of being highly interrupt driven. Most of the other development teams relied on them to provide support for any emergencies that they were dealing with. This team's planning meetings were almost always resulting in plans they couldn't follow as an emergency would invariably pop up for one of the other teams and the team would have to throw out its sprint plan. Without explicitly changing methodologies from Scrum to Kanban, Ultimate overlaid the Kanban principles on top of the current Scrum process. Limiting WIP and visualizing work had an almost immediate effect on the team. They were able to serve the rest of the organization more efficiently. They were also able to invest in process improvement activities that helped them become increasingly productive over time.

After the success of this first experiment, Ultimate rolled out Kanban to all the teams in the organization. One of the first actions that management took when switching to Kanban was merging the previously small Scrum teams into larger teams of up to 30 people. Now, with a single product owner managing their backlog, these larger teams were able to deliver the highest priority features for the organization, even within the committed/desired model.

The first wave of Kanban adoption was facilitated through the training of the leads of the teams that were being moved over to the new Kanban system. This was similar to the initial implementation of Scrum, where the Scrum master of every team was trained in the methodology. The leads then drove the adoption of the principles by the team. While this was a pattern that seemed to have worked well in the past, we were still not able to achieve the gains that would qualify as hyper productivity. We definitely were able to get a greater understanding of how the teams functioned and where work was not moving forward as the leads helped the teams visualize and track their processes. Even at this point something was missing.

Results with Kanban

In late 2014 Ultimate redoubled its focus on Kanban. This time instead of just training leads, entire teams were trained on the importance of flow metrics and of Kanban principles. Trainings were focused on the benefits of explicitly mapping out and visualizing process, limiting Work In Progress and managing for flow. Teams were asked to be collectively and directly responsible for their own processes and policies. Following the training, the teams implemented WIP limits on their boards and for the first time actively managed work according to those limits. The results were far better than expected and are detailed in the individual team case studies below.

ACES

- Greenfield development of new Pay Calculation Engine
- 60% reduction in Cycle Time for stories from 35 days @ the 85th percentile (using Scrum) to 14 days @ the 85th percentile (using Kanban)
- 10% increase in story Throughput from 170 completed in five months to 186 stories completed in five months despite losing almost half of the team

ACES started in 2013 as a 16-member Scrum team whose sole responsibility was the development of a new Pay Calculation Engine. In those early days, the team was widely considered successful because it delivered a consistent velocity (from a Scrum perspective). Upon examining the team's data in the light of flow metrics, however, the team discovered that there were extreme inefficiencies in the process, which when remedied, could result in higher productivity and greater predictability.

Figure 13.1: ACES Team Board

The team started visualizing their cycle time data using a Cycle Time Scatterplot. This visualization immediately showed the team that their process was not as optimal as they believed. They started applying the principles of Kanban and Flow to address these problems. The Scatterplots below contrast the performance of the team before and after adjusting their processes based on Kanban principles:

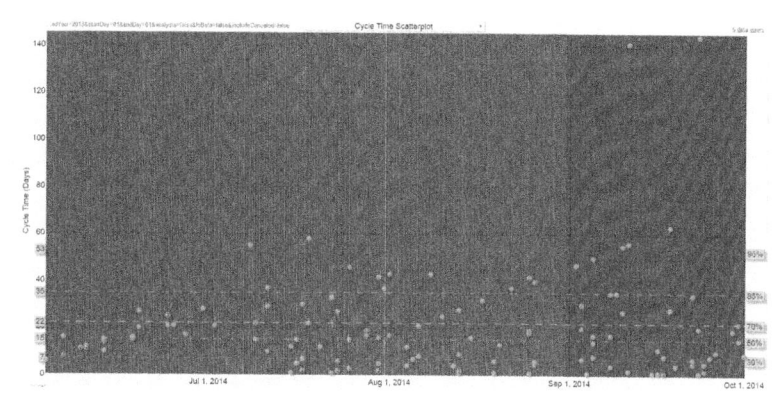

Figure 13.2: ACES Team Cycle Time Scatterplot Before Kanban

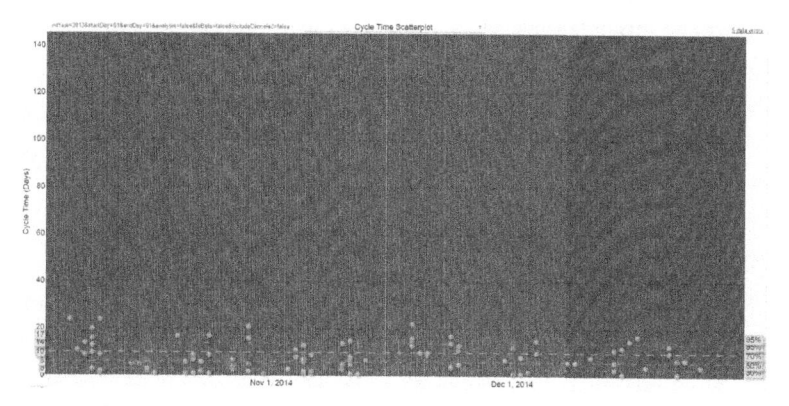

Figure 13.3: ACES Team Cycle Time Scatterplot After Kanban

Figure 13.2 above shows that when the team was using Scrum practices, 85% of their stories took 30 days or less to complete. A 35-day Cycle Time by itself is not necessarily bad, unless you put it in the context of the fact that the team was running 14-day sprints. A more detailed analysis reveals that 50% of the stories completed in that same time frame took 15 days or less to complete. What that means is that stories that started at the beginning of the sprint only had about a 50% chance of completing within that same sprint. This is not the picture of predictability that the team's velocity would lead us to believe.

After analyzing the scatterplot, the team began to dive into the reasons why stories were taking longer to complete than expected. They discovered that most of the stories that took a long time to complete were sitting in the "Ready for QA" column for extended periods of time. The team realized this as a problem because "Ready for QA" was a queuing column where stories are not actively worked on—yet the Cycle Time clock that measures how long it takes work to complete keeps on ticking. The team decided to attack this column first by putting a WIP limit of 5 on that column. The team also chose to prioritize concentrating on work that has been in progress the longest to achieve a consistent cadence of finishing work rather than allowing stories to age indefinitely.

The result of these policy changes were almost immediate. From that point forward the team was able to get 85% of their stories done in 14 days or less. Throughput for ACES also increased from 1.07 stories per day to 1.41 stories per day. It should be pointed out that process modifications did not involve changing the size of stories or working overtime. The team continued to hone the flow-focused process by further lowering the WIP limit on the Ready for QA column and encouraging the various disciplines on the team to help each other out in order to make sure none of the items on the board age beyond their 85th percentile.

The improvements achieved by the ACES team continue to this day.

Payroll Team

- Responsible for core payroll functionality in a context characterized by frequent interrupts of urgent customer requests.
- 79% reduction in average queuing time for stories from 8.84 days to 1.88 days
- 69% reduction in story Cycle Time from 36 days @ the 85th percentile to 11 days @ the 85th percentile

The Payroll team maintains and develops the core payroll capabilities for Ultimate Software's flagship product, Ultipro. The current incarnation of this 30-person team was formed in 2009 by combining three separate Scrum teams. The team had a consistent history of being interrupted by urgent customer issues (think about how upset you might be if your paycheck was not calculated correctly or distributed on time). Due to the urgent nature of these issues, only the experts in the given area were the ones troubleshooting and fixing them, causing deepening knowledge silos.

After re-training in Kanban principles in 2015, the team immediately changed the way they worked. Payroll did not merely limit WIP, they in fact lowered their WIP limits below the number of people in certain areas. The idea behind this change was to promote pairing and removal of knowledge silos. This also left slack in the system to allow for the team to deal with emergency customer issues when they came up. The result of embracing these policies was immediately visible in how long it was taking the team to complete their stories. The amount of time stories spent in queuing states decreased dramatically over time and as a result the Cycle Times for the team went through a dramatic decrease. The table below shows the faster Cycle Times since the team's training at the end of March 2015.

MONTH	AVERAGE TOTAL CYCLE TIME (days)	AVERAGE QUEUING TIME (days)	TOTAL CYCLE TIME 85th PERCENTILE (days)
January	18.49	8.84	36
February	20.72	11.41	34
March	12.77	5.74	27
April	4.24	0.68	7
May	9.21	1.91	18
June	7.83	1.91	13
July	6.94	2.23	12
August	6.39	2.63	11
September	5.05	1.13	10
October	7.23	1.56	12
November	8.08	1.88	11

Figure 13.4: Payroll Cycle Times vs. Queuing Times

The net active time that the team was spending on stories did not change. By limiting their WIP, the team was able to cut down the time the story was just sitting on the board. As the team got more efficient in the use of a Kanban system and started tweaking their process policies, they were able to gain greater consistency in story completion times (at the 85th percentile—see Figure 13.3).

The greater predictability of Cycle Times had two immediate effects. First, the team was able to deliver value to the product owners and customers faster and more regularly. Second, when an emergency issue did come up, the team could ask the question of "Can this wait until we finish one of the items we are currently working on?". As work items were getting done faster, there was a regular cadence of people freeing up to pick up the next item. With a team member freeing up on a daily basis, the team could ask the requesting party to hold off for a couple of hours or till the next morning. The same question could not be asked if the team was taking upwards of 20 days on average to finish work items. In case of absolute emergencies though, the paired-up team members could break the pairs in order to deal with the escalations. In fact, the inability to ask the question and lack of slack in the system was one of the major reasons for driving up the time taken to finish stories.

The manager of the team had this to say about their experience with Kanban principles:

"At first we laughed at the thought of intentionally limiting our Work In Progress and simplifying our Kanban board. We truly believed that this approach would "never work for our team". That was before March's Kanban training. We transformed our board, changed the format of our Standup and implemented sensible WIP limits and the way we work changed forever.

Before Kanban 2.0, we thought we must be "slacking" if we had fewer than 40 stories on the board. Today we rarely break 20. Much to our surprise we discovered that the ideas from our training really do work for us! Now we can focus more clearly on taking each story from open to close, more as a team, and in about half the time. This lets us adjust our feature work more rapidly and deliver higher quality features. As a manager, it's now possible for me see to all of the team's work at a glance and pinpoint areas of concern before catastrophe strikes! Finally, having stable Cycle Time and Throughput data allows us to truly predict our capabilities for future release planning and emergency requests from Production.

Today we laugh, or cry, when we think about the way we worked before!"

-Leighton Gill, Manager of Software Engineering

Business Intelligence

- Responsible for business intelligence capabilities across all Ultimate Software products.
- 73% reduction in story Cycle Time from 63 days @ the 85th percentile to 17 days @ the 85th percentile
- 60% increase in story Throughput from 203 stories completed per 10 months to 324 stories completed per 10 months

Chapter 13: Case Study - Ultimate Software

The Business Intelligence (BI) team provides reporting capabilities for all Ultimate Software products. As a rule, the team would release their reporting module along with the major product releases for the flagship Ultipro product. The BI team is another example of the major improvements that Ultimate's Kanban adoption brought to teams. The BI team was re-trained on Kanban principles in mid-November of 2014. The graph below shows the performance of the team from January 1st to November 15th of 2014. The team completed 203 work items in this time period. 85% of these work items took 63 days or less to complete. The team was highly unpredictable with when they would be able to get a story done as stories were taking more than 2 months to complete, with multiple items taking more than 100 days.

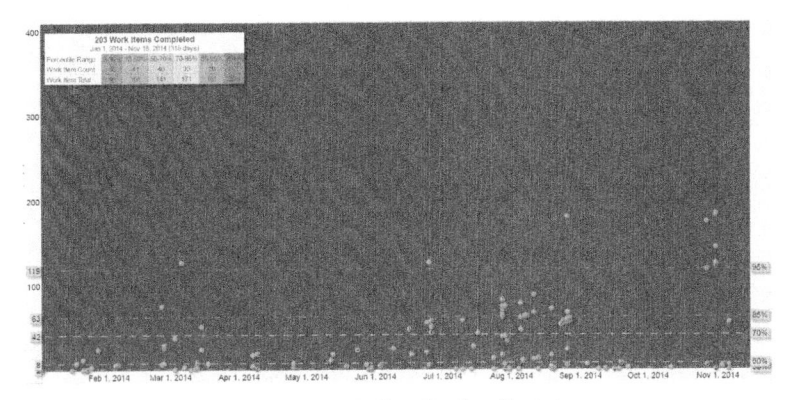

Figure 13.5: BI Before Kanban Training

In contrast, the following graph shows the performance of the team in 2015 for the same time period. The team was able to accomplish 324 work items in this time period with 85% of these items taking 17 days or less. The team increased its productivity by over 50% in this time period. Along with the increase in productivity and predictability, the team was completing work items at a more regular cadence.

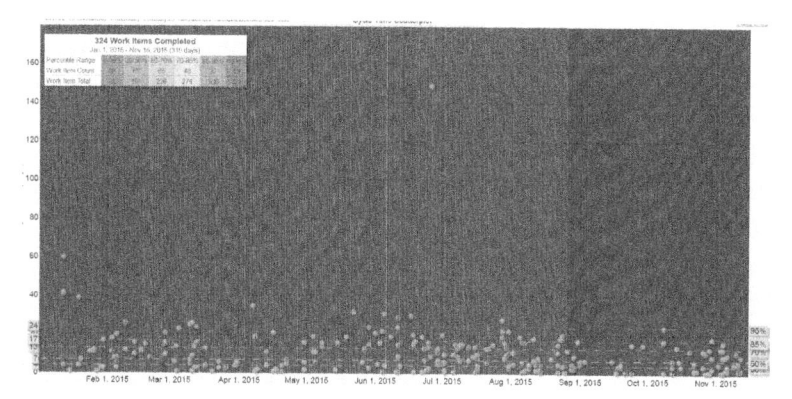

Figure 13.6: BI After Kanban Training

One last benefit for BI resulting from the switch to Kanban: prior to a more flow-based approach, the team released on a semi-annual basis only. Because of the dramatic reduction of Cycle Times, BI was able to increase the frequency of their releases to every other month. The more frequent releases resulted in faster customer feedback, less defects, and overall increased customer satisfaction.

Organization Wide Impact

The improvements outlined above were not limited to just these three teams. In fact, the advances shown here were largely exhibited by all teams across the entire development organization. There was a marked increase in both the number of stories completed and the number of features completed between 2014 and 2015. The shorter story Cycle Times translated into faster completion of features. Faster completion of features translated into a dramatic increase in the total number of features delivered to customers: from 176 in 2014 to 411 in 2015. Looking at the month over month comparisons, every month in 2015 was more productive than the same month in 2014.

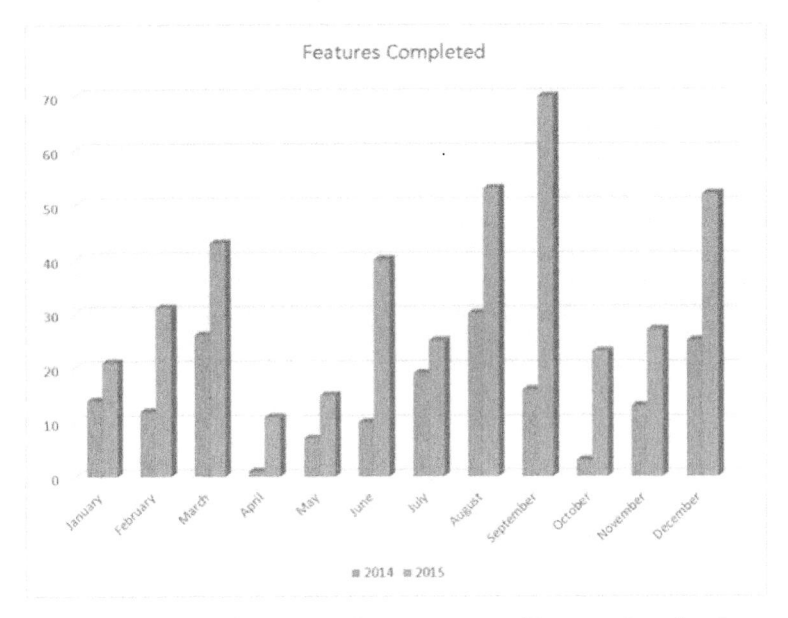

Figure 13.7: Month Over Month Comparisons of Features Completed

These organization-wide improvements had the ultimate effect of streamlining the release planning process. Predictable Cycle Time and stable Throughput allowed teams to experiment with more sophisticated planning techniques. The most important of which was Monte Carlo Simulation.

Probabilistic Release Planning (Monte Carlo)

Monte Carlo is a forecasting technique where past data and performance is used to simulate a system's future performance. Monte Carlo simulations assume that the upcoming days would produce daily Throughput that are similar to the ones from the past few days. The simulations produce results that can initiate the conversation about forecasts in the light of risk levels that the business is willing to accept.

Let us say a team is trying to figure out how many stories they can complete in the next 30 day release. We would run the Monte Carlo Simulation for the team in the following way. We would simulate Day 1 of the release by picking a random day from the team's recent history (last 60 days) and assigning its Throughput to Day 1. We next assign a random day's Throughput to Day 2 of the release. We continue doing this for the 30 days of the release and finally sum up the Throughput for all the days in order to get a single simulation result for how many stories the team an get done over the course of the release. If we repeated the process again, due to the randomness in the simulation we would very likely get a different number of stories as a result. Now, if we ran these simulations a few thousand times, we would get a distribution of results that would look a bit like the graph below.

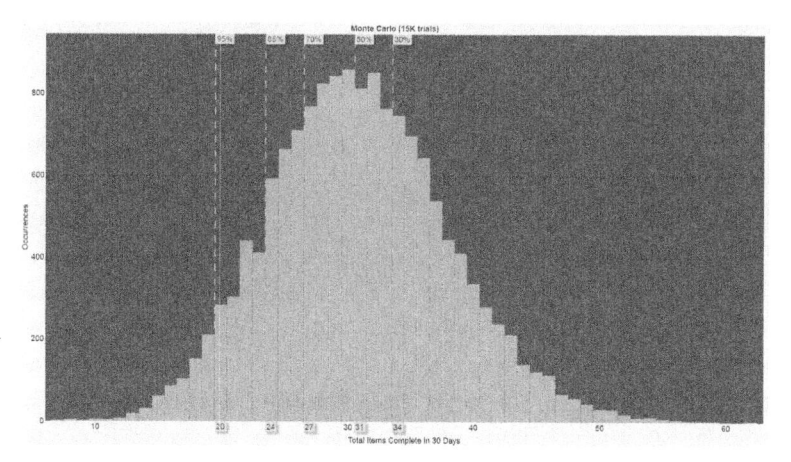

Figure 13.8: Monte Carlo Simulation Results Histogram

Along the x-axis of the graph is the total number of items completed in 30 days and along the y axis is the number of occurrences of that result in the simulations. In the above case we ran 15,000 simulations to get the graph shown here. What this graph also tells us is the probability of getting a certain number of items done in the upcoming 30 days. The vertical dotted lines are the percentile lines we can use as guides in the probability conversation. According to this set of Monte Carlo simulations, the team has a 50% chance of getting 31 items done in the next 30 days. The same team also has an 85% chance of getting 24 stories done and a 95% chance of getting 20 stories done over the same time period.

With these probabilistic results at hand, teams are able to start having the conversation in terms of how much risk are they willing to take. A conservative product owner may plan a feature that is about 20 stories to be delivered for this 30 day release. On the other hand, if the team is not working on highly critical items, they might plan with a 50% risk and try to get 31 stories done. This process moves the conversation from a deterministic one to a probabilistic one leading to a better understanding of the risk we are taking when we are planning features of a certain size. Having the simulations based on real data at hand also results in simpler planning conversations as opposed to 3 hour planning sessions.

Release Tracking

Monte Carlo simulations can also be used to figure out the probability of meeting a certain delivery date, given the number of stories in the release. We can figure out what percentage of the simulations have the team completing the required number of stories in a fixed time frame. This can be done in order to plan the release and also, in order to track the progress of the team towards the release goals. As a team makes progress in a release, we can start running simulations at regular intervals using their latest data. The simulations, run at different points in the release, can provide a temperature check on the status of the release. It can tell us if the team is falling behind on its commitments, is on track or can pull more work into the release.

At Ultimate Software, teams can send out releases independent of each other. Different teams follow different release schedules. This means each team has its own code freeze and release dates. Each team has also made commitments to their product strategy counterparts. Ultimate can take the story level commitment number, the release date and the recent performance of a team to run Monte Carlo simulations. These simulations can then tell us the probability of finishing the release on time for each team. Ultimate runs these simulations on an hourly basis and publish the results to an open URL. Both the development teams and their counterparts in product strategy can review the report. In order to get the most relevant simulation results, they use the last 30 days of the team's Throughput data. This produces simulations that can be trusted for the upcoming release as they take into account any changes that could have happened on the team of late.

Below is a screenshot of the Monte Carlo release tracking dashboard that gets updated every hour to reflect the completion likelihood for every release. The information here also includes the code freeze date for the release, stories remaining to be closed and the date where we can say with 95 percent confidence that the team will be done with the stories in the release.

MonteCarlo

Team	Release	Code Freeze Date	Stories Remaining	85% Completion Date	Completion Likelihood
Recruiting	June 2016	06/30/2016	9	06/29/2016	93.15%
Hiring Integration	June 2016	06/30/2016	5	07/29/2016	4.95%
Onboarding	June 2016	06/30/2016	13	07/11/2016	22.65%
TWIST	June 2016	06/30/2016	9	07/01/2016	76.70%
Platform Services	June 2016	06/30/2016	15	07/27/2016	0.05%
UTA	UTA 6.1.3v15	07/01/2016	5	07/05/2016	80.50%
UTM	UTM-2.7	07/01/2016	16	07/08/2016	32.70%
Talent Management	July 2016	07/08/2016	18	07/12/2016	79.90%
Recruiting	July 2016	07/15/2016	36	07/29/2016	6.85%
Business Intelligence	August 2016	07/28/2016	30	08/11/2016	19.50%
Workforce Management	WFM-Beta	07/29/2016	33	07/06/2016	99.99%
ACES	ACES-ENTCR	08/01/2016	16	07/13/2016	99.95%
Hiring Integration	August 2016	08/11/2016	11	10/11/2016	2.80%
SPS	SPS-Beta	08/31/2016	65	08/17/2016	99.80%
Compliance	V12.1.2 (R2 - Fall/YE 2016)	09/07/2016	216	08/10/2016	99.99%
Hiring Integration	V12.1.2 (R2 - Fall/YE 2016)	09/07/2016	1	10/18/2016	24.55%
SPS	V12.1.2 (R2 - Fall/YE 2016)	09/07/2016	1	08/17/2016	99.99%
Global Benefits	V12.1.2 (R2 - Fall/YE 2016)	09/07/2016	30	08/18/2016	99.70%
Payroll	V12.1.2 (R2 - Fall/YE 2016)	09/07/2016	57	07/29/2016	99.99%
Talent Management	V12.1.2 (R2 - Fall/YE 2016)	09/07/2016	40	06/30/2016	97.00%
Global HR and Compensation	V12.1.2 (R2 - Fall/YE 2016)	09/07/2016	110	09/01/2016	96.15%
TWIST	V12.1.2 (R2 - Fall/YE 2016)	09/07/2016	1	07/05/2016	99.99%
Platform	V12.1.2 (R2 - Fall/YE 2016)	09/07/2016	99	09/08/2016	82.80%

Figure 13.9: **Monte Carlo Dashboard**

The dashboard above becomes the focal point of the discussions around commitments and strategies that need to be employed to make sure the team has a good chance of completing the release. The color coding on the dashboard is as follows – Greater than 90% possibility is considered green, 70-90% is yellow and anything lower than 70% is red.

Daily Product Review

The Daily Product Review (DPR) is Ultimate Software's successor to the Scrum of Scrums. The DPR acts as a focal point where teams bring up dependencies and impediments, share important information and collectively review a couple of key metrics. The DPR acts both as a point of confluence for the development teams and also a meeting where the managers of the teams hold themselves accountable for the progress of their releases and the state of the stories that have gone way beyond the team's SLA. The teams do this collectively to reinforce a culture of accountability. They also highlight cross team dependencies that slow teams down and put releases at risk. The meeting is held every workday at 10:00 am, following daily standups for most teams. This gives team members the opportunity to bring up impediments in standups, which can then be escalated to DPR.

The SLA metrics, Monte Carlo simulations and the DPR are the core components of the scaling of Agile practices at Ultimate Software. The DPR, which is a 15 minute daily meeting, brings together the key metrics of Cycle Time and release completion likelihood in one place to provide the overall scorecard for the development organization. It reinforces the metrics and practices we care about on a daily basis. Below are some pieces of the DPR board that help reinforce and scale these practices.

The first piece is the general announcements section. This section is accessible to everyone in the organization. The section can be updated with notes before or during the meeting so that all major announcements, whether coming from the teams or from upper management can be shared amongst the teams.

Figure 13.10: General Announcements

A slightly modified version of the Monte Carlo dashboard also finds its way to the DPR board. The main difference between the two Monte Carlo views is that the DPR view includes deltas from the previous day. This view is updated only once a day in the morning and for the Stories Remaining and Completion Likelihood columns contains the changes since the same time on the previous day. When a team's release starts to go red or starts slipping further into red they usually respond with any combination of the following three strategies –

- Reducing scope of the release.
- Moving the date for the release.
- Working extra hours to bring the remaining stories count down.

Monte Carlo

Team	Release	Code Freeze Date	Stories Remaining	85% Completion Date	Completion Likelihood
UTB	UTB-2.23.0	06/22/2016	2 (-5)	06/22/2016	99.99% (53.54)
PlatformServices	June 2016	06/30/2016	26 (-1)	08/19/2016	4.91% (0.00)
OnboardingV14	June 2016	06/30/2016	17 (0)	07/14/2016	3.25% (-5.80)
HiringIntegration	June 2016	06/30/2016	5 (0)	07/29/2016	5.45% (0.20)
RecruitingV14	June 2016	06/30/2016	13 (0)	07/04/2016	55.15% (0.60)
TwIST	June 2016	06/30/2016	9 (0)	07/01/2016	79.35% (21.90)
TalentManagement	June 2016	06/30/2016	1 (0)	06/21/2016	99.95% (0.00)
UTM	UTM-2.7	07/01/2016	15 (+2)	07/13/2016	13.40% (-6.00)
UTA	UTA-6.1.3v15	07/01/2016	6 (0)	07/05/2016	73.65% (3.60)
TalentManagement	July 2016	07/08/2016	16 (0)	07/11/2016	84.90% (5.00)
RecruitingV14	July 2016	07/15/2016	35 (4)	08/03/2016	1.20% (-6.80)
BusinessIntelligence	August 2016	07/28/2016	28 (0)	08/19/2016	33.40% (9.45)
WorkforceManagement	WFM Beta	07/29/2016	34 (3)	07/07/2016	99.99% (0.00)
ACES	ACE%ENTCR	08/01/2016	12 (3)	07/08/2016	99.99% (0.00)
HiringIntegration	August 2016	08/11/2016	11 (1)	10/31/2016	2.30% (-3.10)
SPS	SPS-Beta	08/31/2016	65 (-2)	04/17/2016	99.75% (8.70)
HiringIntegration	V12.1.2 (R2 - Fall/YE 2016)	09/07/2016	1 (0)	10/19/2016	25.60% (-6.00)
Platform	V12.1.2 (R2 - Fall/YE 2016)	09/07/2016	100 (-3)	09/08/2016	81.56% (1.55)
GlobalHR	V12.1.2 (R2 - Fall/YE 2016)	09/07/2016	110 (3)	09/02/2016	94.26% (1.80)
TalentManagement	V12.1.2 (R2 - Fall/YE 2016)	09/07/2016	41 (-2)	08/31/2016	96.95% (-2.85)
GlobalBenefits	V12.1.2 (R2 - Fall/YE 2016)	09/07/2016	30 (0)	08/19/2016	99.55% (0.00)
ACES	V12.1.2 (R2 - Fall/YE 2016)	09/07/2016	24 (0)	09/08/2016	99.95% (-9.94)

Figure 13.11: **Monte Carlo Dashboard**

Another part of the DPR board are the individual Team Updates tiles. These tiles are color coded green, yellow or red based on the number of stories that the team has above the 95th percentile of the Cycle Times for their stories. The team can add notes to their tiles with the dependencies that are causing the stories to take a long time and the course of action they are taking to address the long running stories. The assumption here is that since the teams are managing to their SLAs which are at the 85th percentile, anything exceeding the 95th is probably something out of the team's control. As can be seen in the updates from the Payroll team below, their first story is blocked due to an external dependency and the second was blocked due to the lack of proper builds. They have also noted the strategies they have moving these stories forward. Teams can also update the tiles with other announcements that don't necessarily fall under the umbrella of General Announcements and are more team specific.

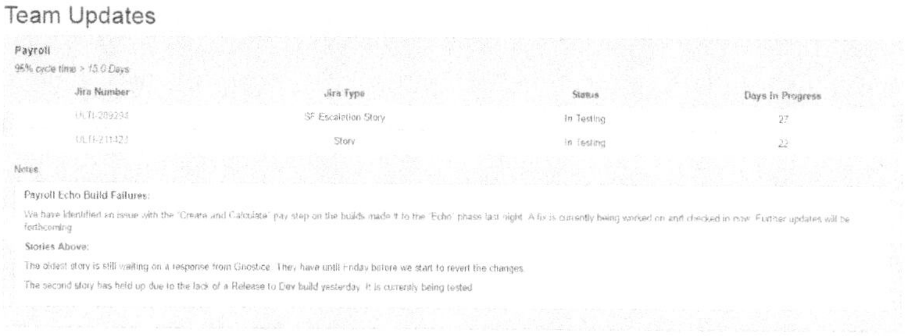

Figure 13.12: Team Updates

The final section of interest for the DPR is the Escalations section that gives a summary of customer raised issues that the teams have not responded to within a reasonable time frame. The Escalations section has three columns that are based on the number of days an escalation has been assigned to a development team without having received an update. In this manner we make sure that not only are we applying the Cycle Time metric to new work, but also to customer issues.

Figure 13.13: Escalations

Feature Visualization

All the visualizations, metrics and simulations that we have talked about so far have been at the story level. It was important for

Ultimate to emphasize flow at the story level so that the developers could stop multi-tasking and teams could get used to finishing items before starting new ones. It also helped in obtaining metrics which directly influenced the ability to be more efficient with day to day processes. Ultimate became very predictable at the story level and were able to make commitments to the product representatives at the story level. There was a fundamental disconnect with this strategy though. Even though the teams were committing by story counts and those were highly predictable, product strategy was committing to customers in terms of features. Ultimate had a layer of feature estimation where each feature was estimated in terms of stories. While this seemed like a simple enough conversion, there were things that were lost in translation.

Every time that the team was off in its estimates, the plans that strategy had laid out and communicated were invalidated. The confidence that the team had with the number of stories they could produce did not translate to the feature level. Teams working on multiple features at a time, could easily meet their story commitments but miss their feature commitments. This would be due to the stories being spread across multiple features instead of having the focus of the team on fewer features and getting a consistent flow of features. In order to alleviate these issues, the first step Ultimate took was to visualize the current state of features across the board for all development teams.

The visualization of features was done on a large three panel wall at the Ultimate Software headquarters. Each of the panels were assigned to the three different domains (Pay and Time, People and Platform) at Ultimate. Within each domain, each team was assigned a horizontal lane on the panel. The columns for the feature wall were the following, repeated on each panel –

- Open – Feature has been assigned to a release, but not started yet.
- Analysis – Analysis and the requirements elicitation process has been started for the Feature.

- In Progress – A story in the feature has been pulled forward to be worked on by a developer.
- Complete – All stories in the feature are done and the feature is marked as done.

The cards themselves contain details about features like total story count, completed story count, priority, projected release date, and dates the feature transitioned between the above states. All the relevant information about any feature in progress within the development organization is now available in one place. The visualization is also enhanced by the fact that the teams can explicitly mark features as blocked and call out dependencies on the board so that the dependencies can be evaluated and subsequently resolved.

Figure 13.14: Feature Kanban Board

The managers of the teams update the feature wall twice a week with any changes that the team has made to its features. The wall is accessible to everyone at headquarters and regularly reviewed by senior management personnel in order to get an idea of which teams need their help overcoming obstacles. Alongside the DPR, the large physical board is one of the primary tools for scaling agile practices at Ultimate Software.

Next Steps

The feature wall brought forth the same issues that had been seen at the story level. While a lot of the issues with flow of stories had been fixed, the same issues became evident as soon as we started visualizing the features that a team was working on. Teams realized that they were working on too many features at the same time. There was not a steady flow of features through the system and this hindered predictability at the feature level.

In order to combat these issues, Ultimate is applying the same strategies that worked well with stories. Teams are being asked to figure out what the correct feature work in progress limit should be. The teams would then hold themselves to the set work in progress limits and only violate them under exceptional circumstances. Teams are also putting a loose upper limit on the size of features. For most teams features should be 25 stories or less 85 percent of the time. Having a size limit and a work in progress limit on features should allow teams to gain stable Cycle Times for features. Once Cycle Times for features are consistent, teams will be able to run Monte Carlo simulations on features to determine the probability of getting a certain number of features done in a release.

The metrics and principles used with stories can now be used with features and to gain higher predictability and Throughput with features, while at the same time eliminating the need for detailed estimation of features. This will remove a key source of uncertainty in Ultimate's planning and road mapping of features. Ultimate Software's development teams have acknowledged repeatedly that they are very inaccurate with their estimates, regardless of the time spent on estimating. Having a single decision point of whether a feature is less than 25 stories or not makes the exercise much easier. It is also expected to provide Ultimate's development teams with a greater predictability than the current feature estimation methods.

Moving Beyond Development

Adopting Agile techniques has provided Ultimate Software the benefits of increased productivity and predictability. For an overall perspective though, Ultimate Software is in a waterfall sandwich. The Agile development organization sits in the middle of traditional sales and support organizations and traditional deployment and activation organizations. As a part of the next evolution of Agile and flow based thinking at Ultimate Software, agile practices are being propagated out to organizations that flank development. Ultimate's culture that encourages managers and employees to experiment and make the right decisions for Ultimate, has aided greatly in spreading the principles outside of core development. Departments within Ultimate Software have started pulling the services of the Agile coaches within development to help them with the same principles.

Development's closer engagement with Product Strategy and the ability to give them higher degree of predictability has vastly improved Development's ability to assist with support issues without interrupting active work. Tier 3 support has also adopted Kanban practices in order to improve their ability to support customers. Product Strategy is able to utilize the predictability and productivity gains of Development to provide better guidance to Sales on upcoming products and features. As Product Strategy and Development continue to improve the predictability that they can provide Sales, they can start creating feature requests and priorities in conjunction with Sales. Features can then be pulled all the way through the value stream and tracking of Cycle Time and Throughput can allow Ultimate to make and keep more accurate commitments to customers.

While the upstream expansion helps Ultimate get better at the creation of value, expanding downstream to deployment and activations is where they can improve the delivery of value to their customers. As Ultimate Software has started working on new products, they have pulled deployment activities onto the teams.

For older products, Ultimate has always done a handoff to the SaaS deployment group. Ultimate broke the "over the wall" mentality by embedding deployment engineers on the development teams for new products and helping them educate the rest of the team on maintaining their own deployment pipelines. The teams were initially concerned about taking on the additional responsibility. Those fears have abated as the teams have realized the support that is available to them from the rest of the organization. This practice has also greatly reduced the occurrences of production environment surprises. Since the teams help build the environments that they deploy code to, the code does not behave unexpectedly when pushed to production. These teams are supported by three groups outside of Product Engineering. Groups that manage the Build and Deployment infrastructure for the products being developed have also adopted Kanban principles and started measuring Cycle Times for making infrastructure available to teams. They have established SLAs for different types of requests and have become predictable with these metrics.

Ultimate can now see a feature make its journey all the way from a request generated in Sales to Product Strategy, to Development and finally to Production. Once the progress of features is tracked in this manner, Ultimate can start identifying opportunities for improvement in the inception-to-delivery cycle. The organization as a whole can identify where features get stuck and apply its understanding of flow to eliminate the time features have to wait in queues across the entire organization.

Another aspect that is downstream from the development and even the deployment group is activations. Activations is the group that helps a new customer go live with Ultimate Software's products. The activation process can take up to a year and can involve multiple teams. Every day that a customer is in the activation phase, Ultimate Software is investing time, but not receiving full revenue. This is an area that can use the benefits that the Development Organization has gained from flow and Agile practices. Development has started working with Activations to share the principles and practices that have made a positive difference in the predictability and speed of completion for deliverables.

Moving Kanban outside the lines is the next large step for Ultimate Software. Ultimate has already started moving in this direction through its work with support and deployment teams. Ultimate continues to scale out its Agile implementation without using any established frameworks. Setting up the right channels of communication and visualizing work in a manner that is easily understood by all is at the crux of how Ultimate has been able to successfully adopt and evolve Agile at scale.

Key Learnings And Takeaways

- Simple Cycle Time metrics can drive valuable conversations and changes.
- Autonomy of process at the team level has major advantages in terms of productivity and predictability
- Scaling Agile practices can be done without implementing expensive pre-defined frameworks
- Probabilistic forecasting can provide early warning signs and streamline planning
- Working in a continuous flow model makes pivoting and responding to information easy

Chapter 14: Case Study - Linear Projections vs Monte Carlo Simulation

Disclaimer: The name of the company discussed in this case study has been withheld as well as some of the details of the project itself, but the data presented below is 100% real and accurate.

The Setup

Back in 2011, I worked for a U.S.-based client who had a contractual agreement to deliver a project by March 1, 2012. If they missed this date, the contract dictated that they would have to pay a significant penalty. The penalty was substantial enough such that any delay in delivery meant that the company would lose money on the project.

At the time, this particular client was using more traditional project management methods: big analysis upfront, big-batch development and delivery, and, of course, forecasting using linear projections. Because they had done all of their analysis upfront, this client determined that the project consisted of exactly 1071 work items (do not even get me started on this deterministic number). The development phase of the project was to start on August 1, 2011 which meant they had precisely 7 months with which to develop and test 1071 work items.

The project started as expected on August 1, 2011. Because of their big batch development process, they did not actually start delivering any work items to "done" until about October 1, 2011. Further, because of their slow development pace, they did not have meaningful data from which to project a possible completion date.

Therefore, the first significant linear projection they did was on November 1, 2011.

They set the start date for their historical data for their linear projection to be October 1, 2011. That is, they ignored the two months of zero Throughput between August 1 and October 1. The point of this case study is not to debate the merits of that decision; rather, it is to explore the effects of different forecasting techniques once a model has been decided. For their purposes, they decided to start their forecast model on October 1, so the rest of this discussion will be based off of that decision.

On November 1, the team had exactly 293 work items finished. Doing the math, 293 work items completed in 31 days is 9.45 items per day. Since they had 778 work items left in their backlog (1071 − 293 = 778), completing 9.45 work items per day would mean they would be done in 83 days (778 / 9.45 = 83). 83 days from November 1, was January 23, 2011, so no problem! Even if you consider the Thanksgiving, Christmas, and New Year's holidays coming up, there was enough schedule buffer between January 23 and March 1 to not cause any concern. So the team plodded on.

Fast forward to December 1, and the team had exactly 490 work items finished. Doing the math again, 490 work items completed in 61 days is 8.03 items per day. They now had 581 work items left in their backlog which means their new completion date based on this updated Throughput was February 11, 2012. This slowdown was to be expected since there would have been a dip in productivity at the end of November due to the Thanksgiving holiday. However, a completion date of February 11 was still no problem!

The next significant date for a forecast was January 3, 2012 (New Year's Day was a Sunday that year which meant the holiday was observed on a Monday). On January 3, the team had 703 items completed which gave a projected completion date of February 22, 2012. This was actually good news because they had come through the productivity slowdown of the holiday season and they were still on track. In fact, they still a week to spare (remember 2012 was a leap year so there were 29 days in February that year).

Lastly, on February 1, the team had 903 items finished which gave a projected completion date of 2/24/2012 so there was nothing to worry about!

The project completed on March 8.

What happened?

The Analysis

It is very easy to say that this was an error in planning or an error in execution, but I believe this was an error in forecasting. Let's re-run each of those forecasts using Monte Carlo Simulation instead of Linear Projection and see what we come up with.

On November 1st when the team had 778 work items left in their backlog, a Monte Carlo Simulation (10,000 runs) that used a historical Throughput range of October 1 – October 31 would have yielded a Results Histogram that looked like:

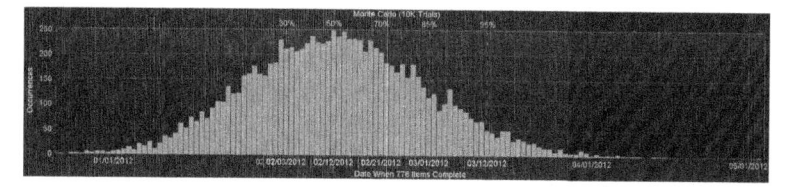

Figure 14.1

The Results Histogram in Figure 14.1 shows that at the time this simulation was run they had an 85% chance of completing on or before the March 1st date. Which is actually not bad. However, given the extreme Cost of Delay associated with this project a more conservative projection is probably in order. You can see that the 95% confidence in Figure 14.1 shows on or before March 12. And you will recall that this does not include the inevitable upcoming holiday slowdown. That March 12 date could easily be a week or more later than that. If you were a team member on this project would you have taken action based on this new information? It would certainly be worth a conversation...

Moving on to December 1st, an MCS that projected forward with updated Throughput numbers and 490 items left in the backlog would have given a Results Histogram that looks like:

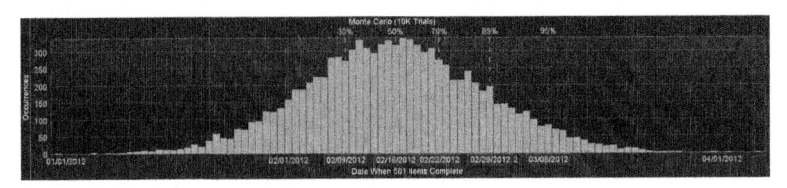

Figure 14.2

Figure 14.2 shows the 95th percentile has not budged from its March 8th prediction. That is good news from the perspective that the Thanksgiving holiday did not slow the team down too much. However, this is still nothing to cheer about as they are still worryingly showing a late date, and they still have the Christmas holidays slowdown to deal with. Ask yourself if now you would have done something?

On January 3rd, the team would have come through its holiday productivity dip. What do you think the MCS would show now? Here it is:

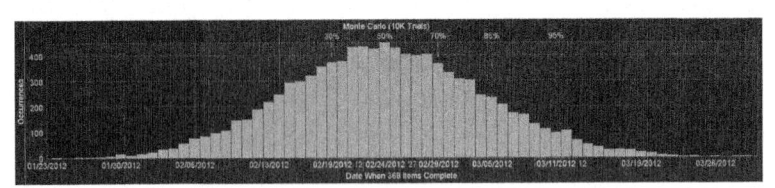

Figure 14.3

Figure 14.3 now shows the 95th percentile at March 11. While they did not take a dramatic hit to the date, they still did take a hit. And, worse, they are still showing late. What would you do now?

The February 1 simulation is much the same story:

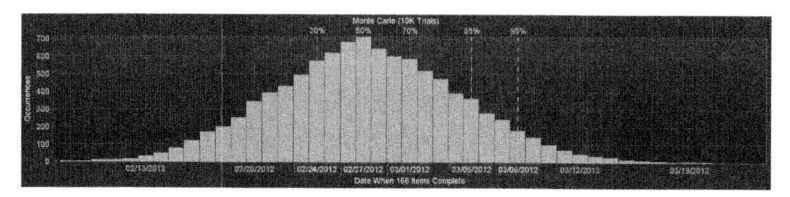

Figure 14.4

You can see the team recovered slightly from their holiday hangover, but they are still showing late at the 95th percentile. Is it reasonable to do something now?

Let's take a look at those projections side by side:

Date Forecast Made	Linear Projection	MCS Projection (95th Percentile)
Nov 1	1/23/2012	3/8/2012
Dec 1	2/12/2012	3/8/2012
Jan 3	2/22/2012	3/11/2012
Feb 1	2/24/2012	3/8/212

Actual Project Delivery Date: March 8, 2012

There are several things that strike me about these results. The first is how accurate MCS was even at a very early date with very little data. As I mentioned in Chapter X, this is without a doubt one of the great strengths of MCS. The second is how consistent the forecasts were even in the face of new Throughput data. Over the course of the project, the team's Throughput was no doubt extremely variable—especially given the multiple holidays. However, even when the MCS model was updated with this updated data, the forecasts did not budge all that much. I have to be careful here because what I am not saying is that these results are typical or even common. But what I am saying is that the power of MCS is its ability to give accurate forecasts even in the face of extreme variability.

Again I want you to ask yourself, had you been using either of these approaches, at what point would you have taken action? Would you have even taken action? My guess is that had you been using the linear projection model you probably would not have made any adjustments to your project schedule. In fact, you might not have even thought to do something until it was too late.

This is the beauty of the MCS approach. You can see in this example that MCS gave you a signal that something was potentially wrong as early as November 1st. As any manager (or customer) will tell you, the earlier you know that a change is needed, the better the chance of that change having an impact. For example, some interventions that we talked about in order affect the outcome of a forecast are:

1. Change scope
2. Change the date
3. Add resources / work longer hours
4. Accept a lower chance of success
5. Some combination of the above

As this was a fixed contract, that eliminated options 1, 2, and 4 above. The only option available to us in this scenario was option 3. However, for option 3 you need enough time for the intervention to take effect. Using the linear projection forecast, we would not have known until very late in February that the project was going to be late. Trying to add resources at that late of a date brings Brooks' law into play, "adding people to a late project only makes it later". Besides, even if the new team members were 100% productive on Day 1, would they have had enough time to make a difference? The same argument goes for working longer hours. There are only so many more extra hours available to work which means you need to know well in advance for that strategy to even work (not to mention the realistically muted impact that overtime has on delivery rates anyway).

Conclusion

Using the linear projection in this case would have provided a warning sign that was too late for any realistic action to be taken. MCS, on the other hand, provided a danger signal almost immediately. Adding people or working extra hours are much more viable options had they been discussed on November 1 as opposed to February 24.

I have provided this short case study as my final argument as to why you should be using some—if not all—of the modern forecasting techniques outlined in this book. They are not hard to get started with and they are not difficult to use. In no time at all you can be on your way to better and more accurate predictions.

Key Learnings And Takeaways

- Linear projections are a classic example of the Flaw of Averages
- Monte Carlo Simulation gives you much more accurate forecasts with much less data
- Needing less data means that you get much more actionable information much sooner
- Having actionable information sooner means that you can make process interventions in a much more timely manner
- Making interventions sooner means that you have a much better chance of your actions having the desired effect (i.e., that those actions make things better).

Chapter 15: Case Study - Siemens HS

Disclaimer: This case study is an exact duplication of the one presented at the end of my previous book, "Actionable Agile Metrics for Predictability". I include it here for those who have not read AAMFP but also as a convenience for those who want a handy reference to one of the better documented case studies on flow metrics. As a reminder, the following is written from the perspective of Bennet Vallet who partnered with me to write up his experience with Actionable Agile Metrics at Siemens Health Services.

Introduction

Siemens Health Services (HS) provides sophisticated software for the Healthcare industry. HS had been using traditional Agile metrics (e.g., story points, velocity) for several years, but never realized the transparency and predictability that those metrics promised. By moving to the simpler, more actionable metrics of flow we were able to achieve a 42% reduction in Cycle Time and a very significant improvement in operational efficiency. Furthermore, adopting flow has led to real improvements in quality and collaboration, all of which have been sustained across multiple releases. This case study describes how moving to a continuous flow model augmented Siemens' agility and explains how predictability is a systemic behavior that one has to manage by understanding and acting in accordance with the assumptions of Little's law and the impacts of resource utilization.

History

Siemens Health Services, the health IT business unit of Siemens Healthcare, is a global provider of enterprise healthcare information technology solutions. Our customers are hospitals and large physician group practices. We also provide related services such as software installation, hosting, integration, and business process outsourcing.

The development organization for Siemens HS is known as Product Lifecycle Management (PLM) and consists of approximately 50 teams based primarily in Malvern, Pennsylvania, with sizable development resources located in India and Europe. In 2003 the company undertook a highly ambitious initiative to develop Soarian®, a brand new suite of healthcare enterprise solutions.

The healthcare domain is extremely complex, undergoing constant change, restructuring, and regulation. It should be of no surprise that given our domain, the quality of our products is of the highest priority; in fact, one might say that quality is mission critical. Furthermore, the solutions we build have to scale from small and medium sized community hospitals to the largest multi-facility healthcare systems in the world. We need to provide world class performance and adhere to FDA, ISO, Sarbanes–Oxley, patient safety, auditability, and reporting regulations.

Our key business challenge is to rapidly develop functionality to compete against mature systems already in the market. Our systems provide new capabilities based on new technology that helps us to leapfrog the competition. In this vein, we adopted an Agile development methodology, and more specifically Scrum/XP practices as the key vehicles to achieve this goal

Our development teams transitioned to Agile in 2005. Engaging many of the most well-known experts and coaches in the community, we undertook an accelerated approach to absorbing and incorporating new practices. We saw significant improvement over our previous waterfall methods almost immediately and our enthusiasm for Agile continued to grow. By September 2011 we had a mature Agile development program, having adopted most Scrum and XP practices. Our Scrum teams included all roles (product owners, Scrum masters, business analysts, developers and testers). We had a mature product backlog and ran 30-day sprints with formal sprint planning, reviews, and retrospectives. We were releasing large batches of new features and enhancements once a year (mostly because that is the frequency at which we've always released). Practices such as CI, TDD, story-driven development, continuous customer interaction, pair programming, planning poker, and relative point-based estimation were for the most part well integrated into our teams and process. Our experience showed that Scrum and Agile practices vastly improved collaboration across roles, improved customer functionality, improved code quality and speed.

Our Scrum process includes all analysis, development and testing of features. A feature is declared "done" only once it has passed validation testing in a fully integrated environment performed by a Test Engineer within each Scrum Team. Once all release features are complete, Siemens performs another round of regression testing, followed by customer beta testing before declaring general availability and shipping to all our customers.

Despite many improvements and real benefits realized by our Agile adoption, our overall success was limited. We were continually challenged to estimate and deliver on committed release dates. Meeting regulatory requirements and customer expectations requires a high degree of certainty and predictability. Our internal decision checkpoints and quality gates required firm commitments. Our commitment to customers, internal stakeholder expectations and revenue forecasts required accurate release scope and delivery forecasts that carry a very high premium for delay.

At the program and team levels, sprint and release deadlines were characterized by schedule pressure often requiring overtime and the metrics we collected were not providing the transparency needed to clearly gauge completion dates or provide actionable insight into the state of our teams.

In the trenches, our teams were also challenged to plan and complete stories in time-boxed sprint increments. The last week of each sprint was always a mad rush by teams to claim as many points as possible, resulting in hasty and over-burdened story testing. While velocity rates at sprint reviews often seemed good, reality pointed to a large number of stories blocked or incomplete and multiple features in progress with few, if any, features completing until end of the release. This incongruity between velocity (number of points completed in a sprint) and reality was primarily caused by teams starting too many features and/or stories. It had been common practice to start multiple features at one time to mitigate possible risks. In addition, whenever a story or feature was blocked (for a variety of reasons such as waiting for a dependency from another team, waiting for customer validation, inability to test because of environmental or build break issues, etc.), teams would simply start the next story or feature so that we could claim the points which we had committed to achieve. So, while velocity burn-ups could look in line with expectations, multiple features were not being completed on any regular cadence, leading to bottle-necks especially at the end of the release as the teams strove to complete and test features. During this period we operated under the assumption that if we mastered Agile practices, planned better, and worked harder we would be successful. Heroic efforts were expected.

In November of 2011 executive management chartered a small team of director level managers to coordinate and drive process improvement across the PLM organization, with the key goal of finally realizing the predictability, operational efficiency, and quality gains originally promised by our Agile approach. After some research, the team concluded that any changes had to be systemic. Other previous process improvements had focused on specific functional areas such as coding or testing, and had not led to real improvements across the whole system or value stream. By value stream in this context we mean all development activities performed within the Scrum Teams from "specifying to done". By reviewing the value stream with a "Lean" perspective we realized that our problems were indeed systemic, caused by our predilection for large batch sizes such as large feature releases. Reading Goldratt (Goldratt, 2004), and Reinertsen (Reinertsen, 2009) we also came to understand the impacts of large, systemic queues. Coming to the understanding that the overtime, for which programmers were sacrificing their weekends, may actually have been elongating the release completion date was an epiphany.

This path inevitably led us to learn about Kanban. We saw in Kanban a means of enforcing Lean and continuous improvement across the system while still maintaining our core Agile development practices. Kanban would manage Work In Progress, Cycle Time, and Throughput by providing a pull system and thus reduce the negative impacts of large batches and high capacity utilization. Furthermore, we saw in Kanban the potential for metrics that were both tangible (and could be well understood by all corporate stakeholders) and provide individual teams and program management with data that is highly transparent and actionable.

We chose our revenue-cycle application as our pilot, consisting of 15 Scrum teams located in Malvern, PA., Brooklyn, N.Y., and Kolkata, India. Although each Scrum team focuses on specific business domains, the application itself requires integrating all these domains into a single unitary customer solution. At this scale of systemic complexity, dependency management, and continuous integration, a very high degree of consistency and cohesion across the whole program is required. With this in mind, we designed a "big-bang" approach with a high degree of policy, work-unit, workflow, doneness, and metric standardization across all teams. We also concluded that we needed electronic boards: large monitors displayed in each team room that would be accessible in real time to all our local and offshore developers. An electronic board would also provide an enterprise management view across the program and a mechanism for real-time metrics collection. Our initial product release using Kanban began in April 2012 and was completed that December. Results from our first experience using Kanban were far better than any of our previous releases. Our Cycle

Time looked predictable and defects were down significantly.

Our second release began in March 2013 and finished in September of that same year. We continue to use Kanban for our product development today. As we had hoped, learnings and experience from the first release led to even better results in the releases that followed.

Actionable Metrics

Now that we had decided to do Kanban at Siemens HS, we had to change the metrics we used so that we could more readily align with our newfound emphasis on flow. The metrics of flow are very different than traditional Scrum-style metrics. As mentioned earlier, instead of focusing on things like story points and velocity, our teams now paid attention to Work In Progress (WIP), Cycle Time, and Throughput. The reason these flow metrics are preferable to traditional Agile metrics is because they are much more actionable and transparent. By transparent we mean that the metrics provide a high degree of visibility into the teams' (and programs') progress. By actionable, we mean that the metrics themselves will suggest the specific team interventions needed to improve the overall performance of the process.

To understand how flow metrics might suggest improvement interventions we must first explore some definitions. For Siemens HS, we defined WIP to be any work item (e.g., user story, defect, etc.) that was between the "Specifying Active" step and the "Done" step in our workflow (Figure 15.1).

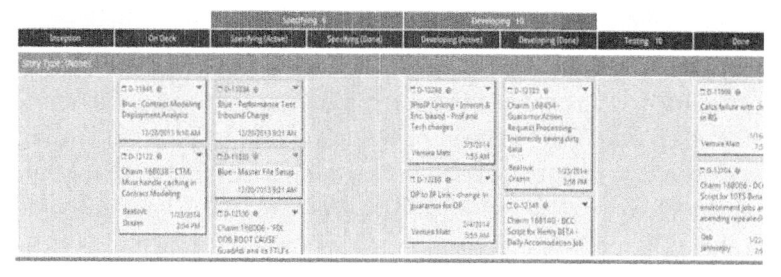

Figure 15.1: Example Kanban Board

Cycle Time was defined to be the amount of total elapsed time needed for a work item to get from "Specifying Active" to "Done". Throughput was defined as the number of work items that entered the "Done" step per unit of time (e.g., user stories per week).

We have stressed throughout this paper that predictability is of paramount importance to Siemens HS. So how was the organization doing before Kanban?

Figure 15.2 is a Scatterplot of Cycle Times for finished stories in the Financials organization for the whole release before Kanban was introduced.

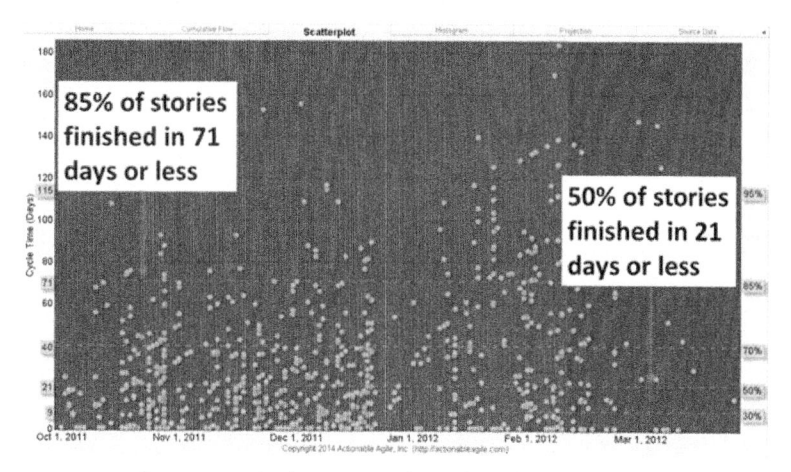

Figure 15.2: Cycle Times in the Release before Kanban

What this Scatterplot tells us is that in this release, 50% of all stories finished in 21 days or less. But remember we told you earlier that Siemens HS was running 30 day sprints? That means that any story that started at the beginning of a sprint had little better than 50% chance of finishing within the sprint. Furthermore, 85% of stories were finishing in 71 days or less—that is 2.5 sprints! What's worse is that Figure 15.3 shows us that over the course of the release the general trend of story Cycle Times was getting longer and longer and longer.

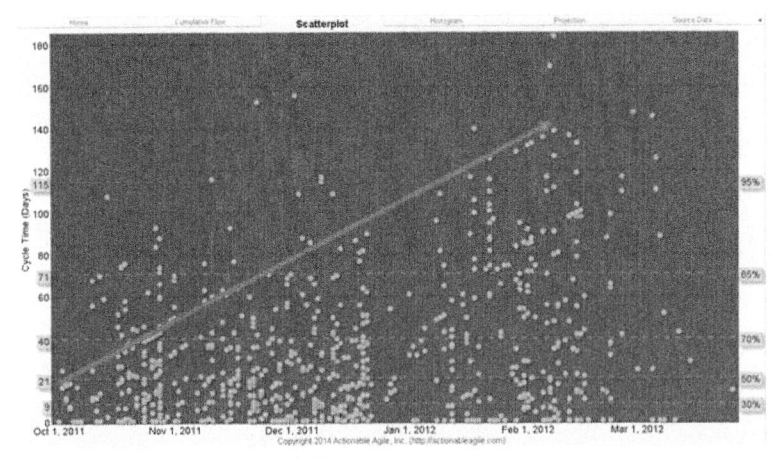

Figure 15.3: General Upward Trend of Cycle Times before the Introduction of Kanban

Figure 15.3 is not a picture of a very predictable process.

So what was going on here? A simplified interpretation of Little's Law tells us that if Cycle Times are too long, then we essentially have two options: decrease WIP or increase Throughput. Most managers inexplicably usually opt for the latter. They make teams work longer hours (stay late) each day. They make teams work mandatory weekends. They try and steal resources from other projects. Some companies may even go so far as to hire temporary or permanent staff. The problem with trying to impact Throughput in these ways is that most organizations actually end up increasing WIP faster than they increase Throughput. If we refer back to Little's Law, we know that if WIP increases faster than Throughput, then Cycle Times will only increase. Increasing WIP faster than increasing Throughput only exacerbates the problem of long Cycle Times.

Our choice (eventually) was the much more sensible and economical one: reduce Cycle Times by limiting WIP through the use of Kanban. What most people fail to realize is that limiting WIP can be as simple as making sure that work is not started at a faster rate than work is completed (please see Chapter 9 as an example of how mismatched arrival and departure rates increases WIP in the process). Matching arrival rates to departure rates is the necessary first step to stabilizing a system. Only by operating a stable system could we hope to achieve our goal of predictability.

Unfortunately for us, however, the first release that we implemented Kanban, we chose not to limit WIP right away (the argument could be made that we were not actually doing "Kanban" at that point). Why? Because early on in our Kanban adoption the teams and management resisted the imposition of WIP limits. This was not unexpected, as mandating limits on work went against the grain of the then current beliefs. We therefore decided to delay until the third month of the release. This allowed the teams and management to gain a better familiarity of the method and become more amenable.

The delay in implementing WIP limits cost us and in retrospect we should have pushed harder to impose WIP limits from the outset. As you might expect, because of the lack of WIP limits, the very same problems that we saw in the previous release (pre-Kanban) started to appear: Cycle Times were too long and the general trend was that they were getting longer.

Taking a look at the CFD (Figure 15.4) in the first release with Kanban clearly shows how our teams were starting to work on items at a faster rate than we were finishing them:

Chapter 15: Case Study - Siemens HS

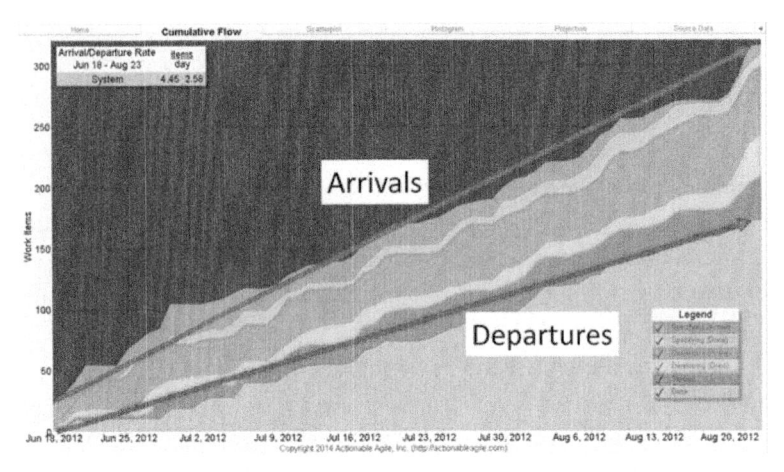

Figure 15.4: CFD Early on in the first release with Kanban

This disregard for when new work should be started resulted in an inevitable increase in WIP which, in turn, manifested itself in longer Cycle Times (as shown in Figure 15.5).

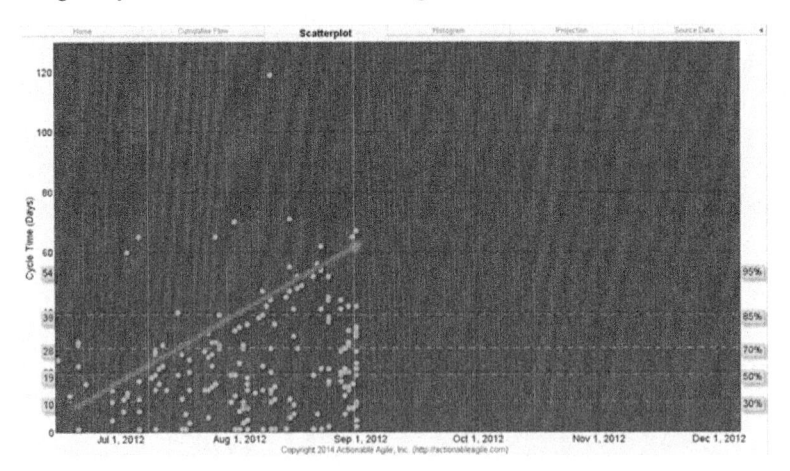

Figure 15.5: Scatterplot early on in the first release with Kanban

Upon seeing these patterns emerge, we instituted a policy of limiting WIP across all teams. Limiting WIP had the almost immediate effect of stabilizing the system such that Cycle Times no longer continued to grow (as shown in Figure 15.6).

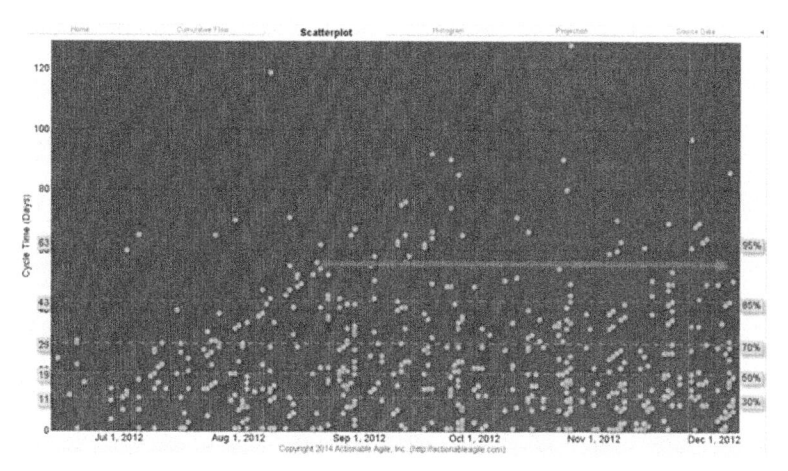

Figure 15.6: Stabilized Cycle Times after introducing WIP Limits

Over the course of our first release with Kanban, the 85th percentile of story Cycle Time had dropped from 71 days to 43 days. And, as you can see from comparing Figure 15.4 to Figure 15.7 (the release before Kanban, and the first release using Kanban, respectively) the teams were suffering from much less variability. Less variability resulted in more predictability. In other words, once we limited WIP in early September 2012 the process Cycle Times did not increase indefinitely as they did the release before. They reached a stable state at about 41 days almost immediately, and stayed at that stable state for the rest of the release.

This stabilization effect of limiting WIP is also powerfully demonstrated in the CFD (Figure 15.7):

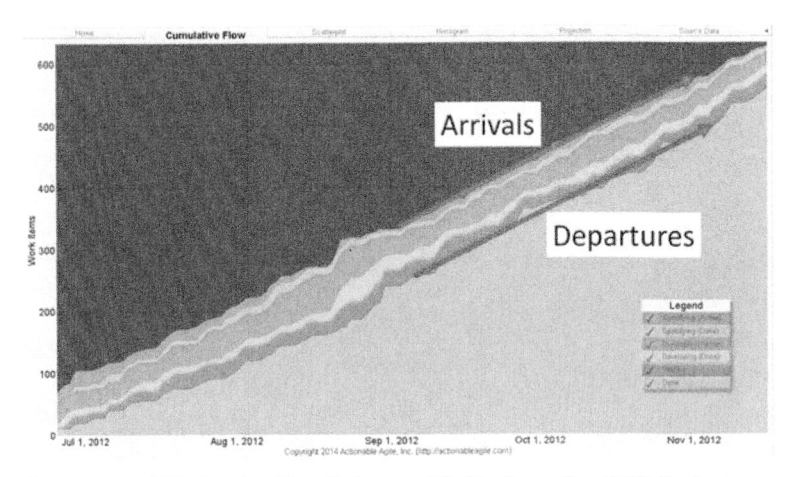

Figure 15.7: CFD in the First Release with Kanban after WIP limits were introduced

The second release after the introduction of Kanban saw much the same result (with regard to predictability). 85 percent of stories were finishing within 41 days and variability was still better controlled. Looking at the two Scatterplots side by side bears this out (Figure 15.8):

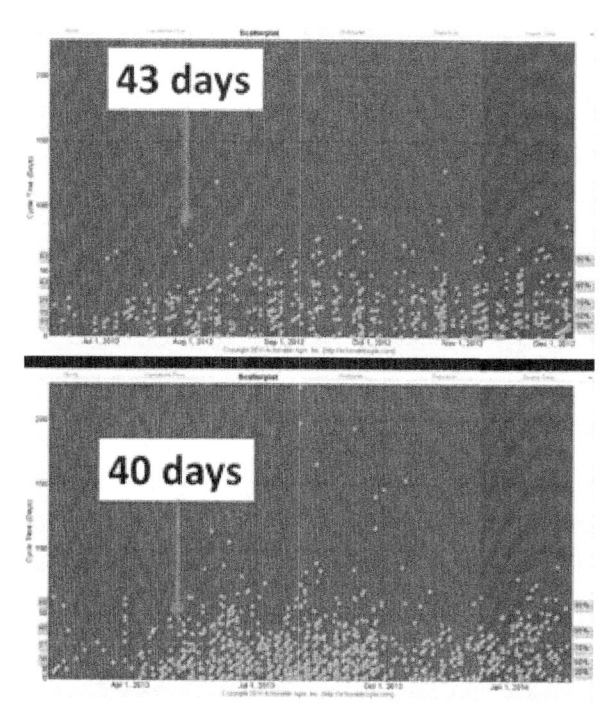

Figure 15.8: Scatterplots of the First Release using Kanban (above) and the Second Release of Kanban (below)

Hopefully it is obvious to the reader that by taking action on the metrics that had been provided, we had achieved our goal of predictability. As shown in Figure 15.8, our first release using Kanban yielded Cycle Times of 43 days or less, and our second release using Kanban yielded Cycle Times of 40 days or less. This result is the very definition of predictability.

By attaining predictable and stable Cycle Times we would now be able to use these metrics as input to future projections. How we did projections will be discussed in more detail in the next section of this chapter.

These shorter Cycle Times and decreased variability also led to a tremendous increase in quality (Figure 15.9):

Chapter 15: Case Study - Siemens HS

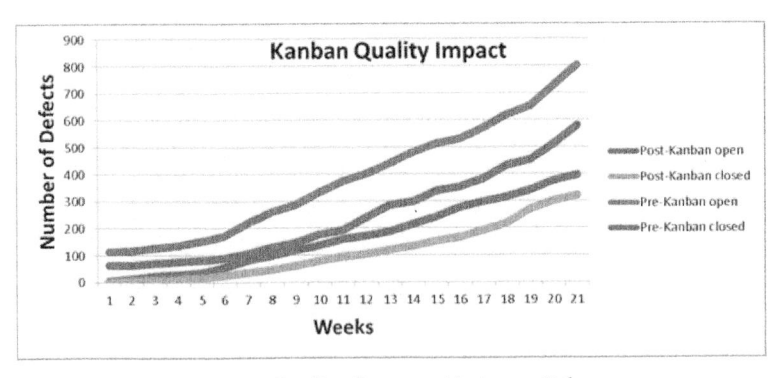

Kanban Quality Impact

(chart showing Number of Defects vs Weeks 1-21, with series: Post-Kanban open, Post-Kanban closed, Pre-Kanban open, Pre-Kanban closed)

Figure 15.9: Quality Compared between Releases

Figure 15.9 shows how Kanban both reduced the number of defects created during release development well as minimizing the gap between defects created and defects resolved during the release. By managing queues, limiting work-in progress and batch sizes and building a cadence through a pull system (limited WIP) versus push system (non-limited WIP) we were able to expose more defects and execute more timely resolutions. On the other hand "pushing" a large batch of requirements and/or starting too many requirements will delay discovery of defects and other issues; as defects are hidden in incomplete requirements and code.

By understanding Little's Law, and by looking at how the flow appears in charts like CFDs and Scatterplots, Siemens HS could see what interventions were necessary to get control of their system. Namely, the organization was suffering from too much WIP which was, in turn, affecting Cycle Time and quality. In taking the action to limit WIP, Siemens saw an immediate decrease in Cycle Time and an immediate increase in quality.

These metrics also highlighted problems within the Siemens HS product development process, and the following section of this chapter will discuss what next steps the organization is going to implement in order to continue to improve its system.

How Metrics Changed Everything

Apart from the improvements in predictability and quality, we also saw significant improvements in operational efficiency. We had "real-time" insight into systemic blocks, variability and bottlenecks and could take appropriate actions quickly. In one case by analyzing Throughput (story run rate) and Cycle Time for each column (specifying, testing and developing), we were able to clearly see where we were experiencing capacity problems. We were also able to gauge our "flow efficiency" by calculating the percentage of time stories were being worked on or "touched" versus "waiting" or "blocked". Wait time is the time a story sits in an inactive or done queue because moving to the next active state is prevented by WIP limits. Blocked time is the time work on a story is impeded, including impediments such as build-breaks, defects, waiting for customer validation etc. The calculation is made by capturing time spent in the "specifying done and developing done" column plus any additional blocked time which we call "wait time". (Blocked or impediment data is provided directly by the tool we are using). Subtracting "wait time" from total Cycle Time gives us "touched time". Calculating flow efficiency is simply calculating the percentage of total touch time over total Cycle Time. Flow efficiency percentage can act as a powerful Key Performance Indicator (KPI) or benchmark in terms of measuring overall system efficiency.

This level of transparency, broadly across the program and more deeply within each team enabled us to make very timely adjustments. Cumulative flow diagrams provided a full picture at the individual team and program levels where our capacity weaknesses lay and revealed where we needed to make adjustments to improve Throughput and efficiency. For example, at the enterprise level using the Cumulative Flow Diagram the management team was able to see higher Throughput in *"developing"* versus *"testing"* across all teams and thus make a decision to invest in increasing test automation exponentially to re-balance capacity. This was actually easy to spot as the *"developing done"* state on the

CFD consistently had stories queued up waiting for the "testing" column WIP limits to allow them to move into *"testing"*. At the team level the metrics would be used to manage WIP by adjusting WIP limits when needed to ensure flow and prevent the build-up of bottlenecks and used extensively in retrospectives to look at variability. By using the Scatterplot, teams could clearly see stories whose Cycle Time exceeded normal ranges, perform root cause analysis and take steps and actions to prevent recurrence. The CFD also allowed us to track our average Throughput or departure-rate (the number of stories we were completing per day/week etc.) and calculate an end date based on the number of stories remaining in the backlog – (similar to the way one uses points and velocity, but more tangible). Furthermore by controlling WIP and managing flow we saw continued clean builds in our continuous integration process, leading to stable testing environments, and the clearing of previously persistent testing bottlenecks.

The results from the first release using Kanban were better than expected. The release completed on schedule and below budget by over 10%. The second release was even better: along with sustained improvements in Cycle Time, we also became much faster. By reducing Cycle Time we were increasing Throughput, enabling us to complete 33% more stories than we had in the previous release, with even better quality in terms of number of defects and *first pass yield* – meaning the percentage of formal integration and regression tests passing the first time they are executed. In the release prior to Kanban our first pass yield percentage was at 75%, whereas in the first Kanban release the pass percentage rose to 86% and reached 95% in our second release using Kanban.

The metrics also gave us a new direction in terms of release forecasting. By using historical Cycle Times we could perform Monte-Carlo simulation modelling to provide likely completion date forecasts. If these forecasts proved reliable, we would no longer need to estimate. In our second Kanban release we adopted this practice along with our current points and velocity estimation planning methods and compared the results. Apart from the obvious difference in the use of metrics versus estimated points, the simulation provides a distribution of likely completion timeframes instead of an average velocity linear based forecast – such as a burn up chart. Likewise Cycle Time metrics are not based on an average (such as average number of points) but on distributions of actual Cycle Times. The Histogram in Figure 15.10 is an example of actual historical Cycle Time distributions that Siemens uses as input to the modelling tool. In this example 30% of stories accounting for 410 actual stories had Cycle Times of 9 days or less, the next 20% accounting for 225 stories had Cycle Times of 10 to 16 days and so forth.

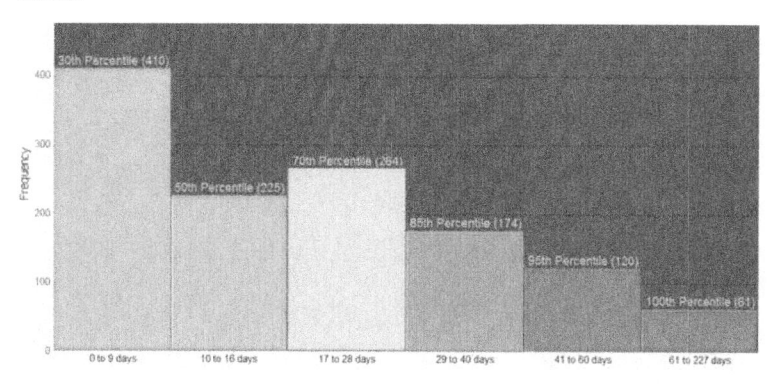

Figure 15.10: Cycle Time Distributions

What we learned was that velocity forecasts attempt to apply a deterministic methodology to an inherently uncertain problem. That type of approach never works. By using the range or distributions of historical Cycle Times from the best to worst cases and simulating the project hundreds of times, the modelling simulation provides a range of probabilistic completion dates at different percentiles. For example see Figure 15.11 below showing likely completion date forecasts used in release planning. Our practice is to commit to the date which is closest to the 85th percent likelihood as is highlighted in the chart. As the chart shows we are also able to use the model to calculate likely costs at each percentile.

Chapter 15: Case Study - Siemens HS

Forecast Date and Likelihood

Likelihood	Date	Workdays	Cost	Cost of Delay	Days of Delay
100.00 %	01-Nov-2013	200	$1,200,000.00	$0.00	0
99.20 %	29-Oct-2013	197	$1,182,000.00	$0.00	0
95.20 %	25-Oct-2013	193	$1,158,000.00	$0.00	0
90.40 %	21-Oct-2013	189	$1,134,000.00	$0.00	0
86.80 %	17-Oct-2013	185	$1,110,000.00	$0.00	0
79.20 %	13-Oct-2013	181	$1,086,000.00	$0.00	0
75.60 %	10-Oct-2013	178	$1,068,000.00	$0.00	0
72.00 %	06-Oct-2013	174	$1,044,000.00	$0.00	0
69.60 %	02-Oct-2013	170	$1,020,000.00	$0.00	0
62.80 %	28-Sep-2013	166	$996,000.00	$0.00	0
52.00 %	24-Sep-2013	162	$972,000.00	$0.00	0
48.00 %	21-Sep-2013	159	$954,000.00	$0.00	0
41.60 %	17-Sep-2013	155	$930,000.00	$0.00	0
32.80 %	13-Sep-2013	151	$906,000.00	$0.00	0

Figure 15.11: Result of Monte-Carlo simulation showing probability forecast at different percentages

Over the course of the release the model proved extremely predictive; moreover, it also provided to Siemens the ability to perform ongoing risk analysis and "what-if" scenarios with highly instructive and reliable results. For example, in one case, to meet an unexpected large scope increase on one of the teams, the Program Management Team was planning to add two new Programmers. The modelling tool pointed to adding a Tester to the team rather than adding programming. The tool proved very accurate in terms of recommending the right staffing capacity to successfully address this scope increase.

At the end of the day, it was an easy decision to discard story point velocity based estimation and move to release completion date forecasts. The collection of historical Cycle Time metrics that were stable and predictable enabled Siemens to perform Monte-Carlo simulations, which provided far more accurate and realistic release delivery forecasts. This was a huge gap in our Agile adoption closed. In analyzing the metrics, Siemens also discovered that there was no correlation between story point estimates and actual Cycle Time.

Siemens also gained the ability to more accurately track costs; as we discovered that we could in fact correlate Cycle Time to actual budgetary allocations. Siemens could now definitively calculate the unit costs of a story, feature and/or a release. By using the modelling tool we could now forecast likely costs along with dates. Moreover, we could put an accurate dollar value on reductions or increases in Cycle Times.

The metrics also improved communication with key non PLM stake-holders. It had always been difficult translating relative story points to corporate stakeholders who were always looking for time based answers and who found our responses based on relative story points confusing. Metrics such as Cycle Time and Throughput are very tangible and especially familiar in a company such as Siemens with a large manufacturing sector.

Implementing Kanban also had a positive impact on employee morale. Within the first month, Scrum-masters reported more meaningful stand-ups. This sentiment was especially expressed and emphasized by our offshore colleagues, who now felt a much higher sense of inclusion during the stand-up. Having the same board and visualization in front of everyone made a huge difference on those long distant conference calls between colleagues in diametrically opposed time zones. While there was some skepticism as expected, overall comments from the teams were positive; people liked it. This was confirmed in an anonymous survey we did four months into the first release that we used Kanban: the results and comments from employees were overwhelmingly positive. Furthermore, as we now understood the impact of WIP and systemic variability, there was less blame on performance and skills of the team. The root of our problem lay not in our people or skills, but in the amount of Work In Progress.

Conclusion

Kanban augmented and strengthened our key Agile practices such as cross-functional Scrum teams, story driven development, continuous integration testing, TDD, and most others. It has also opened the way to even greater agility through our current plan to transition to continuous delivery.

Traditional Agile metrics had failed Siemens HS in that we did not provide the level of transparency required to manage software product development at this scale. Looking at a burn-down chart showing average velocity does not scale to this level of complexity and risk. This had been a huge gap in our Agile adoption which was now solved.

Understanding flow—and more importantly understanding the metrics of flow—allowed Siemens to take specific action in order improve overall predictability and process performance. On this note, the biggest learning was understanding that predictability was a systemic behavior that one has to manage by understanding and acting in accordance with the assumptions of Little's law and the impacts of resource utilization.

Achieving a stable and predictable system can be extremely powerful. Once you reach a highly predictable state by aligning capacity and demand; you are able to see the levers to address systemic bottle-necks and other unintended variability. Continuous improvement in a system that is unstable always runs the risk of improvement initiatives that result in sub-optimizations.

The extent of the improvement we achieved in terms of overall defect rates was better than expected. Along with the gains we achieved through managing WIP; we had placed significant focus on reinforcing and improving our CI and quality management practices. Each column had its own doneness criteria and by incorporating "doneness procedures" into our explicit policies we were able to ensure that all quality steps were followed before moving a story to the next column – for example moving a story from "Specifying" to "Developing". Most of these practices had predated

Kanban; however the Kanban method provided more visibility and rigor.

The metrics also magnified the need for further improvement steps: The current Kanban implementation incorporates activities owned within the Scrum Teams; but does not extend to the "back-end process" – regression testing, beta testing, hosting, and customer implementation. Like many large companies Siemens continues to maintain a large batch release regression and beta testing process. Thus begging the question; what if we extended Kanban across the whole value stream from inception to implementation at the customer? Through the metrics, visualization, managing WIP and continuous delivery we could deliver value to our customers faster and with high quality. We could take advantage of Kanban to manage flow, drive predictable customer outcomes, identify bottlenecks and drive Lean continuous improvement through the testing, operations and implementation areas as well. In late 2013 we began our current and very ambitious journey to extend the Kanban method across the whole value stream.

Finally it is important to say that the use of metrics instead of estimation for forecasting has eliminated the emotion and recrimination associated with estimation. Anyone wishing to go back to estimating sprints would be few and far between, including even those who had previously been the most skeptical.

Key Learnings and Takeaways

- Traditional Agile metrics were not working for Siemens HS as those metrics did not provide the transparency and predictability required by Siemens HS' customers and management.
- Siemens HS decided to dump Story Points and Velocity in favor of WIP, Cycle Time, and Throughput.
- After that shift, Siemens HS quickly discovered the root of their problem was not people or skillsets but too much WIP.

- By controlling WIP, Siemens HS was able to reduce Cycle Time from 71 days at the 85th percentile to 43 days at the 85th percentile.
- Controlling WIP also increased the quality of the HS releases dramatically.
- The second release after limiting WIP produced story Cycle Times of 40 days at the 85th percentile.
- Having predictable Cycle Times allowed Siemens to mostly abandon their old estimation practices.
- The use of metrics instead of estimation for forecasting has eliminated the emotion and recrimination associated with estimation.
- Predictable Cycle Times have also allowed Siemens HS to begin to utilize more advanced forecasting techniques like the Monte Carlo Method (see Chapter 8).

Acknowledgments

As any author will tell you, there may be one name on the front cover, but a book is only possible due to the hard work of numerous people. If I may, I would like to call your particular attention to the efforts of the few of those listed here.

Don't tell him I said this, but **Prateek Singh** is probably the best practitioner of Kanban out there. There are few who understand this stuff better than him and fewer still who have the ability to coach others with competence.

Steve Reid refuses to allow his organization to stagnate. In his mind there is always room for improvement and to his great credit he allows his team members the room to experiment and innovate. Thanks, Steve, for letting me be a part of that ride.

Bennet Vallet is one of those rare individuals who constantly—and I mean constantly—pushes himself to learn and get better. Combine that with his willingness to do whatever is needed to get the correct result and you get a formidable force. He has been and continues to be a great mentor to me. Without his prodding this book may never have seen the light of day. True to form, he is already asking for the next version that covers the more advanced topics.

Dennis Kirlin is one of those guys who you can sit down with and solve world hunger over a cup of coffee—or a whisky as the case may be. There is a reason his Agile teams are the envy of his whole city.

For those of you who don't know, **Darren Davis** is the true "Father of Kanban". It was his matter-of-fact approach to solving real-world problems that got the movement off of the ground. I was fortunate enough to learn from him as he guided me through the process of shedding the shackles of sprints. Because of him I've never looked back.

To my twin sister, **Dina Vacanti**. I frequently forget how rare it is to be a twin–what a terrible brother I am! You don't get to choose your siblings, but if I could, I would choose you every time.

Al and **Pat Vacanti** are the whole reason I was able to write this book. How do you ever say thanks enough for that?

As always, **Todd Conley** remains my wizard behind the curtain. Todd never wavered in his belief when I first pitched the idea of a flow analytics tool to him several years ago, and he has been tireless in his pursuit of perfection in developing that product ever since. Todd has a no-nonsense approach to building software and is without a doubt the best developer I have ever known. He is a trusted advisor, invaluable colleague, and great friend.

Last, but absolutely not least, I'd like to thank my wife, **Ann**. For her role in all of this, she deserves top billing and the "and". She deserves the EGOT. For putting up with me, she deserves both the Nobel Prize and sainthood. No matter how preoccupied, absentminded, or just plain stupid I've been she has always supported me. In the whole time that I've known her, whenever I've wanted to take risks both professionally and personally, she has never said no. I can't imagine a better partner. Nor would I want to.

All of the people listed above have been great collaborators for me. If this book falls short, then I can't fault any of them. That blame lies solely with me.

And, lastly, to you, the reader. Thanks for reading!

Daniel S. Vacanti
February 2018

About the Author

Daniel Vacanti has been working in software for over 20 years and got his start as a Java Developer/Architect. He has spent most of the last 15 years focusing on Lean and Agile practices. In 2007, he helped to develop the Kanban Method for knowledge work. He managed the world's first project implementation of Kanban that year, and has been conducting Kanban training, coaching, and consulting ever since. In 2011 he founded Corporate Kanban, Inc., which provides world-class Lean training and consulting to clients all over the globe—including several Fortune 100 companies. In 2013 he co-founded ActionableAgileTM which provides industry leading predictive analytics tools and services to any Lean-Agile process. Daniel holds a Masters in Business Administration and regularly teaches a class on lean principles for software management at the University of California Berkeley.

Bibliography

Bertsimas, D., D. Nakazato. *The distributional Little's Law and its applications.* Operations Research. 43(2) 298–310, 1995.

Brumelle, S. *On the relation between customer and time averages in queues*

Deming, W. Edwards. *The New Economics.* 2nd Ed. The MIT Press, 1994

Deming, W. Edwards. *Out of the Crisis.* The MIT Press, 2000.

Glynn, P. W., W. Whitt. *Extensions of the queueing relations $L = \lambda W$ and $H = \lambda G$.* Operations Research. 37(4) 634–644, 1989.

Goldratt, Eliyahu M., and Jeff Cox. *The Goal.* 2nd Rev. Ed. North River Press, 1992.

Heyman, D. P., S. Stidham Jr. *The relation between customer and time averages in queues.* Oper. Res. 28(4) 983–994, 1980.

Hopp, Wallace J., and Mark L. Spearman. *Factory Physics.* Irwin/McGraw-Hill, 2007.

Hubbard, Douglas W. *How to Measure Anything: Finding the Value of Intangibles In Business.* John Wiley & Sons, Inc., 2009.

Little, J. D. C. *A proof for the queuing formula: $L = \lambda W$.* Operations Research. 9(3) 383–387, 1961.

Little, J. D. C., and S. C. Graves. "Little's Law." D. Chhajed, T. J. Lowe, eds. *Building Intuition: Insights from Basic Operations Management Models and Principles.* Springer Science + Business Media LLC, New York, 2008.

Magennis, Troy. *Forecasting and Simulating Software Development Projects.* Self-published, 2011.

Reinertsen, Donald G. *Managing the Design Factory*. Free Press, 1997.

Reinertsen, Donald G. *The Principles of Product Development Flow*. Celeritas Publishing, 2009.

Ries, Eric. *The Lean Startup*. Crown Business, 2011.

Roubini, Nouriel, and Stephen Mihm. *Crisis Economics*. Penguin Books, 2010.

Savage, Sam L. *The Flaw of Averages*. John Wiley & Sons, Inc., 2009.

Shewhart, W. A. *Economic Control of Quality of Manufactured Product*, 1931.

Shewhart, W. A. *Statistical Method from the Viewpoint of Quality Control*, 1939.

Stidham, S., Jr. $L = \lambda W$: A discounted analogue and a new proof. Operations Research. 20(6) 1115–1126, 1972.

Stidham, S., Jr. A last word on $L = \lambda W$. Operations Research. 22(2) 417–421, 1974.

Vacanti, Daniel S. and Bennet Vallet. "Actionable Metrics at Siemens Health Services". *AgileAlliance.com. 1* Aug 2014.

Vallet, Bennet. "Kanban at Scale: A Siemens Success Story." *Infoq.com*. 28 Feb 2014.

Vega, Frank. "Are You Just an Average CFD User?" *Vissinc.com*. 21 Feb 2014.

Vega, Frank. "The Basics of Reading Cumulative Flow Diagrams". *Vissinc.com*. 29 Sep 2011.

Wheelan, Charles. *Naked Statistics*. W. W. Norton & Company, 2013.

Wheeler, Donald J., and David S. Chambers. *Understanding Statistical Process Control*. 2nd Ed. SPC Press, 1992.

Wikipedia "Monte Carlo method." *Wikipedia.com* 01 Aug 2014.

Wikipedia "Uniform Distribution." *Wikipedia.com* 01 Aug 2014.

Wikipedia "Uniform Distribution (discrete)." *Wikipedia.com* 01 Aug 2014.

Titanic. (2015). [video] USA: National Geographic. https://en.wikipedia.org/wiki/RMS_Titanic

https://en.wikipedia.org/wiki/RMS_Olympic
http://www.goldsim.com/Web/Introduction/Probabilistic/MonteCarlo
http://hackaday.com/2015/09/11/fermiac-the-computer-that-advanced-the-manhattan-project
National Hurricane Center Product Description Document: A User's Guide to Hurricane Products March 2016
http://www.nhc.noaa.gov/pdf/NHC_Product_Description.pdf

Printed in Great Britain
by Amazon